3D MODELING &

SURFACING

Bill Fleming

Morgan Kaufmann

AN IMPRINT OF ACADEMIC PRESS
San Diego   San Francisco   New York   Boston
London   Sydney   Tokyo

This book is printed on acid-free paper. ∞

Academic Press
A division of Harcourt Brace & Company
525 B Street, Suite 1900, San Diego, California 92101-4495, USA
http://www.academicpress.com

Academic Press
24–28 Oval Road, London NW1 7DX, United Kingdom
http://www.hbuk.co.uk/ap/

Morgan Kaufmann
340 Pine Street, San Francisco, California 94104-3205
http://www.mkp.com

Library of Congress Catalog-Card Number: 98-83120
International Standard Book Number: 0-12-260490-3

Printed in the United States of America
99 00 01 02 03   IP   9 8 7 6 5 4 3 2 1

Contents

Introduction

There are many art techniques, but none quite as powerful and flexible as 3D graphics. There is truly no limit to what can be accomplished with 3D graphics if you understand the tools and how they are applied. There are many 3D graphics tools, which can make it very confusing to determine which tools are best to use. To make things worse, there is a plethora of misinformation about these tools that has flooded the industry and a mind-blowing volume of marketing hype disseminated by the developers of 3D programs. All of this can make the world of 3D graphics appear very daunting and far more challenging than need be. Fortunately, this book is designed to bring clarity to an otherwise chaotic situation.

Although 3D graphics is most certainly a technical art form, it is not as complicated as you might think. There are literally thousands of technologies and tools to explore, which can be quite intimidating, but they are all relatively simple as long as you take them one at a time. I was more than overwhelmed when I first began working with 3D graphics about 3 years ago. I thought I'd never be able to create the very same quality of graphics that I now produce on a daily basis. While it was a bumpy road getting to where I am today, it wasn't as bad as I thought it would be. It's all about exploring each tool or technique one at a time, until you've mastered it, then moving on to the next one. You'd be surprised at how fast you can gain a complete mastery of 3D graphics with this simple approach.

I've written this book to make your process of learning 3D graphics a great deal easier than it was for me. In this book we'll be exploring the many modeling and surfacing techniques that are available in most 3D programs. Of course, this won't do much for us unless we also explore when and where they should be applied. For example, there is no single modeling technique that works for all projects. In fact, each project requires a unique approach, which all depends on the nature of the project. Countless myths have been spread by "so-called experts" and slick marketing people about the "best modeling tools." Of course, these are people who have never been in the trenches, forced to produce mind-blowing 3D models daily.

That's where this book takes a departure from what you might have come to expect with 3D books. We're not talking hypothetical here but actual practice. Each chapter on modeling covers a unique method, and where and when it should be used, and then closes with a walk-through that illustrates how the technique is applied. There is no guesswork in this book. The strengths and weaknesses of each modeling method are explored in detail so you can make an educated decision on which tool you should use for a given project. There is no bias given to support marketing dollars or my own personal preferences. It's a purely objective exploration of each method and their strengths and weaknesses. Understanding these strengths and weaknesses is the most important step in beginning 3D graphics, or even mastering them. Selecting the proper tool can save you days, if not months, of time wasted trying to get the wrong tool to do the job.

If you are a beginner, this book will be instrumental in helping you to choose the right program for your specific 3D graphics goals. If you are an intermediate/advanced 3D artist, this book will give you the foundation to choose the right tool for the job, every time. You can easily see how this single step is the most critical in the 3D graphics process. It's the starting point on your 3D graphics journey, and getting off to a bad start will only lead to more pain as the journey progresses.

All of the figures shown in this book are mirrored in color on the companion CD-ROM. I recommend that you check out the CD-ROM and view the images while you are reading the book. There will be details and references to color in the figures that you can't see in the grayscale printed images.

While I can't promise that this book will make your exploration of 3D graphics a painless journey, I can guarantee that it will save you countless hours of painful experimentation, and who knows how many bottles of aspirin. Simply put, this book takes away the guesswork, making it possible for you to enjoy the art of creating 3D graphics, rather than tarnishing your enthusiasm with failed experiments and dead ends.

Well, that's probably enough ranting. Let's dig in and get our feet wet with an entertaining exploration of 3D modeling and surfacing.

PART I

An Introduction to 3D Graphics

Nothing is quite as challenging as jumping headfirst into entirely new territory, and 3D graphics is definitely new territory for most of us. The industry is only about ten years old. Yes, that may seem like quite a while, but when you consider the age of nearly every other form of graphics, you'll see that it's quite young. Fortunately, the industry has made great strides in the past five years, opening the doors with new technology that enables us to realize our virtual dreams. We've also seen the price of 3D software, and computers that can run it, drop to a point where just about every enthusiast can afford to enter the industry.

Of course, this presents a large number of problems as well. Just exactly where do we enter, and with what software and tools? Well, that's what this book is about. It's designed to give you all the knowledge you'll need to make an informed decision as to which software and hardware to purchase to realize your 3D goals.

Now, it's important to note that this book doesn't sugarcoat anything. It tells it like it is. I find that far too many times a book will glamorize the industry and the tools, making you think it's easier than it is. Well, that won't happen here. In this book you get the straight dope. Yes, 3D graphics are challenging, and it does take a serious commitment and a good amount of time, but the rewards are infinite. Whether you are seeking a career in the industry, looking for a challenging hobby, or just interested in realizing your imagination in 3D, this book will show you how to make it happen.

Well, what are you waiting for—dig in!

CHAPTER 1

Getting to Know 3D Graphics

So what are 3D graphics? Simply put, they are images that represent simulations of three-dimensional space—basically, a simulation of the depth we see in reality. This, of course, comes with a few complications. The first is that we are developing and visualizing 3D objects in a 2D environment. It's quite a challenge to become accustomed to manipulating things in a 3D world, on a 2D monitor.

3D graphics can be found in every medium today. They have taken the creative world by storm. In the past, the cost of the necessary hardware and software limited the market for 3D graphics, but today it's an entirely different story. Affordable 3D programs and technology have opened the doors to the whole creative community. Print graphics are now exhibiting more 3D technology. It's now the staple of architecture and product design. Movie special effects are saturated with 3D technology. In fact, there are now 3D stunt men who are capable of doing things a real stunt man never could (or would). 3D graphics are the backbone of nearly every computer game, and they even permeate educational titles. The range of possibilities for this new medium has barely begun to be explored. Just look at the exposure of 3D on the Internet.

It's safe to say that we are seeing just the beginning of the dominance of 3D graphics. You can expect to see a great deal more 3D graphics in print media in the near future. In fact, 3D comic books are now becoming more popular; there's even a photorealistic 3D comic now. Tell me that won't have a huge impact on the comic industry. The growth of the 3D graphics industry is staggering, and it won't slow down. Two-dimensional graphics are the eight-track player or even LP record of yesteryear. They will be soon replaced by 3D graphics as more of you perfect the art. Of course, this requires a bit of work on your part.

Creating 3D graphics on a computer can be rewarding and frustrating because we are constantly drawn into a 3D world that is being represented in 2D space. Most of us are very comfortable with two dimensions on our computer, particularly the X (left/right) and Y (up/down). These are the dimensions we have been using on our computers since we began. In fact, they are the dimensions we use when we draw on paper.

The tricky part comes when we add that third dimension, *depth*, to the picture. Now we have to navigate in a dimension that we cannot touch and feel. Unlike clay sculpting, we don't have the benefit of simply grabbing the model and beating it into shape, though that urge comes quite frequently after you've been modeling for a while. Instead, we have to manipulate the model with foreign tools such as a mouse or stylus (pen). While these aren't foreign to us in regard to daily use, they are certainly not the tools of choice for sculpting, which is what you are basically doing when you create 3D graphics.

Of course, once you finally get a handle on the mouse or stylus, you need to learn a myriad of complicated tools so you can actually accomplish something in 3D. OK, so it would seem I've painted a rather bleak picture of 3D graphics, but that's not the case. I'm just letting you know that 3D graphics will be a foreign world to anyone who is just beginning. It can be daunting at first and at times rather frustrating, but perseverance is the key to the Promised Land. Dedication to the craft will reward you.

All too often a newcomer to the world of 3D graphics will stop short of the mountaintop out of sheer frustration. This is a real pity since the view from the top of the mountain is extraordinary, as you can see by Figure 1.1.

Quite extraordinary isn't it? Well, it's what waits for you at the end of discovery. The key to achieving your goals in 3D graphics is to fully understand the tools that are available so you can determine the proper choice for your 3D projects. Too many times I've seen 3D artists spend weeks on a project that should have taken days because they chose to use the wrong tool for the job. While all of the 3D tools have their merits, they also have their weaknesses, so you need to be fully aware of what each tool has to offer. That's exactly why this book exists. It's the tool that will help you make the right decisions so you don't find yourself in complete frustration,

FIGURE 1.1 *The reward of perseverance*

slouched over your computer with a bottle of aspirin in one hand and a mouse in the other.

In this book we will explore each of the modeling and surfacing techniques and tools so you can make an informed decision on which program and tools to use for each project you undertake. I can't stress enough how important this is to your sanity. I know—I used the wrong tools many times when I was just beginning my 3D career, and it cost me a large number of brain cells. That's why I created this book. I had a very difficult time trying to find answers when I started in the business, and it's still very difficult for newcomers today. So I thought I'd pack all of the most common answers into this book and its companion, *3D Staging, Lighting, and Animation.*

In this book we'll start the exploration of 3D graphics by taking a look at how we select the proper computer. Then we'll dig right in and examine the actual methods and techniques for creating 3D graphics. Finally, we'll take a moment to determine how we select the right program, depending on what we want to accomplish in the 3D industry.

Before we look at how we choose the right computer, let's take a brief moment to reflect on the history and future of 3D graphics.

A Little History

3D graphics have come a long way over the past ten years, particularly in the past five. We've seen the introduction of such technologies as motion capture, fluid dynamics, bones, morphing, splines, NURBS, subdivision . . . well, you name it—it's probably been introduced in recent history.

The 3D industry began in 1985 with the Amiga computer. There probably aren't too many of us who remember the Amiga, but it was the computer that started the graphics revolution. It was light-years ahead of the other computers available at the time. It had full-color graphics, killer stereo sounds, and a multitasking operating environment.

The original 3D programs launched on the Amiga were Caligari (true-Space), Turbo Silver (imagine), and LightWave. These are the granddaddies of the 3D industry and the pioneers of nearly all the tools we use today in various programs. While they weren't nearly as powerful as today's software, they certainly excited our imaginations with things we never could have dreamed before they came along.

I started using Imagine when it was Turbo Silver back in 1986. Actually, I used it for about 3 months before I sold my Amiga. While I didn't use the program very long, I certainly fell in love with 3D graphics. Unfortunately, it would be more than 10 years before I'd have a chance to work with a 3D program again. Figure 1.2 shows the first model I created back in 1986.

He is, of course, a 3D PacMan. I had no idea what I was doing when I created him, but somehow I managed to make it work fairly well. Back then there weren't that many modeling tools. In fact, it was just plain impossible to do anything quickly. Today the situation is very different. I created a 3D PacMan because about the only thing being done back in 1986 were chrome balls. I figured he was an improvement on the ball.

In 1997 I made my return to 3D graphics and, of course, the first model I created was a remodeled PacMan. It was just after watching the inspirational movie *Jurassic Park,* so naturally I felt compelled to create a prehistoric PacMan. Figure 1.3 shows my Jurassic Pac.

JP, as I fondly call him, was created with the more advanced tools of 1997. It was a great deal easier to add subtle details, and the surfacing capabilities of today's software are astounding compared to those of 1986.

FIGURE 1.2　*A 3D PacMan from 1986*

FIGURE 1.3　*Jurassic Pac of 1997*

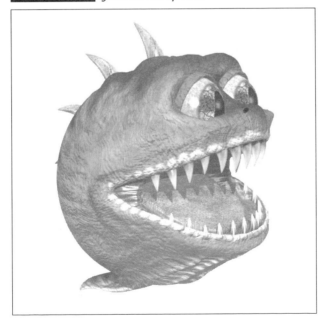

JP was created in LightWave, which is one of the oldest 3D programs—it's also one of the most powerful.

As technology advanced in 3D programs I found there was literally nothing I couldn't create, as long as I stuck with it. Of course, to honor the origin of my art I decided to once again remodel PacMan in 1998. This time I went amphibian and created a character named Munch, shown in Figure 1.4.

Munch, who is also nicknamed Spike for obvious reasons, shows the true capabilities of the 3D programs of today. Munch was created in Light-Wave, but the same technology used to create him also exists in most 3D programs.

The evolution of 3D technology has been erratic, but some consistency has evolved. Most of the 3D programs today seem to adopt very similar technology at about the same time. This is obviously a competitive move, but it's a real blessing to those who use the tools. It means we can all use the same or similar techniques to develop our work. Since the 3D commu-

FIGURE 1.4 *The Munch of 1998*

nity is a tight group that constantly communicates, this makes it possible to share techniques across different programs.

The 3D industry is maturing at a rapid pace thanks to the support the users provide each other. Until recently there hasn't been a quality source of educational information for the 3D enthusiast, but that is changing now. There are more high-quality, informative books and magazines being published on the topic of 3D graphics—not just by writers, but by the actual people who work in the industry, using the technology every day in their professional life. Growth is always a difficult proposition for any industry, but it appears that the 3D industry is off to a good start. Speaking of growth, let's take a brief look at what the future holds.

The Future of 3D Graphics

So what does the future hold? Well, plenty of innovations, no doubt. 3D technology is evolving on a daily basis. There are now 100 times as many companies involved in the industry as there were back in its humble beginning in 1985.

In the near future we can expect to see much more fluid means of character animation. The bones we use today will be the relics of tomorrow. Future character animation systems will likely lose the bones in lieu of an improved animation technique such as freeform metamation or possibly arbitrary deformation matrix. Either process would avoid all of the inherent problems found with bones. You can bet these solutions are right around the corner. In fact, they may even become available before this book is printed. That's how fast this industry moves.

You can also expect to see more virtual modeling methods. It's not likely that we will soon see the modeling glove that allows you to model clay and have the same thing mirrored in your modeling program, but you can bet there will be techniques that are very close. We've only recently seen the addition of subdivision and metashape modeling, which have advanced the modeling process tenfold over previously existing technology.

We're on somewhat of a proving ground in the industry right now. There are countless new innovations being tested in the new products. Some of them will prove useful, while others will be lost by the next release. It's a constant race to see who will come up with the next greatest innovation. This is both good and bad for us as users. Good because eventually they will hit the ball out of the park and provide us with a great tool, but bad because we are the unfortunate guinea pigs in this experiment. We have the pleasure of trying to make sense of the new innovations. As I said, it's still a young industry, and it will improve as it matures.

While the future may hold some exciting revelations, you are better off focusing your energy on the present. Don't worry about what is coming next. Spend your time perfecting what you now have so you're ready to tackle the next greatest thing. Far too many 3D artists get caught up in the excitement of new tools and toys, forgetting to focus on the basics. Don't lose sight of your goals. Keep your nose to the grindstone and wait patiently for the rest of the 3D universe to prove a tool works before you put it to use in your projects. You'll be happy you did.

Selecting a Computer

This is the most important step you'll make. If you select the right computer configuration, you'll be thrilled; if you select the wrong one, you'll probably become homicidal. When you select your computer configuration you need to take into consideration what you'll be doing. What are your goals with 3D graphics? Is it a hobby or a business? This will have an impact on your decision, since speed is very important to a business. You don't want to sit around and wait for something to render—time is money.

Of course, there are other considerations such as the type of computer and operating system you will be using. Will it be a PC with Windows 98, a Macintosh, or a Unix computer? Well, odds are, you already have a computer, so you'll need to work with what you have. If you are getting a new computer, or another one, you'll need to first determine the software you want to use and your budget.

It may be that the software best suited for your needs runs on a Mac, which means that will be your computer of choice. In the last chapter of this book I'll cover the different software programs, their strengths, weaknesses, and best application. This will make it easier for you to decide on the appropriate application.

In regard to the actual computer configuration—well, it's pretty much the same, no matter what type of computer you are using. Below is a minimum recommended computer configuration for a hobbyist, and below that is the professional configuration.

Hobbyist Configuration:

CPU: 200MHz or better
RAM: 64MB or better
Video card: 4MB OpenGL
Hard drive: 3GB
CD: The current fastest speed

Professional Configuration:

CPU: 400MHz or better
RAM: 128MB or better
Video card: 8MB OpenGL
Hard drive: 9GB
CD: The current fastest speed

These configurations apply to both PCs and Macs. You can see how the cost between these configurations will vary dramatically. If you are a hobbyist, you'll need something that can manage relatively complex and demanding graphics, but you won't have a real need for blinding speed. Well, there actually isn't anything remotely similar to blinding speed in 3D graphics, but there are some fast computers. The problem is, the more complicated the image, the slower the computer becomes.

Now if you are a serious enthusiast who likes to push the limits or a professional who is paid to push the limits, you'll want a little more power—particularly in the area of RAM, since you'll need to load a great deal more information into RAM to create complex animations and visual effects.

In the end, you are always better off getting the fastest and most powerful thing you can afford. As your skills grow, so will the demand on your computer.

Wrap-up

OK, that's probably enough of the small talk. Now it's time to get into the real meat of 3D graphics. In the next part we'll be discussing the different 3D modeling methods. This is the most important part of the book since it's the foundation for your 3D graphics. The model is where it all begins. Every project starts with a model, and if you choose the wrong technique, you'll end up kicking yourself. So be sure to read this chapter thoroughly.

PART II

Modeling Techniques

3D graphics can be a complex and daunting proposition. There are many unique segments of 3D graphics to consider. The best thing to do is start at the beginning and work your way forward. I know the tendency is to jump around and explore all of the exciting tools, but this will only serve to defeat you. You'll probably become overwhelmed by the complexity, which will only make the task of learning 3D graphics more difficult. This book is written to take you logically through the segments of 3D graphics so you gain a complete and linear understanding of the tools and their application. It's a lot easier to climb a mountain one step at a time.

In this part we'll explore the first stop on our 3D journey—modeling. Modeling is where it all begins. Without a model, well, we won't have much of an image in the end. The first step in understanding 3D graphics is to explore the different types of modeling methods and tools. This is a critical step because it will give you the knowledge to make the best decisions—decisions that will save you time and money.

Understanding the modeling methods and tools will help you to decide which modeling technique is best for the particular task you are undertaking. Selecting the wrong method can lead to wasted time and a serious need for aspirin, so you want to start off on the right foot with a confident modeling method selection.

In this part we will explore the different modeling methods and where they are best used. Then, in the second section we will dig a little deeper into 3D modeling and explore the common modeling tools you'll find in most 3D programs.

OK, let's get started.

CHAPTER 2

Modeling Methods: How and When to Use Them

There are a number of modeling methods you can use to create your 3D objects. It's important to fully understand each method so you can determine which one is best suited for the project you are developing. While each method has its strengths, some are better suited for specific applications.

In this chapter we will explore the first of seven common modeling methods:

- Polygon
- Patch
- MetaNurbs
- MetaBalls
- MetaShapes
- Spline
- NURBS

We'll be starting with the polygon method, which happens to be the granddaddy of all modeling methods. It dates back to the very beginning of 3D graphics, more than 10 years ago. Let's take a look at the one that started it all.

Polygon Modeling

The polygon method is not only the oldest, but also the most powerful method of modeling. A number of modeling methods have been created in the past five years, but none of them offer the power and flexibility of the polygon.

A polygon is a 3D building block. Well, it's not actually a block, but rather a two-dimensional plane in space. A polygon is defined as a closed plane bounded by straight lines. Simply put, it's a flat plane with straight edges. There are no curved lines in a polygon. This can be both a good and bad thing, which we'll explore later in this chapter. First, let's take a look at the common components of a polygon shown in Figure 2.1.

(A) Vertex or Point: This is the foundation of a polygon. It all starts with a point. The most common and reliable polygon has three points. Nearly all 3D programs work with three-point polygons, though there are a few that can handle four-point and greater polygons such as Light-Wave and trueSpace. A four-point polygon has a few advantages when modeling, but we'll get into those later in this chapter.

(B) Vertex or Edge: This is the side of a polygon. It's the line that connects two points. You are typically required to have three vertexes to make a polygon, but a program such as LightWave will allow two-point polygons, which creates a single-vertex polygon. Well, it actually isn't a polygon in the typical sense, but it does render—it just doesn't hold surface details such as image maps. A vertex doesn't hold surface attributes. It merely creates the edge of the polygon.

(C) Face: This is the visual representation of the polygon. It's what we will see when we render the object. It's also the portion of the polygon that reflects the surface attributes. A face is made of three or more vertexes, though only a couple programs can handle more than three vertexes.

As you can see, a 3D polygon is a relatively simple element. Of course, there are a number of great examples of polygons in reality. In fact, any flat plane such as a piece of wood is a polygon, but there are more creative examples that really help to explain the polygon modeling process such as, well, Tinkertoys.

Tinkertoys have been keeping kids constructively occupied since Woodrow Wilson was in the White House. Eighty-six year ago Hasbro, Inc., introduced Tinkertoys, a splendid toy that perfectly illustrates the principles of polygon modeling. Have you ever used Tinkertoys? Well, they just happen to have all of the main components of a polygon, as shown in Figure 2.2.

FIGURE 2.1   *The components of a polygon*

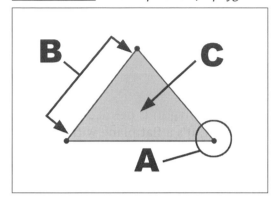

FIGURE 2.2   *A real-world polygon*

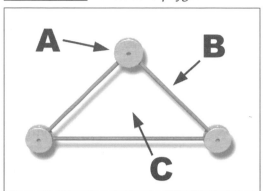

(A) Spinner Spool: This element represents the point or vertex.

(B) Rod: This is the edge or vertex.

(C) Center: This, of course, is the polygon.

Yes, it's a bit of a whimsical example, but think about it for a moment. Have you ever seen a Tinkertoy construction? Well, let's take a look at how one compares to a 3D polygon model. Figure 2.3 shows a simple polygon cube compared to a Tinkertoy cube.

The similarities are amazing, aren't they? Notice how both have points with vertices between them, forming polygons that make the cube. The good news is that if you've ever had the fortune to work with Tinkertoys, you'll have very little trouble grasping the polygon modeling method. Of course, there are a few important considerations when creating polygons.

FIGURE 2.3   *A comparison of polygon models*

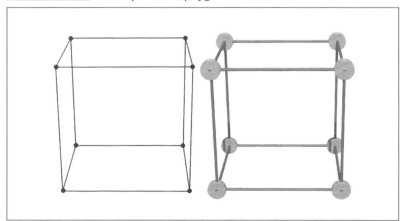

The Face Direction

A polygon is single-sided, meaning it faces one direction. If you view the polygon from the opposite direction, it will be invisible. This is done to expedite the render. We can typically see only one side of the polygon, so there is no need to render the side we can't see. When you are modeling your objects, you'll need to be aware of which direction the polygon is facing. Typically, your 3D program will give you a visual indication such as the one shown in Figure 2.4.

The dotted lines extending from the center of each side of the cube show the facing direction of the polygon. In this case, all of the polygons are facing outward, making all surfaces of the cube visible. If we were to flip one of the polygons so it faced the opposite direction, it would vanish like the one in Figure 2.5.

As you can see, the polygon that is now facing inward is invisible. It hasn't really vanished but is now facing the opposite direction. If we were inside the cube we would see the polygon. Of course, we wouldn't see any of the other polygons, since they are all facing outward. This is a valuable aspect since, we don't want to render what can't be seen. Computing 3D images is hard enough without adding unnecessary complications.

Of course, you can make a polygon double-sided so both sides render, but this only makes sense when you're using a thin object where both sides need to be visible, such as a blank page of paper. There are actually very few cases where you would need to render double-sided polygon, but if the need should arise, your 3D program will have a selection in the surfacing attributes to make the surface double-sided.

Now that we understand the facing direction of a polygon, let's take a look at a unique problem encountered with polygon modeling—nonplanar polygons.

Nonplanar Polygons

An important thing to consider when modeling with polygons is the integrity of the polygon. If you twist a polygon at an awkward angle, you'll end up creating a nonplanar polygon, which will cause an error when you render. A nonplanar polygon creates a hole in the object. It's not a physical hole, but rather a polygon that doesn't render because it's twisted.

Remember our definition of a polygon? It's a "flat" plane bounded by straight lines. The key word is flat. For a polygon to render properly it must be flat, with no bends. Now I know what you're thinking—"How do we make complex object when all of the polygons need to be flat?" Well, to explain this concept, let's examine a common object, the cover of a

FIGURE 2.4 *Facing direction of polygons*

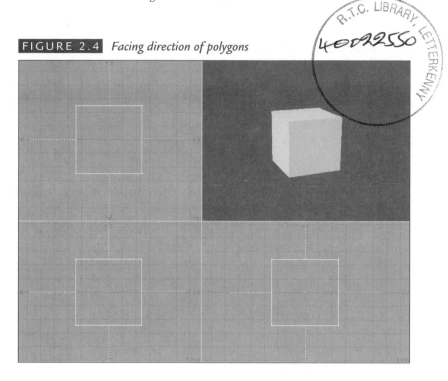

FIGURE 2.5 *A flipped polygon has vanished*

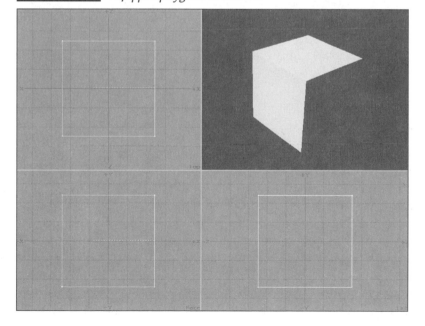

hardbound book. A book cover is a polygon. It's a flat plane bounded by straight lines. When a book cover is manufactured it starts as a completely flat plane, as shown in Figure 2.6.

As you can see, the cover to the left is perfectly flat. This, of course, will not work, since we need the cover to be wrapped around the book. To accomplish this, and still maintain the polygon integrity of the cover, we need to divide the cover into several polygons, which can be rotated to wrap around the pages as shown in Figure 2.7.

Notice how the cover is now perfectly wrapped around the pages, yet all of the polygons that comprise the cover are still planar. The polygons of the cover are still flat—they're just rotated. Dividing the cover into segments allowed us to rotate portions of the cover and still keep the polygons planar. It's the same thing that is done to real book covers. When they manufacture the cover they crease the cover in two places to allow it to be bent, effectively dividing it into three unique planar surfaces.

To maintain polygon integrity we need to do some proper planning. Now, some 3D programs have accomplished this for us by limiting us to three-point polygons. A three-point polygon will never be nonplanar, since no matter where we place any one point, they will always form a per-

FIGURE 2.6   *A flat plane book cover*

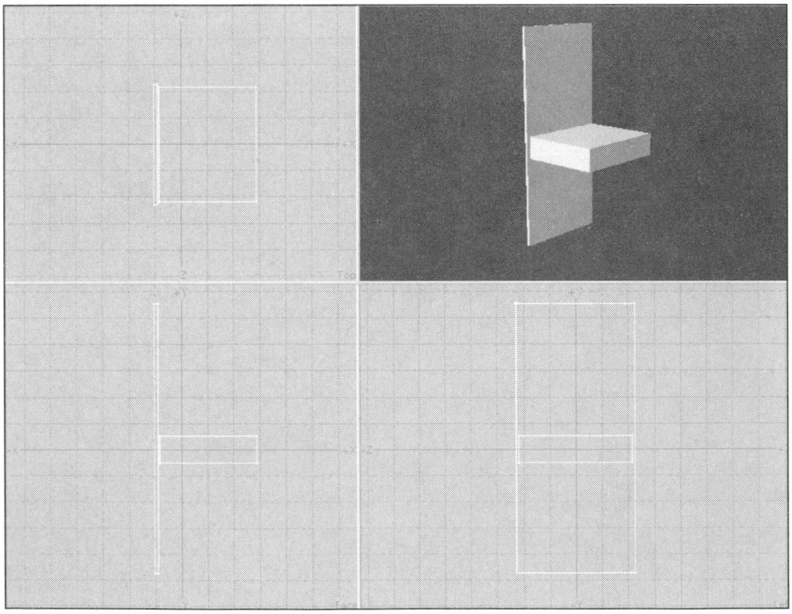

FIGURE 2.7 *Dividing a polygon to permit rotation*

fectly flat plane. This is both good and bad. You see, limiting us to three-point polygons will reduce the flexibility of our modeling. There are many modeling techniques that require four-point polygons, such as Metaform and Metanurbs. We'll be discussing these polygon modeling techniques later. For now, let's take a look at how a four-point polygon becomes nonplanar. Figure 2.8 shows an example of a nonplanar polygon.

Here we have a simple cube that's been divided into twenty-four polygons (four on each side). What I've done is to pull one point back into the cube. This has created a nonplanar polygon, which has been selected. If you take a look in the OpenGL preview window in the upper right, you'll see there is a hole where the nonplanar polygon is located. This is because the polygon has been twisted to the point where it is no longer a flat plane. For the polygon to remain a flat plane, all of the points must be aligned.

The way to correct the problem is to divide the nonplanar polygon into two three-sided polygons, as shown in Figure 2.9.

By splitting the four-sided polygon into a pair of three-sided polygons we have resolved the problem. A three-sided polygon cannot become nonplanar, so this easily corrects the problem. There are, of course,

FIGURE 2.8   *A nonplanar polygon*

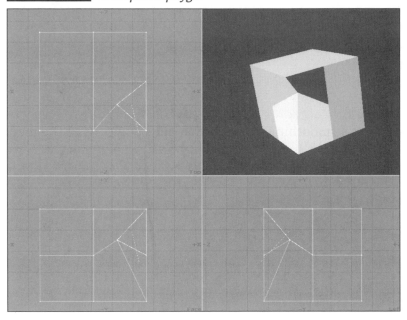

FIGURE 2.9   *Splitting the nonplanar polygon*

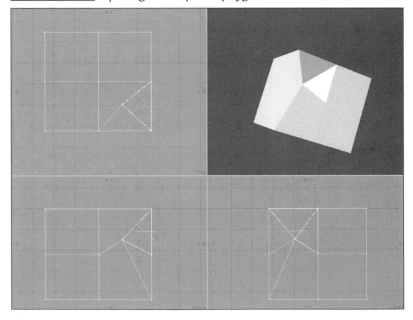

circumstances where a nonplanar polygon isn't a problem you need to manually correct. This is the case when using subdivision technology to smooth your mesh with MetaNurbs or Metaform. Let's take a look at how these techniques correct the problem. In Figure 2.10 we have a character head created with simple polygons.

As you can see, there are a large number of nonplanar polygons on this model, which have been circled. These polygons don't present a problem because they are automatically corrected by subdivision technology. Subdivision is a smoothing function that adds polygons to the model to round off the angular lines. Splitting a nonplanar polygon into several smaller polygons eliminates the nonplanar problem. Each of the new, smaller polygons has a smaller rotation, which means they won't be nonplanar. Figure 2.11 show the result of applying subdivision to the character model.

As you can see, the nonplanar polygons are all removed and the model is now very smooth. When you're modeling with subdivision technology, you don't need to be concerned about nonplanar polygons.

Of course, even if your program used four-point polygons, you'll still need to convert the model to three-point polygons to render it properly.

FIGURE 2.10 *Nonplanar polygons on a character model*

FIGURE 2.11 *Subdivision correcting nonplanar polygons*

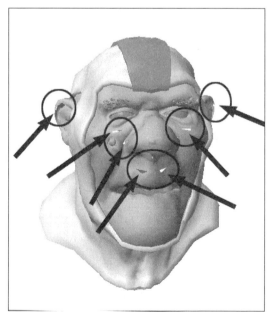

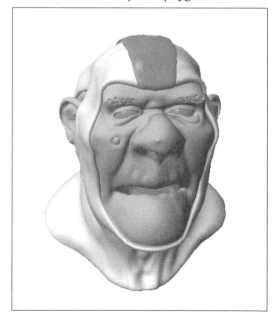

Why? Well, if you're going to use bones or morph target to animate the model, you'll be deforming the model, which will rotate the polygons. This can create nonplanar polygons. If you convert the model to all three-sided polygons, you won't have a problem, since they can never become nonplanar. Most programs have a function called "Triple" that divides all polygons into three-point polygons.

OK, now that we have a handle on polygon faces and nonplanar polygons, we can take a close look at the pros and cons of polygon modeling.

The Pros and Cons of Polygon Modeling

Each modeling method has its strengths and weaknesses. Before you embark on a modeling campaign, you'll need to identify the best modeling method to use for the project. This is a critical step, since it will save you countless hours of trying to work around the shortcomings of the wrong modeling method. We'll be discussing the pros and cons of each modeling method as it's covered in the following chapters. We'll also cover the best and worst applications of each modeling method so you know which one to use for each project you undertake.

In this chapter we'll explore the pros and cons of polygon modeling.

Polygon Pros

- **Low-Resolution Modeling:** The main advantage of a polygon is that you can model the object in low resolution and push a single button that makes it a high-resolution organic shape. This technique is called subdivision, and it's only available with polygons. Figure 2.12 shows a low-resolution model of a human head on the left and the result of subdivision on the right.

  You can see how subdivision has transformed the simple low-resolution model into a very realistic and organic head. To create the same high-resolution model with splines and NURBS, you'd need to manually create the entire high-resolution mesh. This is why polygon modeling is much better for editing highly detailed organic shapes such as human heads.

- **Varied Mesh Density:** Polygons are very flexible and allow you to add the highest amount of surface detail. You can vary the density of the mesh depending on where you want the detail. Unlike spline and NURBS modeling, polygons allow you to create specific areas of high density, such as the human ear shown in Figure 2.13.

FIGURE 2.12   *Low-resolution modeling*

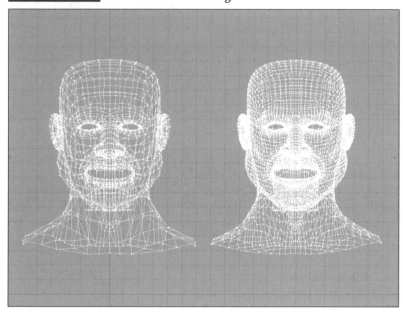

FIGURE 2.13   *Varied mesh density*

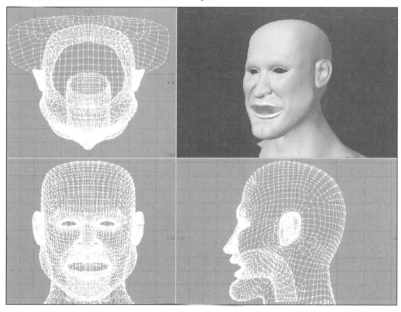

Notice how the ear has a mesh density that's twice that of the head. This is because the ear has plenty of fine detail, unlike the general shape of the head. If you were modeling with splines and NURBS, you'd need to make the head the same mesh density as the ear, creating plenty of unnecessary detail that only slows down your rendering and makes editing difficult.

• **Surface Details:** Polygons allow you the greatest degree of surface detail. Since you can create varied surface density and work with a low-resolution mesh, you can rapidly create incredible surface details that would take significantly longer in modeling methods such as splines and NURBS. For example, if you want to create hair follicles on a creature, you can simply sweep polygons back into the head to create the holes as shown in Figure 2.14.

As you can see, the little hair follicle holes really add an amazing amount of depth to the character and it only took about 30 minutes to create all of them. You'll notice the back of the head has a higher polygon volume so we could create enough hairs. The varied levels of density made it possible to create the follicles and subdivision-shape the model so it would appear realistically organic.

FIGURE 2.14   *Creating minute details with polygons*

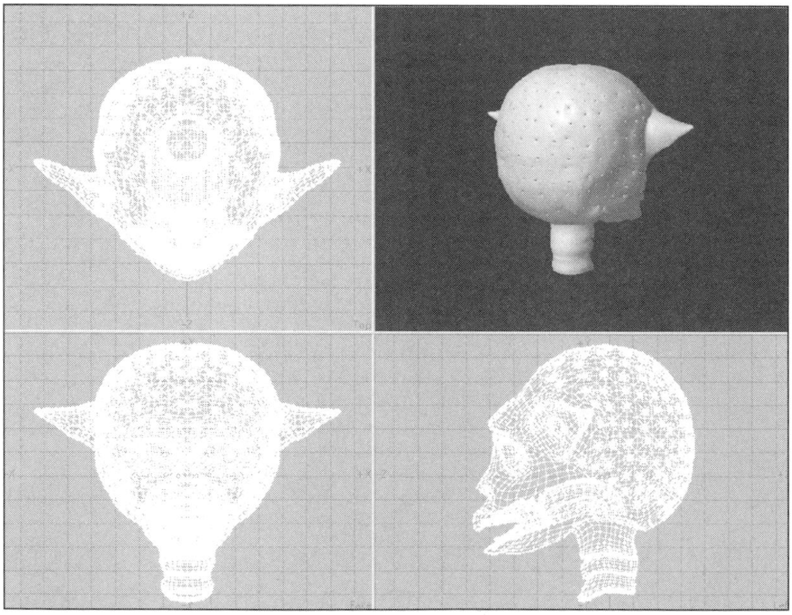

Polygon Cons

• **Smooth Curves:** Smooth curves are a real problem with polygons. It's not that you can't make them; it's just that editing the curves is a pain in the neck, because you end up with numerous points to edit. Figure 2.15 illustrates the difference between a polygon and a spline curve.

As you can clearly see, there are significantly more points on the polygon curve. In fact, there aren't enough to make the curve as smooth as the spline below. A spline creates curves between two points. These points act as controls for the shape of the curve. Each control has a handle you pull out that controls the curvature. This allows you to create very clean curves without a large number of editing nodes. On the other hand, a polygon is nothing but a straight line. To create a curve you need a large number of polygons to create the illusion of smoothness. It can be done, but remember, if you want to change the curve you need to manually drag each point, whereas you only need to manipulate a single handle to do the same with a spline.

Polygons can create smooth curves, but this is best handled with subdivision. You start with a very rough curve and smooth it by applying subdivision. We'll talk about the specifics of subdivision technology in a coming chapter.

• **Curve Accuracy:** This relates to the inability of a polygon to form a smooth curve. If you are modeling very specific details such as technical plans for a car or any other precise mechanism, you'll need to be extremely accurate with your curves. This is a shortcoming of polygons. While they're extraordinary for creating detailed organic shapes, they aren't accurate enough for creating smooth flowing lines.

FIGURE 2.15   *Comparing a polygon and spline curve*

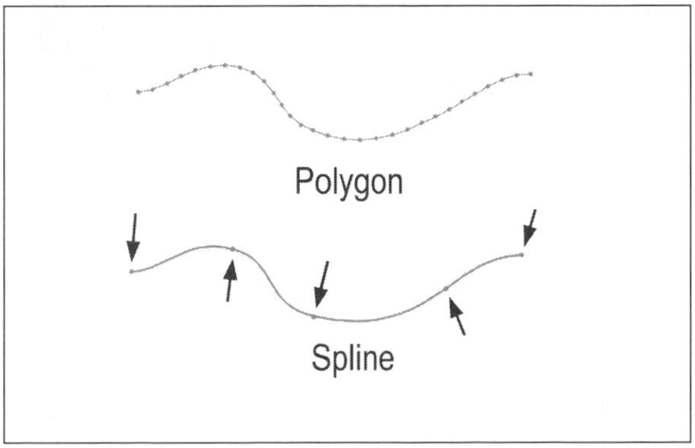

Where and When to Use Polygons

You can see how polygons have some very strong capabilities that make them the obvious choice for creating complex, natural organic shapes. The operative word in that sentence was "natural"—meaning anything Mother Nature might have created. This is an important distinction because these objects have no particular need for curve accuracy. They aren't machined or manufactured, so the lines don't need to be flawless. While polygons are a fabulous modeling method, they are not a wise choice for anything that requires machined curves, such as car bodies, engines, or mechanical gears. If you are creating technical designs for industrial use, you should use splines or NURBS, which produce very accurate curves of infinite resolution. We'll cover both splines and NURBS later in the book.

Let's take a look at some of the places where you should use polygons and those where you shouldn't.

When to Use Polygons

- **Detailed Creatures and Characters:** This is where polygons really shine. The ability to work with low-resolution models, create varied density, and apply minute details makes polygons the hands-down winner in the category of character and creature modeling. Sure, if you plan to create a simple character you can use splines and NURBS, but if you want something really complex, such as the character shown in Figure 2.16, you'll need to use polygons.

  This character is named Chakan. He's a world famous comic book character designed by Robert Kraus. I modeled him with polygons for the *Platinum 3D* comic book. Chakan is a great example of the detail you can quickly create with polygons. He shows a tremendous number of wrinkles on his face and neck, not to mention plenty of wrinkles on his clothing. These can be created in a few minutes with polygons, but take much longer with splines and NURBS.

  If you build a great model, you'll have the foundation for a killer render. Just take a look at Figure 2.17, which shows the Chakan character with surfacing applied to the detailed model.

  As you can see, the results are very impressive indeed. A model literally comes to life when you apply the proper surfaces, which is something we'll be covering later in this book. Before you begin modeling a complex character, remember to use polygons so you can achieve the infinite detail they offer.

- **Natural Organics:** This would include all forms of plant life. Polygons are great for creating flowing leaves, tree branches, rocks; terrain such

FIGURE 2.16 *A complex character created with polygons*

FIGURE 2.17 *Chakan with surfacing applied*

as mountains, valleys and lakes; and natural structures such as wood buildings, adobe huts, rock walls, cobblestone roads, and log cabins.

Polygons allow you to create very detailed natural organics, which is essential. Nothing looks more artificial than a perfect leaf or branch. All elements in nature have chaotic surfaces and details. These details are easily added with polygons. Figure 2.18 shows several examples of natural organic models.

You can see that these objects already look realistic—and they don't even have surfaces yet. That is due to the high level of model detail. The rough protrusions on the trunk of the palm tree are very quickly created with polygons by sweeping out the polygons on the trunk. The same technique was used to make the stubs protruding from the wood branch. The lumpy organic surface of the branch was created by simply applying a jitter to the low-resolution model and then applying subdivision to smooth it. All of these techniques and tools will be covered in Part 3, Modeling Tools.

- **Linear Models:** Linear models include such objects as furniture, computer equipment, multimedia components, buildings, and city streets. These are items that have relatively flat surfaces with the occasional curve and do not require precision curves. Figure 2.19 shows the lobby of a movie theater, which is a perfect application for polygons.

  Notice how most of the shapes in the room are flat. This is the obvious strength of polygons. There are some curves, but they tend to be round, which is a simple polygon shape. The stands for the velvet ropes are a simple lathe, and most of the detail was created with boolean actions, which are another strength of polygons that we will cover in Part 2.

There are thousands of practical applications for polygons; using them is the most diversified and flexible of the modeling methods. You can't go wrong by using polygons—that is, unless you plan to use them for mechanical organics.

When Not to Use Polygons

- **Mechanical Organics:** This includes anything in the industrial design area, such as car bodies, complex engines, and mechanical gears—anywhere you are prototyping an object that requires infinite resolution curves. Figure 2.20 shows a car modeled with NURBS.

  Notice the clean, flowing lines of the car. While these can certainly be created with polygons, it takes a great deal longer to ensure the lines are smooth and free of flaws. It's also an inaccurate means for technical

FIGURE 2.18 *Natural organic models*

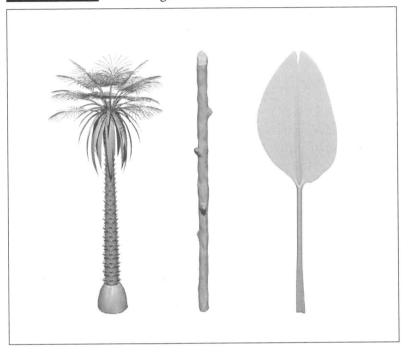

FIGURE 2.19 *Using polygons for architectural construction*

FIGURE 2.20 *A car modeled with NURBS*

design, since the curves of a polygon are not infinite resolution. Instead, they are a number of small, straight lines that create the illusion of a curve. If you zoomed in on the model, it would become more jagged the closer you came. This, of course, isn't usually much of a problem, since we don't often zoom in that close to a model, but if you were creating technical schematics for industrial design, you'd end up with a rather rough curve with polygons.

Well, there you have it: where and when to use polygons. It's easy to see that polygons can be used just about anywhere with maximum efficiency.

Now that we have a handle on polygons, we're ready to see how it all works. We're going to walk through the development of a model using polygons, step by step, so you can see how it's done.

A Polygon Modeling Walk-through

There are a number of methods for polygon modeling. Not all programs approach it in the same manner. Some will allow you to manually place points on a page and create your own polygons. Other will provide you with polygons that you need to weld together to create your model. And some will even require you to start from a primitive shape such as a sphere or cube. The important thing to note is that there are a number of ways to get your model started, so don't limit yourself to one way of thinking. To get where you want to go in the 3D world, you'll need to be a creative thinker.

In the following walk-through, I'll be showing you how a cartoon character is created. Actually, I'll be showing you how to create Chuckie, a character I created for a children's book. Chuckie is a relatively simple character, but he still has a lot of personality. Modeling a character is a rather involved process, but it's not actually that hard. It's just a bunch of repetitions and an understanding of the tools.

The purpose of this section is to illustrate the process of modeling with polygons. It's not quite a tutorial, but rather a walk-through. I'll be building a model and explaining briefly how and why the modifications were made.

Modeling Chuckie

To create Chuckie I will be using several common modeling tools such as Drag, Move, and Scale. I will also be using some unique tools such as Sweep/Smooth Shift and Magnet. I'll explain all of these tools as we walk through the modeling process. This will help you to gain a better understanding of their application. It will also introduce you to the world of tweaking. Creating a 3D model requires constant tweaking. It's like modeling with clay. You start with a very primitive object and tweak it until you have something familiar, adding lumps of clay as you go to create the details. This is exactly how you model in the 3D world. What you start with will never look anything like what you finish. It takes patience and an imagination to create 3D models.

The modeling method used in this walk-through can be used in such 3D programs as LightWave, trueSpace, 3D Studio Max, Cinema 4D, and FORM*Z. Many of these programs have polygons editors, but the technique used in this walk-through requires subdivisions, a feature that isn't available in all programs. However, it's a complete necessity for detailed organic modeling. Another thing to note is that programs such as 3D Studio Max only work with three-point polygons. This walk-through is based on four-point polygons. The only difference is that you'll have twice the polygons in 3D Studio Max. The process of modeling is still the same.

One last note before we get started. This exercise isn't a tutorial, but rather an example of the modeling process. If it were a tutorial I'd spend more time illustrating the details. What I want to accomplish with this walk-through is to demonstrate what you can expect to go through when modeling with polygons. Often it's very difficult to get started because you don't know where to begin. This walk-through will show you the entire process of modeling from beginning to end.

OK, enough chatter, let's get started with the walk-through.

Walk-through: Creating Chuckie

In this walk-through we'll be starting with Chuckie's head, and then we'll tackle his body. To create the head we first need to create our basic object. When modeling with polygons this is quite often a simple cube, as is the case with this tutorial. All programs have some form of primitive object generator that allows you to create a cube. The model starts with a simple cube that has one polygon on all six sides as shown in Figure 2.21.

The next step is to add polygons to the cube. This is accomplished with subdivision smoothing, which is often called Metaform or Meshsmooth. This will round the cube into a ball. Why not start with a ball and save the extra step? That's a great question. The problem with a ball is that it has polygons wrapped around a single point at the top and bottom of the object. This will make it impossible to properly model Chuckie. We need to have equally sized and shaped polygons on all sides of the ball. Subdivision makes this possible by dividing the cube and rounding it at the same time. Figure 2.22 shows the difference between the subdivided cube and a sphere.

As you can see, the subdivided cube has very uniform polygons, while the sphere is pinched at the top and bottom. Now that we have our subdivided cube, with plenty of polygons, we can begin shaping it into Chuckie's head. The first step is to delete half of the ball from the front. Why? Because it makes the modeling process easier. When you model complex objects that are basically the same on both sides, you start by completely modeling one half; then you mirror the object to create the other half. This saves you half the time it would take to model both sides individually. You need to work hard and smart when creating 3D objects.

Once half of the ball is deleted, we can use the Magnet tool to shape the jaw. A Magnet tool is exactly what it sounds like: It acts like a magnet, pulling or pushing the mesh. Magnet tools allow you to adjust the size of the magnet and its range of influence so you can achieve more precise control. In the case of Chuckie, a magnet half the size of his head was used to pull the lower half of the ball forward and out to the side, as shown in Figure 2.23.

You'll notice I gave the ball some color. Actually what I did was assign it a surface. When you model with polygons, you need to give the unique

FIGURE 2.21 *The basic cube*

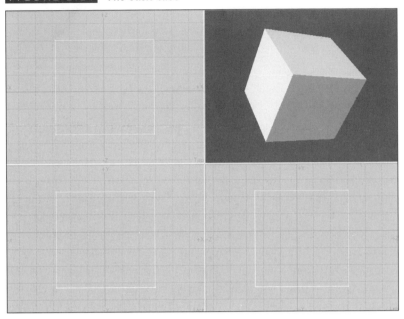

FIGURE 2.22 *A comparison of a subdivided cube and a sphere*

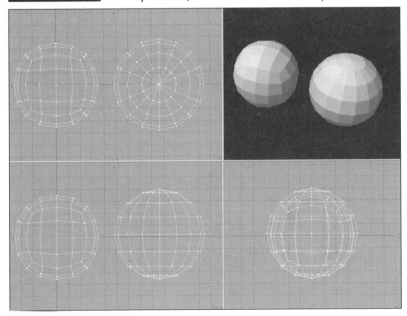

FIGURE 2.23   *Shaping the jaw with a Magnet tool*

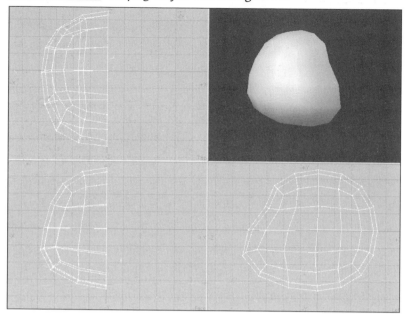

parts of your model different surface names so you can properly surface them later. For example, the label on a bottle of wine would be one surface, while the bottle itself would be another. The way you assign surfaces varies from program to program, but the result is the same. When I model I like to assign a surface color to my object that resembles the final look. Making Chuckie's head a skin tone makes it easier to visualize him.

The next step is to shape the mouth. This is where the real tweaking begins. The first thing is to move the points on the ball to form the basic outline of the mouth as shown in Figure 2.24.

You can see how the selected polygons make the ridge of the mouth. Now the depth needs to be added. This is where the Sweep/Smooth Shift tool is used. The selected polygons are swept and scaled down as shown in Figure 2.25.

This defines the upper and lower lips. A Sweep/Smooth Shift takes the selected polygons and moves them away from the object, creating new polygons to connect them. This is the most valuable tool in your polygon-modeling arsenal. Of course, once the polygons are moved you'll need to do some tweaking to align them properly. A sweep is great, but it won't do all of the work for you.

FIGURE 2.24 *Creating the outline of the mouth*

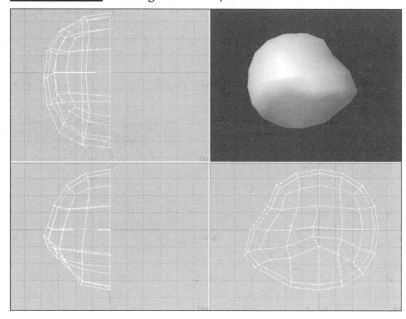

FIGURE 2.25 *Sweeping the mouth back into the head*

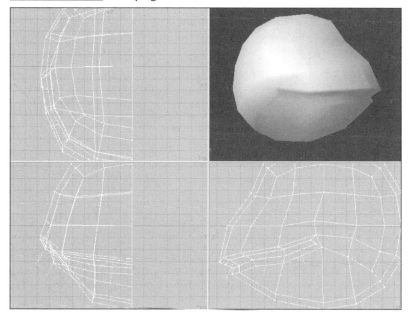

The next step in creating the mouth is to build the little bulge of skin at the back of the mouth. This is the element that makes Chuckie appear cute. To create this bulge, the polygons at the base of the mouth are first shaped by dragging the points. A Drag tool does exactly what its name states: It allows you to drag around points and polygons, depending on what you've selected. Once the polygons are shaped, the Sweep tool is used to shift them out. Then they are rotated so the front of the polygons are moved away from the head, as shown in Figure 2.26.

This creates a thick ridge around the back of the jaw. It may look rough now, but when we're done with the model, we push that magic Subdivision button and the model is transformed into a smooth, organic object. That's the beauty of polygon modeling. We work on a low-resolution model, then push a single button to make it high-resolution perfection.

OK, that does it for the mouth for now. The next step is to create the nose. This is very simple now that we have a handle on sweeping polygons. To create the nose, the second polygon up from the mouth is selected and swept. It's then scaled down and swept three more times, scaling the polygons each time until the nose is complete, as shown in Figure 2.27.

You can see how it's not really that difficult to add details to a polygon model. It just requires a bit of tweaking and patience. Speaking of tweak-

FIGURE 2.26   *Creating the fold at the base of the mouth*

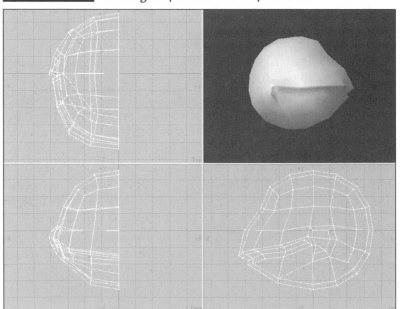

FIGURE 2.27   *The completed nose*

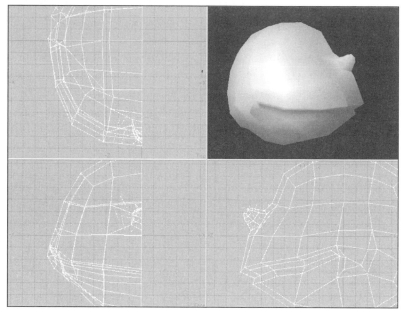

ing, the mouth needs one more tweak before it's perfect. The back of the mouth needs to be rotated upward to create the smile. Also, as long as we're tweaking, the forehead needs to be rotated forward so the eyes can be created. The polygons directly behind the forehead also need to be rotated forward to reinforce the forehead, as shown in Figure 2.28.

Now Chuckie is starting to take shape. It's a tricky process to model 3D objects. You can see that we have barely started the head, yet we've made a number of changes. Modeling can be very enjoyable—just don't get any false hopes about creating objects in a few strokes. I'm not saying it's a *nightmare*, just that you need to expect to work a bit to make a good model. As you gain experience you'll find the models come a great deal faster and with greater ease. When I first started modeling it would take weeks to make a complex character model. Now it takes a little over a day! Perseverance pays off, so don't get discouraged by the length of this walk-through.

OK, back to business. Now that the eyebrow ridge is created, the eye sockets can be shaped. This is more easily accomplished by hiding the back of the head. Many 3D programs will allow you to hide selections of polygons so you can gain a clear view of the model. Once the back is hidden, the polygons on the front of the face can be manipulated to form the general shape of an eye socket as shown in Figure 2.29.

FIGURE 2.28   *Making the smile and the eyebrow ridge*

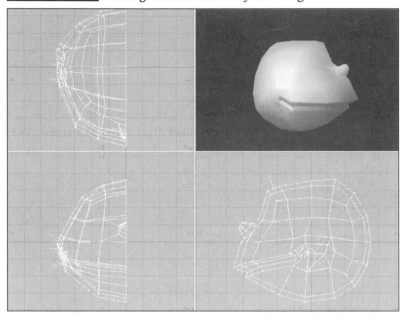

FIGURE 2.29   *Shaping the eye socket*

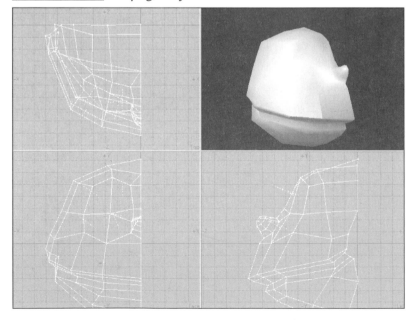

We now have a good start on the eye socket. The next step is to build the ridge around the eye. This is where we get creative in our thinking. We want to reinforce the edge of the eye socket without adding polygons to the front of the eye socket. To do this, the polygons around the eye are selected and swept as shown in Figure 2.30.

Now for the tricky part. The points on the back of the new polygons are moved forward as shown in Figure 2.31.

This is what we want, but the problem is that we now have a line of points on the front of the eye socket that we don't need. We moved the points along the back of the polygons but not the front, so now we have points sitting on top of each other. To resolve this problem we merge the points using a Merge or Weld tool, depending on the program. This, as it implies, merges the points so they become a row of single points again.

Once the points are merged, the polygons in the middle of the eye socket are selected and swept back to complete the eye socket. The next step is to create the ear. We could create the eye first, but that's an easy step and I like to get the complicated steps out of the way first. It's always nice to end on an easy step.

Creating the ear is very similar to the last step we just covered. The polygons just behind the skin-bulge at the corner of the mouth are shaped

FIGURE 2.30   *Building the ridge around the eye socket*

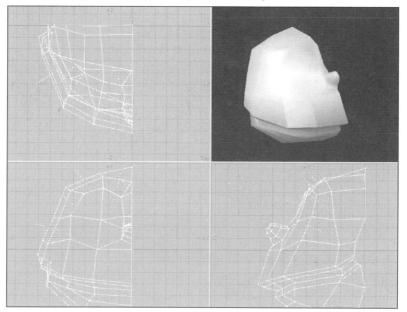

FIGURE 2.31   *Moving the points forward*

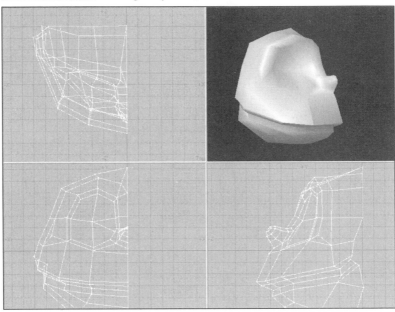

to form an outline of the ear. Then they are selected and swept, but not moved. Instead, they are rotated outward in the back, using the front of the ear as the pivot point. Now they are swept again and rotated as before to create the ear foundation shown in Figure 2.32.

Now we have the same problem as before with overlapping points. There are now three layers of points on the front of the ear. The easy solution here it to select the points and merge weld them. This is different from before because the points don't share the exact same space, so they need to be manually selected and welded. The top point on the front of the ear is selected, which also selects the two points below it, and welded to create a single point. The same is done for the lower point on the front of the ear. Now the basic ear shape is formed. The last step is to add the ridge around the top of the ear.

Once again, this is the same process we followed to create the ear. The polygons along the edge of the ear, from the side, are selected and swept. Then they are rotated outward and the points at the beginning and the end of the ridge are welded so the ear looks like Figure 2.33.

OK, now the only thing left to create is the eye. This is easily accomplished by selecting the polygons in the middle of the eye socket, giving them a new surface name and color, then Sweeping them outward a few times, scaling them down each time to create the eye shown in Figure 2.34.

FIGURE 2.32   *The ear foundation*

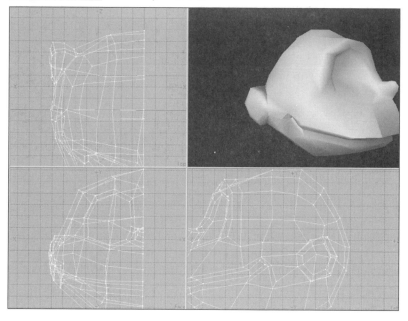

FIGURE 2.33   *The completed ear*

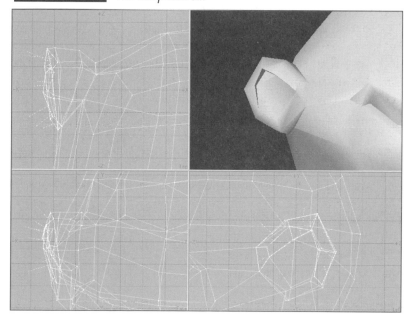

Well, we now have half of Chuckie's head. The final touch would be to add the neck. This is easily accomplished by selecting the polygon on the bottom of the head and sweeping it down once to make it smaller, then two more times, moving them each time to create the neck shown in Figure 2.35.

Now that the head is complete the model can be mirrored to form the entire head. Once it's been mirrored along the center axis, the points are merged and the object is Subdivided to smooth it. When completed, the model looks like the one in Figure 2.36.

As you can see, we now have a very smooth, organic head created with polygons. It took a few steps to complete, but it wasn't all that bad when you consider the head was basically repetition. We performed one sweep after another to add detail to Chuckie's head. Of course, if we wanted to reach perfection, we'd need to do a bit of tweaking, but that's consistent with any modeling project you undertake, regardless of the method.

Well, that was a typical example of modeling with polygons. Any modeling method will seem daunting at first, but if you take your time and explore the tools, you'll find it's not rocket science—just plenty of repetition.

FIGURE 2.34   *The completed eye*

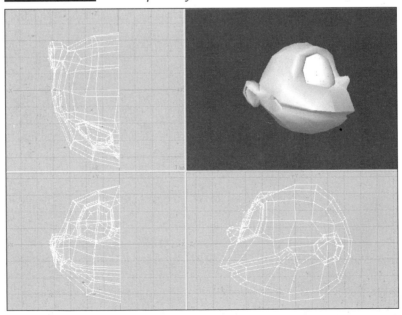

FIGURE 2.35   *The neck*

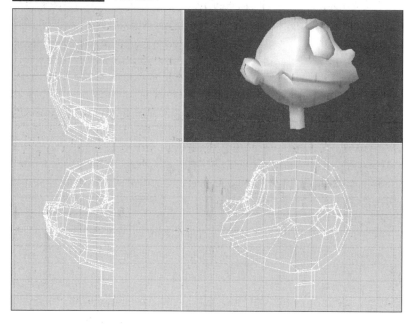

FIGURE 2.36   *The completed head*

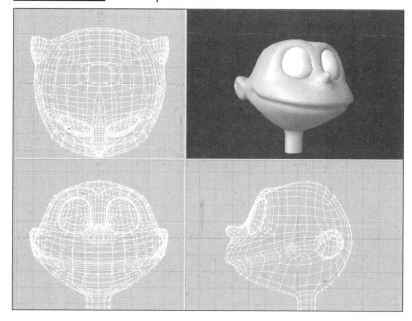

Wrap-up

Polygon modeling is both challenging and rewarding. It's truly the most flexible method of modeling. The important thing to remember is where and when to use polygons. Fortunately, polygons are perfect for nearly every modeling project, with the exception of those that require curves with infinite resolution for technical applications.

In Part 3 we will dig deeper into polygon modeling by examining the most common and useful editing tools. You'll be amazed at how easily you can create complex objects if you have the right tools. Right now let's take a look at another form of 3D modeling—subdivision.

CHAPTER 3

Subdivision and MetaNurbs Modeling

Subdivision and MetaNurbs are basically one and the same, but they are applied differently and at different times. Subdivision is actually more of a tool than a method, while Metaform is a modeling technique that incorporates Subdivision technology. Confused yet? Well, let me put it this way. Subdivision is the smoothing and shaping tool that is applied after you are done with the model, while MetaNurbs is a modeling method that incorporates real-time Subdivision feedback as you model. We've briefly covered Subdivision in Chapter 2, but let's get into it a little deeper so we can fully understand how it's used as a modeling method.

Subdivision

Subdivision is basically a mathematical algorithm that adds polygons to a model in an effort to smooth the rough edges. There are actually three common forms of Subdivision: Faceted, Smoothing, and Metaform. Let's take a look at each of these and how they are used.

Facet Subdivision

This form of Subdivision merely splits the polygons into four parts. Basically it triples the polygon count of your model without applying any

FIGURE 3.1 *Faceted Subdivision*

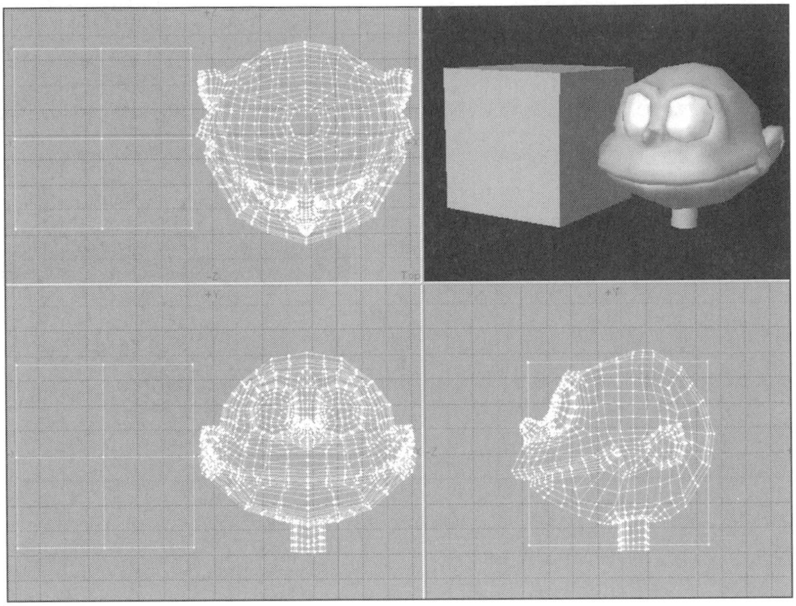

smoothing. Figure 3.1 shows an example of Faceting on a simple cube and the Chuckie object from Chapter 1.

Notice how the sides of the simple cube have been divided into four polygons. That's because it was split vertically and horizontally. The shape of the cube hasn't changed, but it now has more polygons. The same has occurred to the Chuckie head model on the right. It now has significantly more polygons. OK, so Facet splits the polygons—but why is this valuable for modeling? Well, it's not the most productive tool, but it does come in handy for increasing the tension of your model before you subdivide it with Smoothing or Metaform. Sometimes you'll want the model to be a bit more rigid and less organic. By adding polygons with Facet you make the density of the polygons greater, which makes it more rigid when smoothed. Speaking of smoothing, let's take a look at Smooth Subdivide.

Smooth Subdivision

This form of subdivision smooths the polygons. What it tries to do is soften the curves. It still divides the polygons like Facet, but also softens the curves. Figure 3.2 shows an example of Smooth Subdivide.

You can see how the cube has been turned into a rough ball. All of its corners have been smoothed. The same has occurred to Chuckie's head.

Smooth Subdivision

Take a close look at the corner of Chuckie's mouth in the OpenGL preview and you'll see that the edge of his skin fold is rather harsh. This is because the edge was sharp to begin with and Smoothing only softened the edge—it doesn't shape it.

There is a setting that often comes with Smoothing that's called Max Smoothing Angle. This field is used to limit the influence of smoothing. Any polygon with an adjoining angle greater than the Max Smoothing Angle will not be smoothed. OK, so what is the adjoining angle? Well, it's the angle where two polygon edges meet. Take a look at Figure 3.3, which will help to clarify this.

The white polygons are examples of adjoining polygons because they share a common vertex. The angle of the polygons along this vertex is called the Adjoining Angle. The two polygons in the upper right have an adjoining angle of 90 degrees since they form a right angle. The polygons in the lower left have an adjoining angle of 180 degrees because they are flat.

OK, now let's take a look at the effect of different Max Smooth Angles when applied to this cube, shown in Figure 3.4.

Here we have two copies of the same cube with Smoothing applied. The cube on the right had a Max Smoothing Angle of 89 degrees while the one on the left had a Max Smoothing Angle of 179 degrees. Notice that the

FIGURE 3.3   *Adjoining Angles*

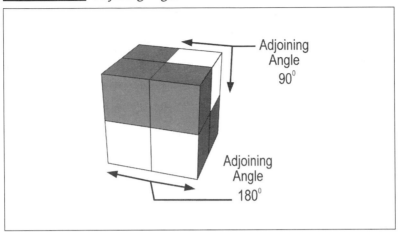

FIGURE 3.4   *The effect of Max Smoothing Angles*

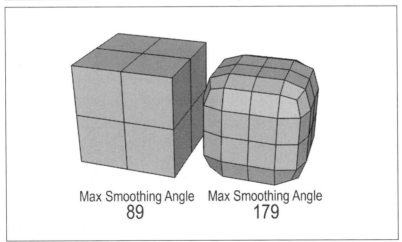

cube on the left remained unchanged. That is because all of its adjoining angles are greater than 89 degrees. On the other hand, the cube on the right was rounded on the corners because all of the corners had an adjoining angle of 90 degrees. The adjoining angles in the middle of the cube were 180 degrees so they remained unchanged.

Once you get a handle on the Max Smoothing Angles, you can plan around them when you model. You'll be able to determine exactly how the Smoothing will take shape when applied. Now let's take a look at the last form of subdivision—Metaform.

Metaform Subdivision

This is the most powerful and useful subdivision you'll find. It's a shaping subdivision, meaning it actually shapes the objects for you. Smoothing rounds the curves, but Metaform rounds everything. It will soften all of the hard lines into curves. It's the perfect tool for polygon modeling because it allows you to model in low resolution and push a single button to convert it to a very organic, high-resolution model, as you saw in our Chuckie modeling walk-through in Chapter 2.

Figure 3.5 shows the effect of Metaform Subdivision.

You'll notice that the cube is very similar to the one created with Smooth Subdivide. That's because it had a limited number of polygons and few adjoining angles. Looking at the Chuckie head you'll soon realize the power of Metaform Subdivide. Notice that there are no rough lines on the model as there were with Smooth Subdivide. The hard edges on the corner of the mouth and the ears are all gone. He now appears perfectly smooth, natural and organic.

Well, there you have the three forms of subdivision. They are all useful, but the real shining star is Metaform. You probably noticed that all of the examples of subdivision were postproduction, meaning they were performed on the model after completion. That is when they are typically applied, though they can often be applied at varied stages of development to

FIGURE 3.5 *Metaform Subdivision*

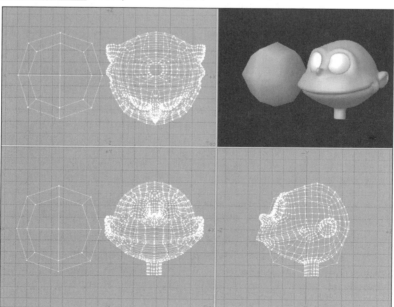

add more polygons so details can be created. For example, when creating a detailed creature you might go though two passes of Metaform before the final one is applied. This allows you to continually add more and more detail.

Now that we have a handle on Subdivision, let's take a look at the pros and cons of Subdivision modeling.

The Pros and Cons of Subdivision Modeling

The pros and cons of Subdivision modeling are nearly the same as those for polygon modeling, since it's actually just another method of polygon modeling. Let's take a look.

Subdivision Pros

- **Low-Resolution Modeling:** The main advantage of a polygon is that you can model the object in low resolution and use Metaform Subdivision to make it a high-resolution organic shape. To create the same high-detail model with splines and NURBS, you'd need to manually create the entire mesh, which would take ten times as long. This makes Subdivision modeling the real champion for creating highly detailed organic objects.

- **Varied Mesh Density:** As with Polygon modeling, Subdivision is very flexible and allows you to add the highest amount of surface detail. You can vary the density of the mesh depending on where you want the detail. Unlike spline and NURBS modeling, Subdivision allows you to create specific areas of high density. This can be very valuable, particularly when creating dense areas of detail like the eyelids on a human or creature.

- **Surface Details:** Polygons allow you the greatest degree of surface detail, so Subdivision also carries this benefit. Since you can create varied surface density and you can work with a low-resolution mesh, you can rapidly create incredible surface details that would take significantly longer in modeling methods such as splines and NURBS.

Subdivision Cons

- **Smooth Curves:** Smooth curves are a real problem with polygons. It's not that you can't make them; it's just that editing the curves is a pain in the neck, because you end up with numerous points to edit. Subdivision does create very smooth curves, but they won't be accurate enough for machine work, and they are not infinite resolution.

- **Curve Accuracy:** This relates to the inability of a polygon to form an infinitely smooth curve. If you are modeling very specific details such as technical plans for a car or any other precise mechanism you'll need to be extremely accurate with your curves. This is a shortcoming of polygons—they're extraordinary for creating detailed organic shapes, but they're not accurate enough for creating smooth flowing lines, since they are merely a series of straight lines. The curve may look smooth, but it will be very rough when it's machined.

- **Three-point Polygons:** Subdivision does work with three-point polygons, but it's best to use four-point polygons. When Metaform is applied, it smooths the surface based on the tension between points. A four-point polygon evenly distributes the tension between all four points. A three-point polygon tends to apply a large amount of tension to a single side, which can create hard creases and pinching when you Metaform. Most of the time you'll need to use a few three-point polygons on a model, but try to keep them to a minimum and definitely keep them away from areas such as the corners of a mouth or the eyes, since they will tend to crease and pinch. It's better to move them away from really detailed areas of the model.

As you can see, the pros and cons of Subdivision are very similar to those of polygons. This, of course, is because Subdivision is based on polygons. However, Subdivision used in a few different circumstances than standard polygon methods. Let's take a look at where and when you should use Subdivision modeling.

Where and When to Use Subdivision

Subdivision is a powerful organic modeling technique. This means it is perfect for organic objects and not a good choice for those that need to be linear. Choosing the right modeling method is a must before you begin any project. You've heard me say it before, and I'll probably say it again a dozen more times before this book is finished. I can't stress enough how important this single decision is.

Let's take a look at some of the places where you should use Subdivision and those where you shouldn't.

When to Use Subdivision

- **Detailed Creatures and Characters:** This is absolutely the best place to use Subdivision. It makes a somewhat daunting process a great deal easier to deal with. The ability to work with low-resolution models, create varied density, and apply minute details makes Subdivision the hands-down winner in the category of character and creature modeling.

- **Natural Organics:** This would include all forms of plant life. Subdivision is great for creating flowing leaves, tree branches, rocks; terrain such as mountains, valleys and lakes; and natural structures such as wood buildings, adobe huts, rock walls, cobblestone roads, and log cabins. It makes it possible to create very flowing and lumpy lines, which are common in natural organics.

When Not to Use Subdivision

- **Linear Models:** Linear models include such objects as furniture, computer equipment, multimedia components, buildings, and city streets. These are items that have relatively flat surfaces with the occasional curve so they do not require a lot of organic shaping. Yes, there are some models such as multimedia components and modern furniture that have flowing lines, but these are actually wiser to create with basic polygon modeling tools, since Subdivision is much better suited for soft-tissue objects.

- **Mechanical Organics:** This includes anything in the industrial design area, such as car bodies, complex engines, and mechanical gears—anywhere you are prototyping an object that requires infinite resolution curves. While Subdivision can create flowing lines, it takes a great deal longer to ensure that the lines are smooth and free of flaws. In fact, it's almost impossible to remove all of the flaws. In addition, for mechanical design you need curves of infinite resolution so you can machine the designs. You don't want mechanical components with rough surfaces.

So now you know where and when to use Subdivision. You'll notice there is one difference between polygon modeling and Subdivision modeling—you'll want to avoid using Subdivision on models with flat surfaces, since that is better left to polygon modeling.

Now that we have a handle on Subdivision, we're ready to see it works in the modeling process. We're going to walk through the development of a model using Subdivision, step by step, so you can see how it's done.

A Subdivision Walk-through

As we discussed in Chapter 2, there are a number of methods for polygon modeling. Subdivision is just another method. Actually, it's more of a technique. When we walked through the development of Chuckie's head, we started with a simple cube. This time we'll be starting with a flat mesh. This technique is referred to as Flat Mesh Modeling, and it's probably one of the best ways to ensure that you model the object with accurate details.

The purpose of this section is to illustrate the process of Subdivision modeling. As before, it's not quite a tutorial—it's a walk-through. I'll be building a model and explaining briefly how and why the modifications were made so you can see how the process of Subdivision modeling works.

The modeling method used in this walk-through can be used in such 3D programs as LightWave, trueSpace, 3D Studio Max, Cinema 4D and FORM*Z. Although many programs have polygon editors, these programs have incorporated Subdivision as a part of the program, or as an available plug-in. With any luck, more programs will begin to incorporate the miracle of Subdivision technology.

All right, let's get started with our walk-through.

Modeling Chuckie's Shirt

Chuckie's shirt is a relatively simple model, but there are a few cool details that can be added to really make it interesting, such as ridges around the sleeves and collar, and possibly a fold of fabric under the arm. To make these details easier to incorporate, we need to plan ahead. Proper planning can save you countless hours of problem solving. One of the most common problems with 3D modeling is that artists tend to jump in and start modeling without planning. This is a bad idea: Quite often they find themselves completely rebuilding the model because they were unable to fix their problems.

Probably the best-planned models are created with the flat modeling technique. Flat mesh modeling is designed to aid in planning the model. Most of the details that will be created in the final model are incorporated into the flat mesh. You add the polygons into the flat mesh that will be used in the specific details of the object. For example, if we want to add ridges to the ends of Chuckie's shirtsleeves, we'll need to add the row of polygons that will become the ridge to our flat mesh. It's a very simple process once you get the hang of it. To make this easier to grasp, let's get started with Chuckie's shirt.

There are a number of ways to build a flat mesh. Probably the easiest way is to manually lay points on the screen and then build your custom polygons by selecting a group of points and pressing the Make Polygon button. Many programs have an Add Point tool that lets you drop points on the screen. These points are usually laid down over a template to help you create the proper shape. The template is usually a picture or a line drawing that is loaded into the background of your modeling program.

Once the points are created, you can select the points in series, one after the other, and make a polygon. To work with Subdivision it's recommended that you make four-point polygons, though you will have to make a few three-point polygons. Figure 3.6 shows a flat mesh I created for Chuckie's shirt.

Here we have the basic shape of a shirt—well, half a shirt, anyway. When modeling objects that have identical sides, you should model one half at a time and them mirror it to complete the model. This will save you a lot of time that would be spent creating the identical thing on the opposite side. Take a look at the figure and you'll see some polygons highlighted on the end of the sleeve, on the bottom of the shirt, and under the arm. These are the polygons that will later be used to create the ridges and the wrinkle. This is why flat modeling is so beneficial when creating models with plenty of details. You have the opportunity to plan well ahead.

Once the flat mesh is created, and it contains all of the necessary polygons for the details, it's time to start adding depth. This is accomplished by extruding the mesh. An Extrude function is similar to Sweep and Smooth Shift with one exception: It only shifts the polygons along one of the axes, X, Y, or Z. This is fine for objects like the shirt, but if you are modeling complex objects with varied angles, you'll need to use Sweep and Smooth Shift. Figure 3.7 shows the result of extruding the flat mesh.

FIGURE 3.6 *Chuckie's flat mesh shirt template*

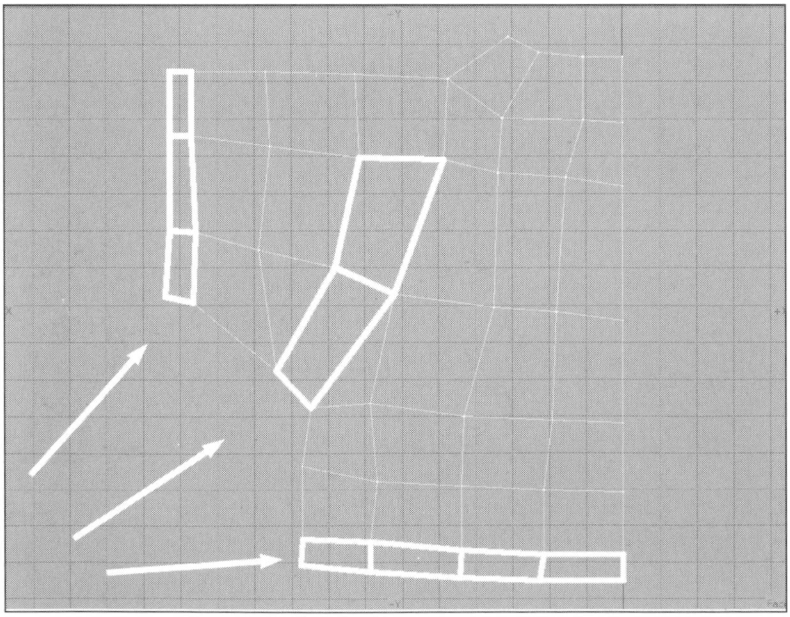

FIGURE 3.7 *Extruding the flat mesh*

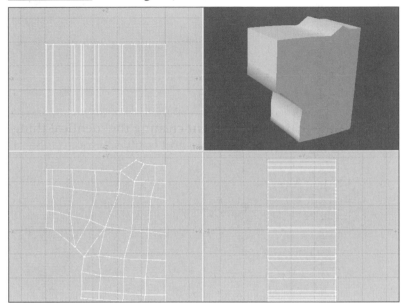

The shirt has plenty of depth now, but it's a bit angular. We need to round it off. This is accomplished by selecting the polygons along the outer edge and stretching them inward as shown in Figure 3.8.

You can see that the shirt is starting to take shape. The Stretch tool does exactly what it suggests. It stretches polygons and points. It's a great tool for editing, particularly when using the flat mesh modeling method. The shirt is looking better, but it needs a little more shape. It's still too flat, particularly around the body. The shirt can be shaped very quickly by dragging the front and back outward with the Magnet tool as shown in Figure 3.9.

This is much better. Now that we have the basic shape for the shirt, we're ready to give it thickness. One of the major shortcomings you'll see in most 3D images is the lack of material depth in objects. 3D is all about depth, so it's important that you add it to all of your objects. To add depth to the shirt, the collar, sleeve ends, and base of the shirt need to be swept. This is accomplished by selecting the polygons on the ends and sweeping them. Then they are scaled down slightly and swept back into the shirt.

Now there is an important thing to consider when doing Subdivision modeling—the tension of polygons. If you don't reinforce your polygons they will oversmooth, creating sharp edges. For example, if the ends of the sleeves were simply Swept back into the shirt a single time as shown in Figure 3.10, the sleeve would Subdivide to a sharp edge as shown in Figure 3.11.

FIGURE 3.8   *Rounding the shirt*

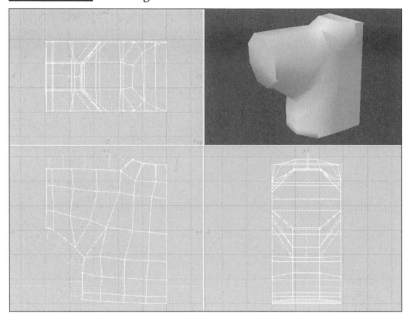

FIGURE 3.9   *Adding depth to the body of the shirt*

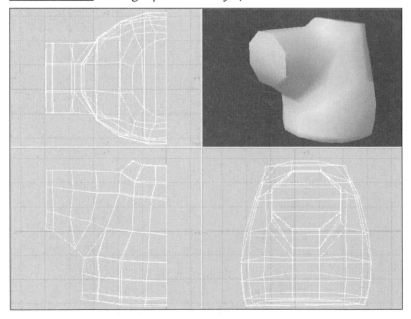

FIGURE 3.10   *A single Sweep inward*

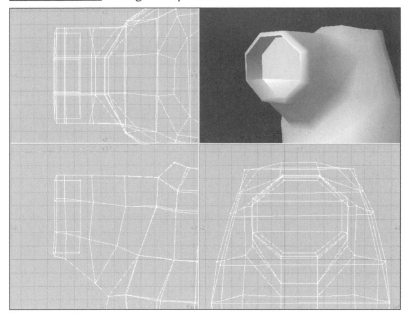

FIGURE 3.11   *The sharp edge created by Subdivision*

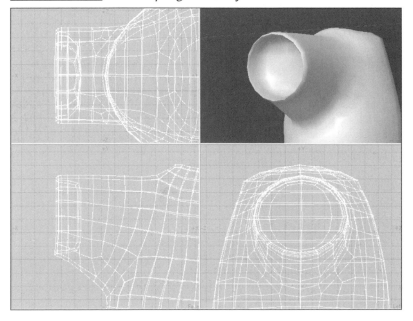

You can see that this is an undesirable result. The way to prevent this is to shorten the distance between the polygons. If you first swept the polygons back into the sleeve a small amount, and then swept them back into the arm, you would have reinforced the end of the sleeve so it wouldn't create a sharp edge when swept. Figure 3.12 shows the shirt with the collar, sleeves, and base swept back into the shirt properly.

The shirt will now hold its edges when Subdivision is applied. The foundation of the shirt is complete now. The next thing to do is add the subtle details that make the shirt interesting. We'll start with the fold of fabric under the sleeve. This is created by selecting the polygons just under the sleeve and sweeping them. Then the new polygons are scaled down and moved out a bit to create the wrinkle shown in Figure 3.13.

That looks pretty good. Now for the final detail—the ridges along the edges of the sleeve and collar. This is part of that original planning we did when the flat mesh was created. The polygons along the edges of the selves are already created, so they simply need to be selected and swept outward as shown in Figure 3.14.

Once the polygons were swept, they were stretched upward and outward to create the thickness of the ridge. They could have been scaled, but they would have ended up being thicker than the base of the ridge, which

FIGURE 3.12 *Adding material depth with Sweeps*

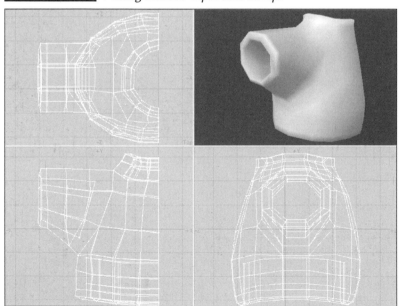

FIGURE 3.13 *Creating the fabric fold under the sleeve*

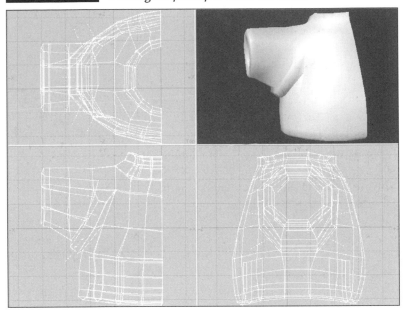

FIGURE 3.14 *Adding the ridges to the sleeves and collar*

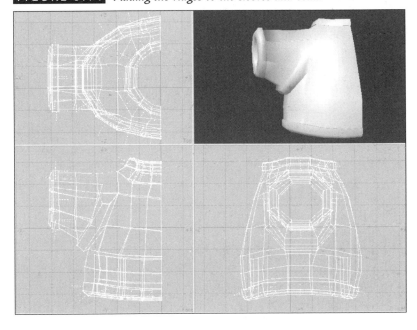

FIGURE 3.15 *The subdivided shirt*

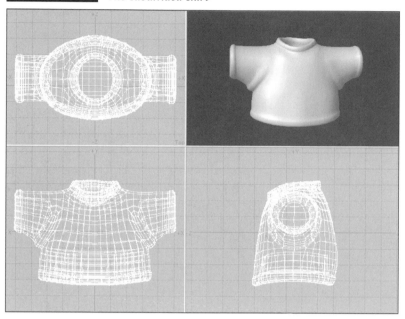

would create an undesirable effect. If we subdivided the polygons with the top wider we would end up with a hard edge on the ridge because the angle would be too extreme. We want angles less than 90 degrees to make the ridge smooth.

The shirt is now complete. To finish it off the model is mirrored along the X axis, then Metaform Subdivided to create the model shown in Figure 3.15.

Well, that looks pretty darn good, doesn't it? As you can see, it didn't take much effort to create a detailed shirt with material depth. It's all about understanding the tools. Subdivision makes modeling objects like this a breeze because we can create very low-resolution models, which are transformed into high-detail masterpieces with the press of a single button.

That was a good example of Subdivision modeling but there is another form of Subdivision modeling known as MetaNurbs. Let's take a look.

Modeling with MetaNurbs

MetaNurbs is a unique form of Subdivision. Actually, it's identical to Metaform, except that the Subdivision is performed in real time on the model as you work. It's the closest thing you'll get to clay modeling on the computer. MetaNurbs is a combination of Subdivision and Splines, which means you're working with primitive polygons that have curved lines. When you activate MetaNurbs on a mesh, the model is surrounded by a cage of control points as shown in Figure 3.16.

Take a close look at Chuckie's head in the lower left view and you'll see little points floating around his head. These are the MetaNurbs control points. They are in the same location as the point, but they work like a spline control point, modifying a curve as you drag it. Basically, the polygon mesh is surrounded by a spline cage that lets you manipulate the polygons as if they were splines, turning the straight lines into curves. Figure 3.17 shows the result of manipulating MetaNurbs control points.

You'll notice that four control points on the top of the head have been pulled out, creating smooth ridges. The smooth lines you see, forming the bumps on the wire mesh, are a part of the MetaNurbs control cage. They represent the spline translation of the polygons. If we disable MetaNurbs, we'll see very sharp points on the top of his head, as shown in 3.18.

A little scary, isn't it? Once the MetaNurbs control cage is removed, we see the actual placement of the points, which appears very exaggerated. When working with MetaNurbs, you need to make very exaggerated gestures with the points to create the details. This isn't always the case, but it

FIGURE 3.16 *A MetaNurbs control cage*

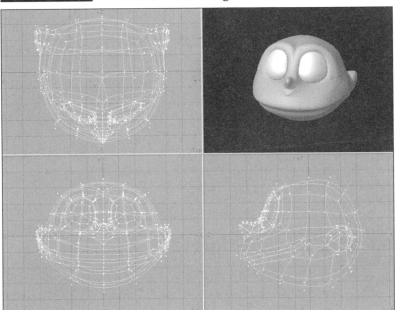

FIGURE 3.17 *Manipulating MetaNurbs control points*

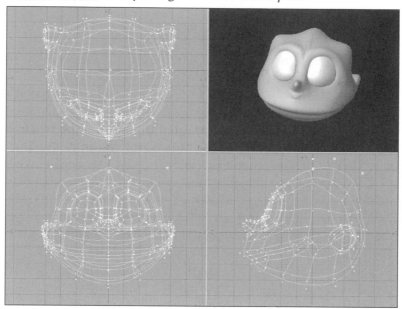

FIGURE 3.18 *The edited mesh without MetaNurbs*

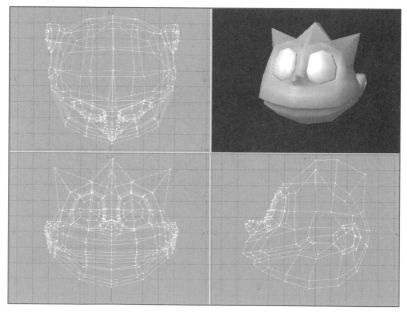

is when you are adding high-altitude details, which are details that move away from the base mesh.

When you're finished editing your model with MetaNurbs, you perform a Freeze action to create the high-resolution, smoothed mesh. When you freeze a MetaForm mesh, you often have the option of choosing the number of divisions. This is how you determine the final resolution of the model. Normal subdivision is a division of two. If you wanted your MetaNurbs model to possess the resolution of a subdivided model, you would set the Divisions to two. If you wanted the mesh to be twice as high, you would set the Divisions to 4, but this is not recommended. It's usually a good idea to keep the Divisions below 4 so your model doesn't become too much of a resource drain when you try to animate it.

Now that we have an idea of how MetaNurbs works, we can do a quick experiment to show how MetaNurbs and Subdivision create the same effect. If we apply MetaForm Subdivision two times to the model it will look exactly as it did with MetaNurbs applied, as you can see in Figure 3.19.

It's a perfect match. The reason we needed to apply Metaform twice is because that's how MetaNurbs translates the mesh. In effect, it performs a real-time double Metaform on the mesh while you edit it. This can be both a benefit and a detriment at the same time. Since we're on the subject of pros and cons, let's take a look at how MetaNurbs differs from Subdivision.

FIGURE 3.19　*The edited mesh with Metaform applied*

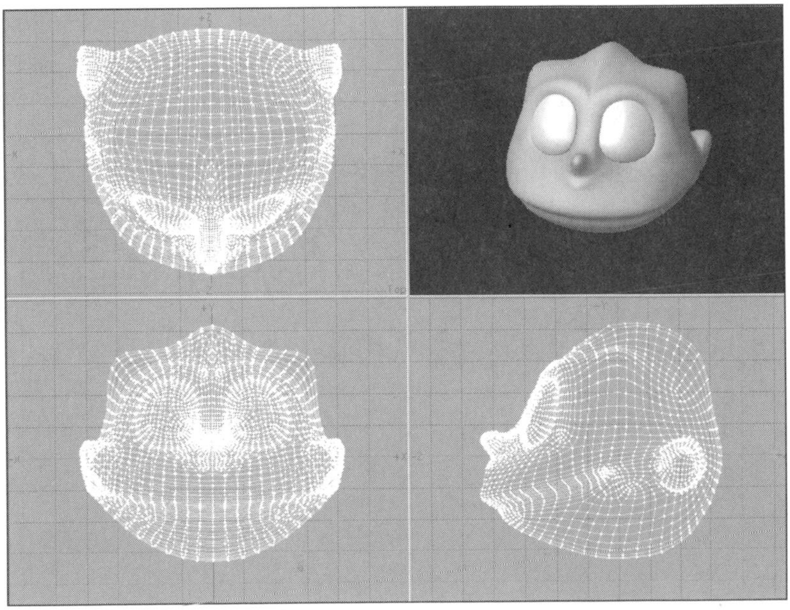

The Pros and Cons of MetaNurbs Modeling

The pros and cons of MetaNurbs modeling are very similar to those of Subdivision modeling, but there are a few differences. Let's take a look at them now.

MetaNurbs Pros

MetaNurbs has all of the advantages of Subdivision, plus one additional advantage—real-time smoothing.

- **Real-time Smoothing:** The main advantage of MetaNurbs is that you can have a real-time preview of your model as it will appear in high resolution. This can be a real benefit when working with models where you'll need to do a lot of Subdivision tests.

MetaNurbs Cons

MetaNurbs has all of the disadvantages of Subdivision, plus a few additional ones, so let's take a look at them.

- **Three-point Polygon Pinching:** MetaForm works perfectly on four-point polygons but has real trouble providing accurate visual feedback with three-point polygons. While the final mesh will be fine, the OpenGL preview will have pinches wherever you have three-point polygons, as shown in Figure 3.20.

  The pinching areas have been circled in the image. You can see the undesirable pinches on the ear, corner of the mouth, around the eye, and under the nose. These appear as errors but they are not. They are only an error in the OpenGL preview. This is a major disadvantage because it will be very misleading. You'll think you have a problem when you really don't. You could spend hours trying to resolve a problem that doesn't exist.

- **System Resource Abuse:** This is the real shortcoming of MetaNurbs. The more polygons you have, the slower your refresh rate in the OpenGL preview. This makes it almost impossible to work on high-detail objects unless you have a very large capacity OpenGL video card, something along the lines of 24 to 40MB of RAM and 200MHZ processors.

As you can see, the pros and cons of MetaNurbs are very similar to those of Subdivision. This, of course, is because MetaNurbs is a form of Subdivision. MetaNurbs can, however, be used in a few different circumstances than standard Subdivision methods. Let's take a look at where and when you should use MetaNurbs modeling.

FIGURE 3.20 *The pinching of three-point polygons*

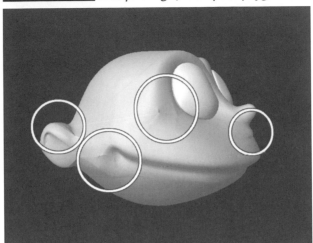

Where and When to Use MetaNurbs

MetaNurbs is a great technique for creating organic objects in a very short time, but it does come with its problems. It's important to understand the limitations of a modeling technique before you use it. As with any modeling method, there are times when the method is very useful and those when it's not. Let's take a look at where and when to use MetaNurbs.

When to Use MetaNurbs

- **Simple Creatures and Characters:** Since MetaNurbs is a lot like modeling with digital clay, it's great for creating creatures and characters. You could easily create the Chuckie head covered in Chapter 2 with Meta-Nurbs. Of course, you'll want to avoid doing characters with really high detail—it will be very slow going, since MetaNurbs is performing a real-time subdivision.

- **Manufactured Organics:** MetaNurbs is great for doing manufactured objects that are fairly organic such as multimedia components, furniture, and cars (as long as they don't need infinite resolution curves).

- **Natural Organics:** This would include all forms of plant life. MetaNurbs is great for creating flowing leaves, tree branches, rocks; terrain such as mountains, valleys and lakes; and natural structures such as wood buildings, adobe huts, rock walls, cobblestone roads, and log cabins. It makes it possible to create very flowing and lumpy lines, which are common in natural organics.

When Not to Use MetaNurbs

- **Detailed Creatures and Characters:** This is not a good place to use Meta-Nurbs, since the OpenGL preview will operate too slowly. It will only cost you time, which is not a good idea. In fact, MetaNurbs will go from real time to a really long time. Subdivision is the best technique for modeling complex creatures because there is nothing to slow you down. When you're modeling with Subdivision, you can use Meta-Nurbs to get a preview of your model so you can see how it will look. I do this quite often.

- **Linear Models:** Linear models include such objects as furniture, computer equipment, multimedia components, buildings, and city streets. These are items that have relatively flat surfaces with the occasional curve so they don't require a lot of organic shaping. Yes, there are some models such as multimedia components and modern furniture that have flowing lines, but it is actually wiser to create these with basic polygon modeling tools, since MetaNurbs is much better suited for soft-tissue objects.

- **Mechanical Organics:** This includes anything in the industrial design area, such as car bodies, complex engines, and mechanical gears—anywhere you are prototyping an object that requires infinite resolution curves. While Metaform can create flowing lines, it takes a great deal longer to ensure that the lines are smooth and free of flaws. In fact, it's almost impossible to remove all of the flaws. In addition, for mechanical design you need curves of infinite resolution so you can machine the designs. You don't want mechanical components with rough surfaces.

Although MetaNurbs uses Subdivision technology, it does have its differences because it tends to be a resource drain, which can be a problem if you're working on a tight timeline. Remember that effective 3D modeling is all about choosing the right tool for the job. MetaNurbs is super for jobs that don't require a ton of detail.

Well, all that's left now it to take a walk-through with MetaNurbs to see how it's used in a modeling project.

A MetaNurbs Walk-through

The purpose of this section is to illustrate the process of MetaNurbs modeling. It's not quite a tutorial but rather a walk-through. I'll be building a model and explaining briefly how and why the modifications were made so you can see how the process of MetaNurbs modeling works.

The modeling method used in this walk-through can be used in two 3D programs: LightWave and trueSpace. Unfortunately these are the only two that possess MetaNurbs technology. Let's hope that more programs begin to incorporate this powerful modeling technology in the near future.

OK, let's get started.

Modeling Chuckie's Diaper

To demonstrate MetaNurbs, I'll be showing you how Chuckie's diaper was modeled. This is a great example because it not only shows off MetaNurbs, but also demonstrates some great modeling techniques. I'll be using the same flat mesh modeling technique that was used to create Chuckie's shirt, since there's just no better way to model the diaper.

The basic shape of the diaper was created by manually laying points on the screen and then creating the polygons by selecting groups of points. This is exactly how the basic shape of Chuckie's shirt was developed. To make the job easier, I created only half of the diaper so it can be mirrored to create the whole model. Figure 3.21 shows the flat mesh of the diaper.

As you can see, it's a simple shape, but it will soon become a complicated object as the really interesting details are added, such as a seam around the edge, a puffy center, and Velcro tabs to hold the diaper on. Before the details can be added, the object needs to be given depth so it can

FIGURE 3.21 *The flat mesh for the diaper*

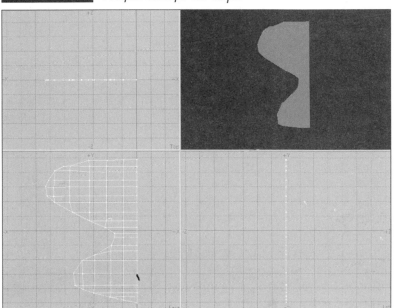

be Metaformed. To accomplish this the mesh is extruded back slightly as shown in Figure 3.22.

Now MetaNurbs can be activated so the details can be added. Once MetaNurbs is activated, the linear diaper turns into a very smooth and organic shape as shown in Figure 3.23.

You can see that the MetaNurbs control cage has been added to the model. Now the details can be added. The first detail to create is the seam. This is easily accomplished by selecting the polygons along the outside edge and sweeping them as shown in Figure 3.24.

Once the polygons were swept, they were stretched to create a thin seam of polygons around the edge of the diaper. Now the diaper is ready for some organic thickness. It's a cloth diaper, so it needs some padding, but not nearly as much as a disposable diaper, which tend to be very large. To add depth to the diaper the inner polygons are selected and swept away from the diaper slightly, which can be seen in Figure 3.25.

The diaper now has some depth, but it's too rigid along the seam. To make the diaper appear more like fabric, the polygons in the center need to be swept one more time, shifted away from the diaper, and scaled slightly as shown in Figure 3.26.

FIGURE 3.22 *The extruded diaper*

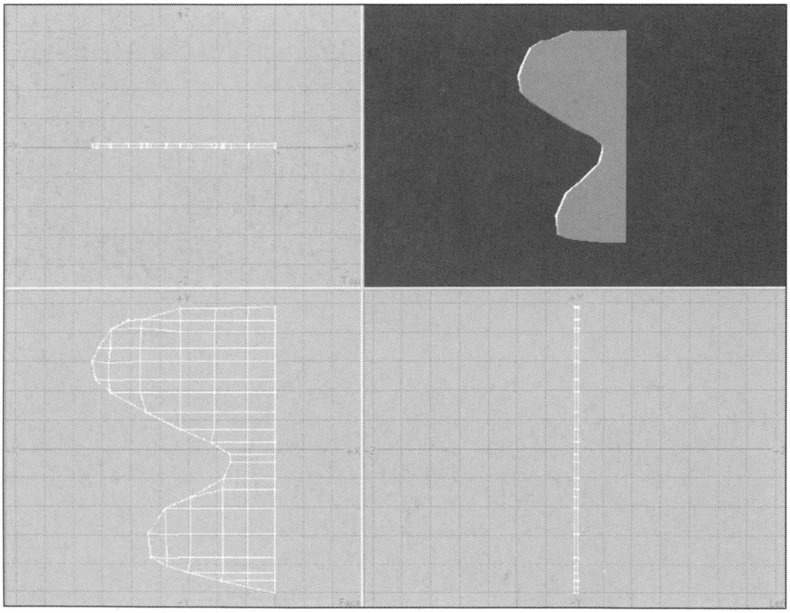

FIGURE 3.23 *MetaNurbs applied to the diaper*

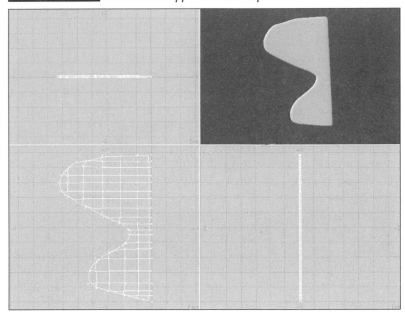

FIGURE 3.24 *Creating the diaper seam*

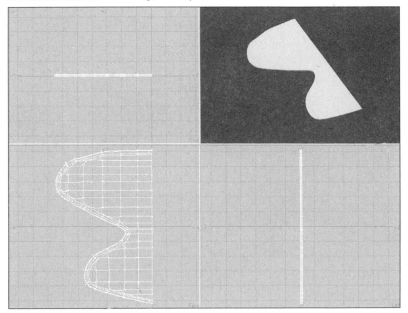

FIGURE 3.25   *Adding padding to the diaper*

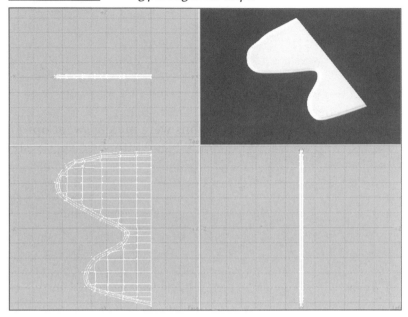

FIGURE 3.26   *Softening the diaper seam*

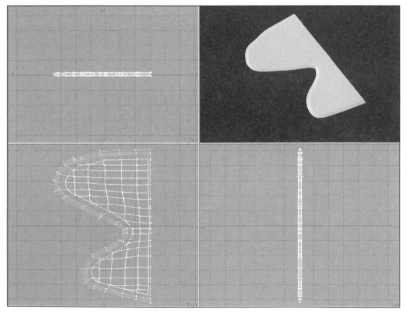

The diaper now has a soft edge before the seam. The next step is to add a little puffiness in the front and back so it looks padded. To do this, the polygons in the middle of both sections are selected and stretched away from the diaper slightly as shown in Figure 3.27.

Great! It's starting to look like a diaper now. The basic diaper form is now complete so the only thing left to add before it's folded is the piece of tape on the winged tabs. This is easy to create but the steps are important if the proper effect is to be achieved. The tape needs to appear as if it's sitting on top of the diaper. If the polygons were merely swept upward it would add some depth, but the tape would blend into the diaper as shown in Figure 3.28.

Notice how the tape is blended into the diaper, as if it had been painted on. This is a common error seen in many 3D objects. The problem is that if you simply sweep the polygon upward, the adjoining angle of the polygon is only 90 degrees, which means it will be smoothed out by the subdivision. What you need to do is use a couple of sweeps to separate the tape from the diaper. The first step is to sweep the polygons for the tape and scale them a bit larger, but not move them. Figure 3.29 shows how the model looks after this step is performed.

FIGURE 3.27 *Adding puffiness to the diaper*

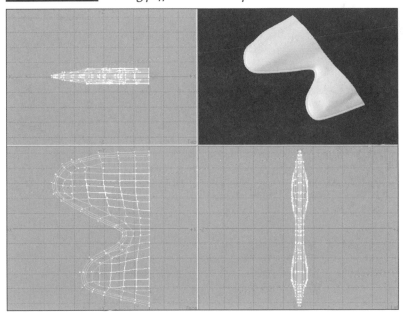

FIGURE 3.28   *The wrong effect*

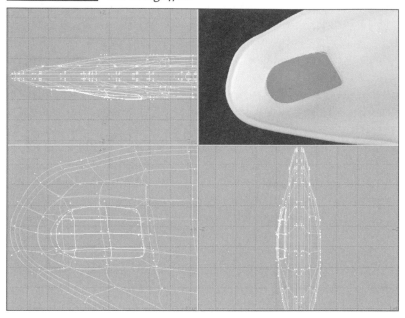

FIGURE 3.29   *The first sweep for the tape*

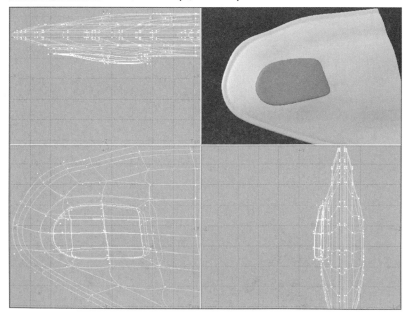

Now a new surface is assigned to the polygons to make them the tape surface. The next step is to sweep the polygons again and move them out a bit to add depth to the tape as seen in Figure 3.30.

That's much better. The tape has depth and looks as if it's sitting on top of the diaper, not a part of it. By scaling the first Sweep larger, we add a little more range for the smoothing. It moves the polygons out far enough that when the Subdivision is applied, the polygons won't be smoothed nearly as much. It's an easy trick that adds a great deal of depth to the models.

Well, that does it for the modeling of the diaper. The next step is to fold it. This is the easy part, and it's a bit of fun as well. To fold the diaper the lower half of the model is selected and a Bend tool is used to fold up the leading edge as shown in Figure 3.31.

The Bend tool is perfect for jobs like this, and it's a simple tool to use. What you do is select the axis you want to bend the model along, determine if it's a positive or negative bend, and then drag the mouse to bend the object. OK, so what the difference between positive and negative? Well, that refers to which end will be bending. The positive end is the one closest to us, or the top, depending on the viewpoint. The negative is the one farthest away from the bottom. In the case of the diaper a negative bend was used because the bottom of the diaper was bent upward.

FIGURE 3.30 *The proper way to create the tape*

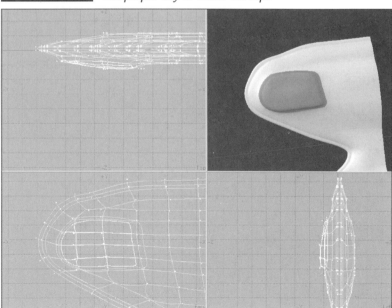

FIGURE 3.31   *Folding the leading edge of the diaper*

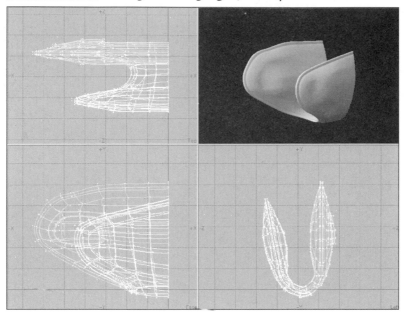

Now that the diaper is folded, the tabs can be turned inward. This is also accomplished with the Bend tool. A negative bend was used to bend the front tab inward as shown in Figure 3.32.

Then the same negative bend is used to warp the back tab around the front as seen in Figure 3.33.

The diaper is nearly complete now. The last step is to shape it, but first it needs to be mirrored so both sides of the diaper can be manipulated. Figure 3.34 shows the mirrored diaper.

Now the shaping begins. This is a simple process, which involves using the Magnet tool to drag the front and back of the diaper outward to give it depth. The Magnet tool is also used to shape the groin and behind. In just a few tweaks the model was transformed into the finished product seen in Figure 3.35.

It looks great, doesn't it? It has all of the details you'd expect to see in a diaper. Well, all of the pleasant ones anyway. Now that the model is complete, it's ready to be frozen into its final state. Since the diaper is a simple object, a Division of 2 will be fine for the freezing, which produces the result seen in Figure 3.36.

Notice how clean the model looks. All of the pinching we saw in the MetaNurbs OpenGL preview is gone. The diaper is now ready for Chuckie to use.

FIGURE 3.32　*Bending the front tab inward*

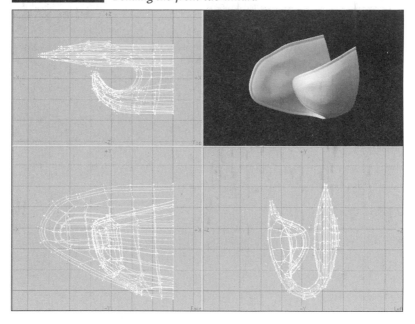

FIGURE 3.33　*Wrapping the back tab around the front*

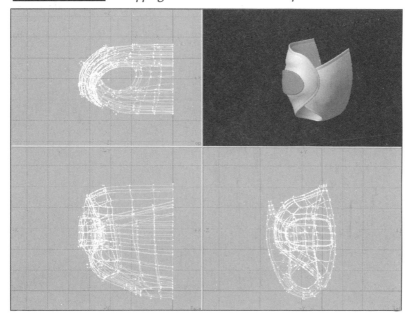

FIGURE 3.34 *The mirrored diaper*

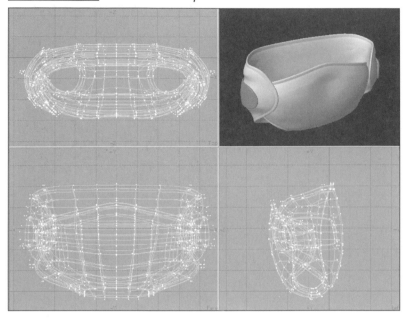

FIGURE 3.35 *The completed diaper*

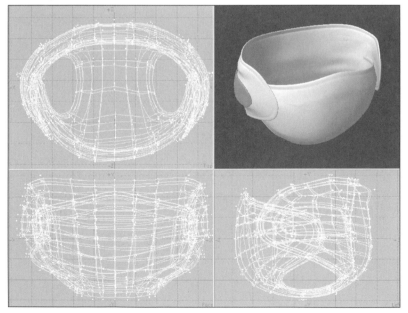

FIGURE 3.36   *The frozen diaper*

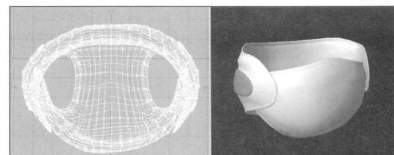

The diaper may have seemed like a bit of a challenge at first because it's all folded up, but you can see how it was actually a rather simple process thanks to proper planning. Starting with the Flat Mesh method made modeling the diaper very easy. In fact, it would have taken much longer with any other polygon modeling method. Good 3D modeling is all planning, planning, planning! Have I said this already? Well, it can't be said too many times.

Wrap-up

As you can see, Subdivision modeling is a real winner when it comes to creating organic shapes. Nothing does it better and in less time. There are those who would argue that Splines or NURBS can do organics better, but that's just not true. Splines and NURBS have their shortcomings, which we'll be discussing in Chapter 4.

Right now it's time to take a look at the last type of polygon modeling—metaballs and metashapes. These are very unique and productive modeling methods that can be a lot of fun to use, so flip the page and let's get started.

Metaballs and Metashapes

Metaballs and metashapes are a rather unique approach to 3D model-ing. They are very similar to building objects with clay. When sculpt-ing with clay you start with a basic glob of clay and then start adding smaller clumps to form the details. With metaballs and metashapes you do nearly the same thing. You start by placing a single ball on the screen; then you add more objects to create the details. OK, so it's not quite the same, but it's very close.

OK, so what are metaballs and metashapes? Well, they are simply poly-gon or spline shapes that are specifically designed to be skinned. There are some differences between metaballs and metashapes, so let's take a look at them one at a time. We'll start with metaballs.

Metaballs

Metaballs consist of a series of subprimitives called "components," which are spherical in shape. Each component has a size and an "attractive" (+) or "repulsive" (–) strength associated with it. The final shape of the metaball is computed based on the position, size, and strength of each component (ball). Simply put, metaballs are spheres that blend together to form a sin-gle object.

The metaball concept originated in 1982 when James F. Blinn described a technique that could be used to approximate atoms by means of Gaussian distribution functions. The idea was proposed to Carl Sagan to create a DNA animation for the Cosmos television series. Blinn called his raytraced creations "blobby models."

Shortly thereafter, people at Osaka University and at Toyo Links in Japan began using blobby models. They called theirs "metaballs." Yoichiro Kawaguchi became a big user of their software and their Links parallel processor machine to create his "Growth" animations, which have appeared in the SIGGRAPH film show over the years. The first time the general public was truly exposed to metaballs was in 1991, when the blockbuster movie *Terminator 2: Judgment Day* introduced the T-1000 Liquid Metal Cyborg. Shortly after the movie, TV commercials started to integrate metaball animation. Well, to make a long story short, metaballs entered mainstream 3D graphics in 1992 when Clay Studio was introduced for 3D Studio. It was the first commercial metaball modeling tool. Now nearly every 3D program has metaballs.

OK, that's enough history. Now let's take a look at how metaballs work.

Metaballs are created by defining an "isosurface." OK, so what is an isosurface? Well, think of it this way. An isosurface is defined by checking for a constant value throughout a region in 3D space. For example, if you place a small heating element in the middle of a room, heat radiates evenly in all directions, with the maximum temperature in the center of the room and a minimum temperature closest to the walls. If you use a thermometer to mark anywhere in the room (including the air) where the temperature is equal to a specific value, the collection of points where the temperature is equal to the specific temperature defines an isosurface ("iso" means "equal" or "the same"). In this example the surface created would be a sphere. This is how a metaball is defined.

OK, so a metaball is the spherical shape where the strength is equal to a set value. Figure 4.1 shows a typical metaball.

The upper left and lower right windows show the wireframe view of a metaball. Most metaball systems use a simple spline sphere rather than a polygon mesh to make it easier to see what you are doing. If you have several metaballs close to each other, a polygon mesh will make it very difficult to select a metaball. The lower left window shows the shaded view of a metaball. It basically looks like a polygon ball. The upper right window shows the skinned metaball. It looks the same as the shaded view because there are no other metaballs to blend with. Now that we understand the concept behind a metaball, let's take a look at how they react with one another.

FIGURE 4.1 *A metaball*

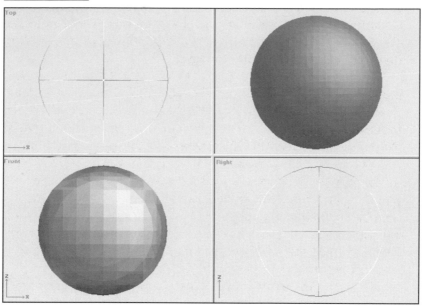

Let's think back to our analogy of the heating element effect. As the heat extends into the room, it loses intensity. The change of temperature throughout the room is called the "density distribution" or "potential distribution." The specific value that defines the isosurface is called the "threshold." In other words, if the threshold value is a large number, the isosurface will be very small (since the higher temperatures are those nearer to the heating element); smaller threshold values would mean that the surface becomes larger. For simplicity, the density can be a number between –1.0 and 1.0 and the threshold 0.0 to 1.0. Figure 4.2 displays an approximation of a metaball's density distribution.

The center of the metaball has the maximum density value, and as we move outward the density goes to a minimum. OK, so what happens when two or more metaballs interact? Well, when two metaballs interact, their density values are added in those places where they overlap. As in the example of the heating element, if you now place a second heating element in the room, there will be places where the heat from each one overlaps, increasing the temperature at that point. This may also increase the chance that the point has a density value equal to or greater than the threshold. When two or more metaballs with positive densities interact, the result is a final shape that creates the effect of "attraction" between the metaballs, shown in Figure 4.3.

FIGURE 4.2 *Metaball density distribution*

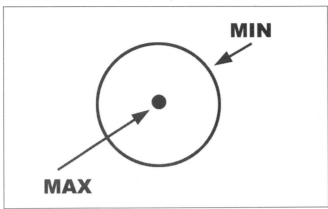

FIGURE 4.3 *A positive metaball influence*

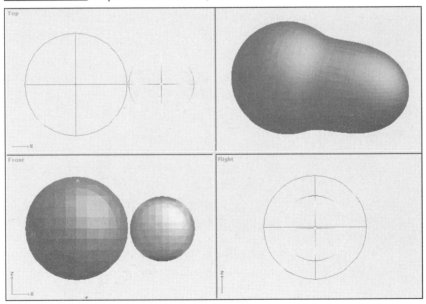

The upper right window shows the blending result of the positive metaball influence. The larger metaball has a smaller threshold, so it's greater in size. The point between the metaballs, where the density distributions meet, is larger than the small metaball because the additive value is lower than the small metaball's threshold. The lower the value, the larger the ball. This is the positive effect of metaballs. There is also a negative effect.

Metaballs can be additive or subtractive, depending on the configuration. A subtractive metaball will push the surface in on an additive metaball. The density value for any point where metaballs interact is calculated by adding up their densities at that point. Since one is positive and the other negative, there will be points where the density will become so low that it will be below the threshold value. This creates the effect of repulsion. The metaball displays a "dent," as if it were trying to repel the other metaball. Figure 4.4 shows the effect of a negative metaball.

You can see that the negative metaball has clearly dented the larger positive metaball. This can be an effective tool for creating cavities in the model, such as sockets for the eyes, or possibly flattening out parts of the model like the soles of a shoe. Take a look at Figure 4.5, which shows a cartoon superhero designed by world famous comic-book artist Robert Kraus.

Here we have a cartoon character made with a combination of metaballs and metashapes. We'll be covering metashapes later in the chapter. For now, let's examine this character. Notice the two metaballs in front of the head. They don't show up in the preview window because they're negative metaballs. They are creating the dents in the front of the head where Space Goon's eyes will be placed. This is a very basic example of negative metaballs. For a more advanced example, let's take a look at his shoes. Notice the flat metashapes under the shoes. These are used to flatten the bottom of the shoe. The sole is primarily made of two metaballs, which are

FIGURE 4.4 *The effect of a negative metaball*

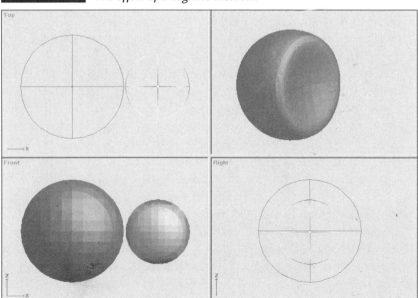

FIGURE 4.5 *Applications for negative metaballs*

round. Since we don't want a round sole, the negative metashapes are used to effectively cut off the bottom of the shoes.

By the way, to give you an idea of how fast you can model with metashapes and metaballs, it took me about 15 minutes to create this character. Although I have some experience with 3D modeling, it really doesn't take that long to model with metaballs. To get a better idea of what you can do with metaballs, take a look at the cartoon dinosaur in Figure 4.6.

This character has about 250 metaballs and took a little under 40 minutes to create. I'm sure you noticed that some of the metaballs in the object are not perfect spheres, such as those in the middle of the body. One thing that makes metaball editing easier is the ability to modify the spherical shape of the metaball. If all you had to work with were balls, you'd have great difficulty creating many organic shapes. To make life easier, metaball editors allow you to stretch, shear, bend, and twist the balls to create a variety of different shapes. Figure 4.7 shows a few of the possibilities.

The metaball in the upper left has been stretched along its Z axis to make it oval. The metaball in the middle has been sheared, and the one in the lower right has been tapered. Although you can't make as many shapes as you can with metashapes, you can certainly do better than a basic sphere.

FIGURE 4.6 *A metaball creature*

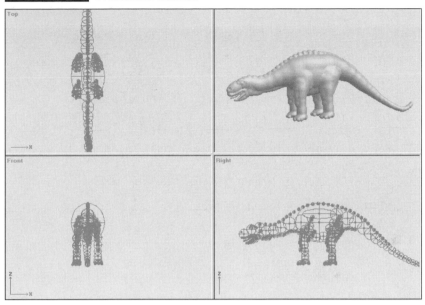

FIGURE 4.7 *Modifying metaballs*

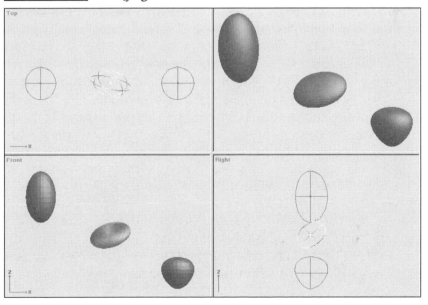

OK, that's about all there is to metaballs. Most of the complexity is in the placement, which we will explore in the metaball walk-through later in the chapter. For now, let's take a look at the pros and cons of metaball modeling to get an idea of where we should use them.

The Pros and Cons of Metaball Modeling

The pros and cons of metaball modeling are nearly the same as those of polygon modeling, since it's actually just another method of polygon modeling. Let's take a look.

Metaball Pros

- **Complex Organics:** The main advantage of metaball modeling is that you can create very complex organic objects without much effort. The blending of metaballs can achieve some highly organic details that are difficult with polygons and nearly impossible with splines and NURBS. Metaball modeling requires the least amount of effort.

- **Rapid Modeling:** Metaballs are one of the fastest modeling methods available. You can very quickly generate highly complex objects without a great deal of effort. Creating the same detail with polygons would take twice as long, and you'd grow old trying to do the same with splines and NURBS.

- **Animation:** One of the best attributes of metaballs is that they are often animatable, meaning you can move the metaballs around to create some very wild organic animation that is completely impossible with polygons, splines, or NURBS. Some of the best uses for Metaball animation would be water effects and liquid metals. Metaballs can easily create the effect of a liquid metal creature such as the T-1000 Liquid Metal Cyborg in the movie *Terminator 2: Judgment Day.*

Metaball Cons

- **Model Visualization:** One of the difficulties with Metaball modeling is trying to determine the placement of the metaballs. Since the metaballs blend together, you need to be creative in the placement. If they are too close, you'll end up with bulges in the mesh. Quite often the metaballs need to be separated by a gap to produce the proper effect as shown in Figure 4.8.

    As you can see, there is a significant gap between the metaballs that create the area around the elbow, yet the skinned mesh looks fine. This

FIGURE 4.8 *Metaball placement*

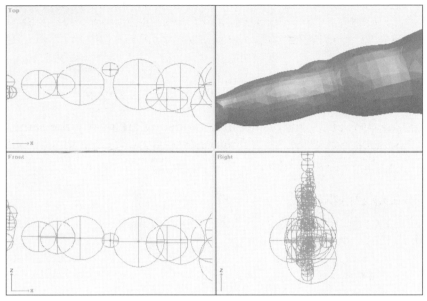

is the problem in visualizing your models with metaballs. You sometimes have to make exaggerated movements, which can be difficult since the tendency is to place the metaballs next to each other.

- **Mesh Quality:** The biggest shortcoming of metaballs is the poor mesh quality. You see, when the skin is created over the metaballs it merely blends the shapes together. It's as if you took two polygon spheres and blended their meshes together. The result is a very disorganized mesh, which often leads to pinching and seams, as shown in Figure 4.9.

   Take a look at the circled areas and you'll see that the mesh is anything but uniform. It's chaotic and full of creases. This is a problem that won't occur with polygons, splines, or NURBS. Of course, these errors can be avoided, but you'll need to output an extremely high-resolution mesh, which is undesirable. A good mesh for a 3D model should be as uniform as possible. Polygons, splines, and NURBS can create very clean meshes, while metaballs tend to be sloppy.

- **Fine Details:** Small details are very difficult with metaballs. The problem lies in the smoothing. Metaballs tend to smooth out the small details. If you try to place little details on the model, you can end up with very rough bumps, since the mesh won't be dense enough for the proper smoothing. Figure 4.10 shows the result of trying to add very small details to a Metaball object.

FIGURE 4.9   *The poor mesh quality of metaballs*

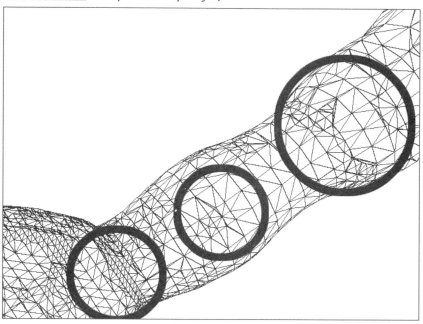

FIGURE 4.10   *The result of adding fine details with metaballs*

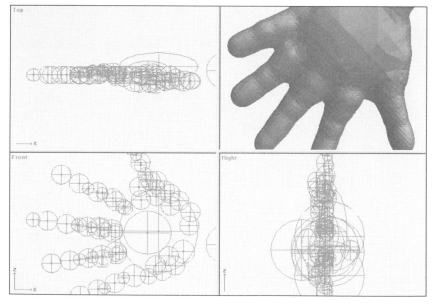

Notice how the fingers tend to blend together. This is because the metaballs are having too much influence over one another. The solution is to use many smaller metaballs or increase the mesh density, but that will just make animation very difficult because your system resources will quickly be depleted by extremely high-resolution models.

• **Lumpy Models:** While it's desirable to add bumps to creatures to simulate muscles, it's not a good idea to have round bumps all over the body. The problem with metaballs is that the models tend to come out looking as if they're made of spheres. Figure 4.11 shows an example of a lumpy mesh created by metaballs.

You can eliminate much of the problem by adding more metaballs between the lumps, but this leads to way too many metaballs in most cases. A detailed metaball model can easily contain more than 1000 metaballs, which makes editing very complicated.

It would appear the pros and cons of metaball modeling are evenly split. There are some very positive effects as well as rather negative ones. This can make it difficult to determine where and when to use metaballs. You might think the cons prevent you from utilizing metaballs, but that's not the case, as you'll soon see.

FIGURE 4.11   *The lumpy look of metaball objects*

Where and When to Use Metaballs

Metaballs are a very powerful and flexible organic modeling technique. This means they're perfect for organic objects and not a good choice at all for linear objects. In fact, you can't achieve a straight line with metaballs.

Let's take a look at some of the places where you should use metaballs and those where you shouldn't.

When to Use Metaballs

- **Detailed Creatures and Characters:** This is absolutely the best place to use metaballs. It makes a somewhat daunting process a great deal easier to deal with. The ability to create flowing curves and details makes metaballs a strong contender for character modeling. Adding details can be as easy as dropping a metaball on the screen.

- **Natural Organics:** Metaballs are great for creating organic natural objects such as trees, terrain, rocks, and water effects. Plants are not necessarily a good idea, since they tend to have an abundance of flat surfaces, which are nearly impossible with metaballs. You'll want to stick to the thicker organics when using metaballs.

- **When Time Is Short:** Metaballs are the fastest organic modeling method, so they're a perfect choice when you're short on time. Quite often you'll be in a rush to create an organic object. Planning an organic model with polygons, splines, or NURBS can often take as long as it would take to create the model with metaballs.

When Not to Use Metaballs

- **Linear Models:** It's impossible to achieve a straight line with metaballs, so you can't use them to create linear models such as furniture, computer equipment, multimedia components, buildings, and city streets. Polygons are the best choice for linear models.

- **Mechanical Organics:** This is an obvious con. Metaballs are a crapshoot when it comes to accuracy. In fact, they are the most inaccurate modeling method. If your project requires precision curves, you'll want to steer clear of metaballs and point yourself in the direction of splines and NURBS.

- **Models that Require Close-ups:** Since metaballs tend to create a chaotic mesh that quite often has errors, you'll want to avoid using them for models that will require close-ups. They're fine if you'll be using standard distant shots, where the objects never occupies the full screen, but if you intend to zoom in close, you'll want to use another modeling method such as splines or NURBS, which have infinite resolution curves.

Well, there you have it: the pros and cons of metaballs. It's obvious that the pros of metaball modeling are significant, but you need to carefully consider the cons when selecting this modeling method. Metaballs can be a real lifesaver or a complete nightmare. It all depends on the project you are undertaking. Be sure to carefully consider your project before selecting the metaball modeling method.

Now that we have a handle on metaballs, we're ready to see it works in the modeling process. We're going to walk through the development of a model using metaballs, step-by-step, so you can see how it's done.

A Metaball Walk-through

The purpose of this section is to illustrate the process of metaball modeling. It's not quite a tutorial, but rather a walk-through. I'll be building a model and explaining briefly how and why the modifications were made so you can see how the process of metaball modeling works.

The modeling method used in this walk-through can be used in such 3D programs as LightWave, trueSpace, 3D Studio Max, Cinema 4D, FORM*Z, Organica, and StrataStudio Pro. The metaball features will vary widely from one program to another, but they all have the basic metaball tools.

OK, let's get started with our walkthrough.

Modeling Chuckie's Arm

Chuckie's arm is a very organic shape. Since he's a baby, he has rather lumpy and pudgy skin, which is perfect for metaball modeling. In fact, metaballs are the perfect choice for creating the lumpy body of a child.

Starting the model is very easy. The arm is started with three metaballs that make the basic shape of the upper and lower arm, as shown in Figure 4.12.

It looks rough now, but it will make more sense after we add the shoulder. To create the shoulder, three metaballs were grouped around the end of the upper arm as shown in Figure 4.13.

Why didn't I just use one metaball for the shoulder? Well, it needed to have more bulk on the back of the shoulder. Using two metaballs for the back of the shoulder makes it possible to control the shape more easily, and one metaball in the front created the portion of the shoulder that would connect to the pectoral muscle. One thing to note is that all of the

FIGURE 4.12   *The start of the arm*

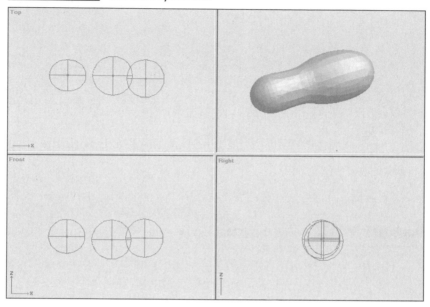

FIGURE 4.13   *Creating the shoulder*

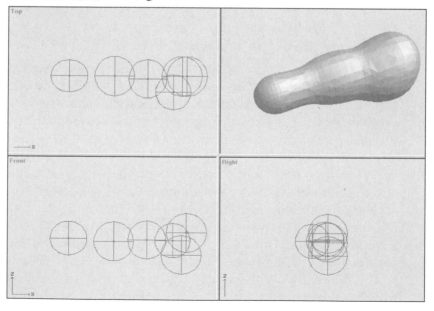

metaballs used in this walk-through have the default setting. No changes were made to the strength of the metaballs. Quite often you can get great results by simply moving and sizing the balls rather than trying to find the settings that work.

OK, now it's time to give Chuckie an elbow by placing a small metaball between the upper and lower arm as shown in Figure 4.14.

The last step in creating the arm is to add some vertical height to the forearm and a bulge to the bicep with squashed metaballs like the ones in Figure 4.15.

These metaballs were flattened on the X axis with the shaping tool. If they were round, the forearm would look as if it had a ball in the middle of it, and the biceps would be too tall vertically. You'll find that the occasional squashing of a metaball really helps to create the proper shapes.

Now that we have the completed arm, we're ready to tackle the hand. The hand is tricky because it requires a large number of metaballs to create the fingers, knuckles, and pads on the palm. The hand is started with two squashed metaballs as shown in Figure 4.16.

The large metaball is the hand and the small one forms the center of the palm. The fingers are created with rows of metaballs that are places on the front side of the palm as shown in Figure 4.17.

FIGURE 4.14 *Creating the elbow*

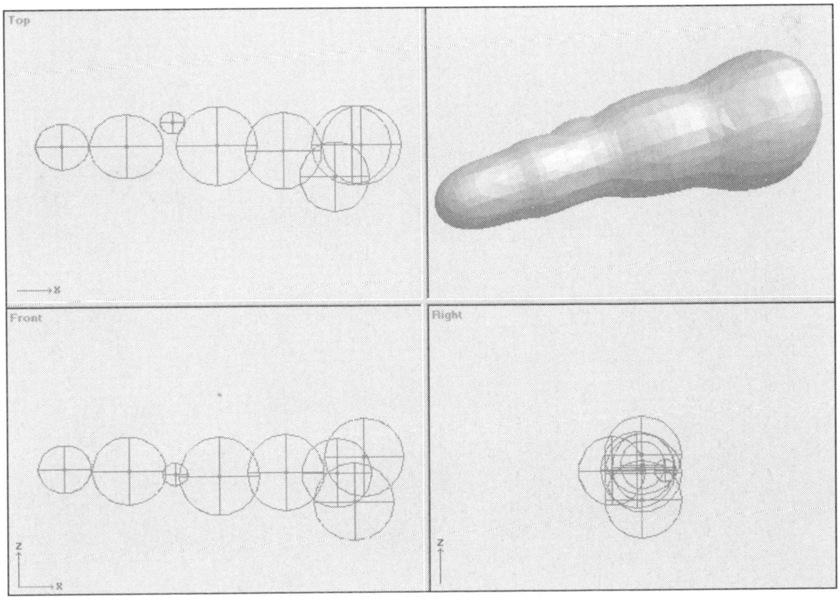

FIGURE 4.15   *Creating vertical depth*

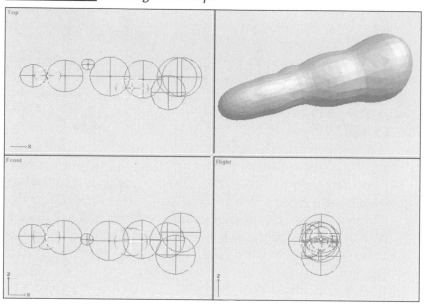

FIGURE 4.16   *The foundation for the hand*

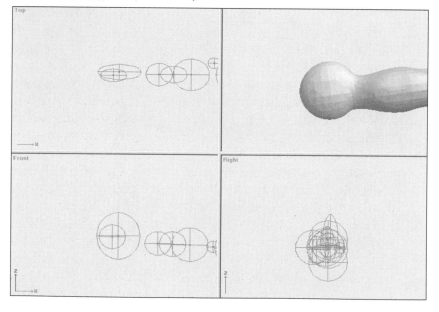

FIGURE 4.17 *Creating the fingers*

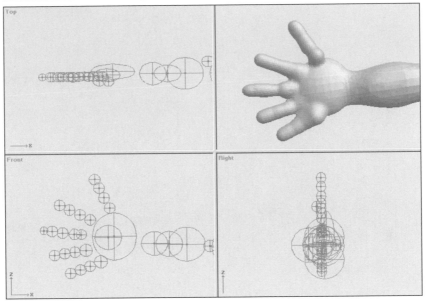

Some of the metaballs are out of alignment and slightly different in size to make the fingers blend properly. This is where the tweaking begins. Your metaballs won't always appear organized. Sometimes you need to move them around to create the proper shape. Now that the fingers have been started, it's time for the palm to be completed. The first step it to group a bunch of metaballs around the left and right sides of the palm as shown in Figure 4.18.

The groups of metaballs form the pad for the thumb and the pinkie. Once again, there is plenty of tweaking involved. There must be enough metaballs to create a smooth surface with a flowing line around the outside of the hand. Once the pads are complete, three small metaballs are added to create the pads at the base of the fingers, like the ones in Figure 4.19.

With the palm completed, the fingers can now be rounded. I'm sure you noticed the fingers were a bit weird. Well, you'll want to wait on completing the fingers until the palm is finished. This is because the metaball of the palm can affect the fingers. It's better to complete the palm and then apply the finishing touches to the fingers. Figure 4.20 shows the completed fingers.

Several small metaballs were added to balance the shape of the fingers. The hand is looking great from the front, but the back is lacking detail. The

FIGURE 4.18   *Creating the palm*

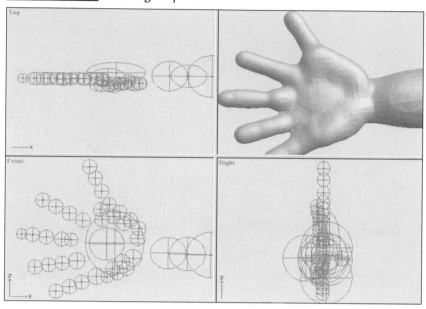

FIGURE 4.19   *Completing the palm*

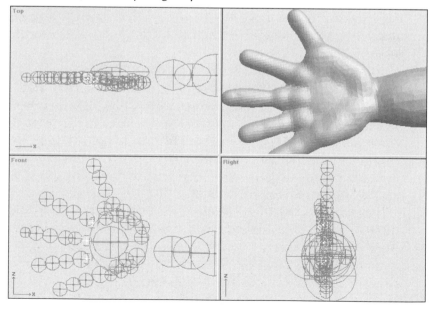

FIGURE 4.20   *The completed fingers*

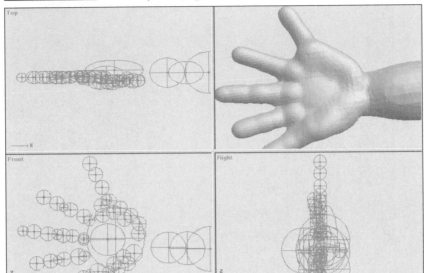

back of the hand needs knuckles and some blending between the back of the fingers and the hand. Figure 4.21 shows the metaballs that were applied to the back of the hand to complete it.

You'll notice that several small metaballs were added to create the knuckles on the back of the fingers and the hand. There were also a few more added to the area opposite the pads on the front to shape the pads from the back. This completes the hand, so now it's time for a look at the whole thing. Figure 4.22 shows the completed arm.

Well, that looks just about perfect for Chuckie's arm. It's a short, chubby child's arm that only took a few minutes to create. As you can see, metaball modeling is a great choice for creating highly organic shapes like the human body. There are those who would argue that splines or NURBS can do organics better, but that's just not true. Splines and NURBS have their shortcomings. They do have numerous strengths, but complex character modeling isn't one of them.

Metaball modeling does require a lot of tweaking, but it's far easier to do than in any other modeling method. It can also be quite enjoyable. You have the opportunity to quickly see the model take shape. Speaking of quickly taking shape, there is one modeling method that actually outshines metaballs for speed—metashapes. Let's take a look at metashapes and see how they differ from metaballs.

FIGURE 4.21   *The back of the hand*

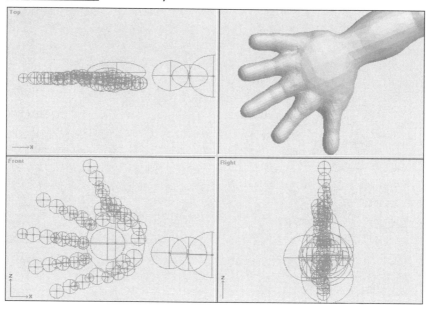

FIGURE 4.22   *The completed arm*

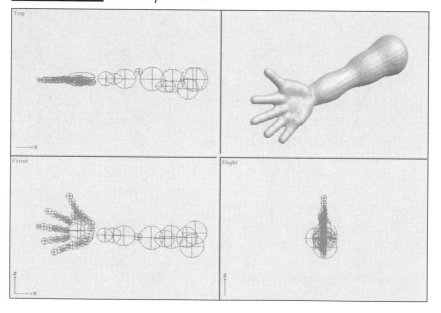

Metashapes

Metashapes are basically the same as metaballs except they have more options. With metaballs you can only use spheres. Yes, you can perform some minor modifications on them, but your shapes are very limited. With metashapes you are provided with an abundance of shapes, which open the door to more possibilities.

Remember our discussion on metaballs and our heating example? Well, the same applies for metashapes. They are also isosurfaces. The difference is that they can be many different shapes, which means their density distribution isn't even throughout 3D space. As with the metaball, the density distribution takes on the shape of the object. For example, the threshold of a cylindrical metaball will be in the form of a cylinder, and the threshold of a cube is in the form of a cube.

There are many possible metashapes. It all depends on the program you are using. Organica from Impulse, inc. has the largest collection of metashapes—25—which are shown in Figures 4.23 and 4.24.

As you can see, there are plenty of metashapes to play with. There isn't much you can't do with these metashapes. They have the advantage of

FIGURE 4.23 *Metashape examples*

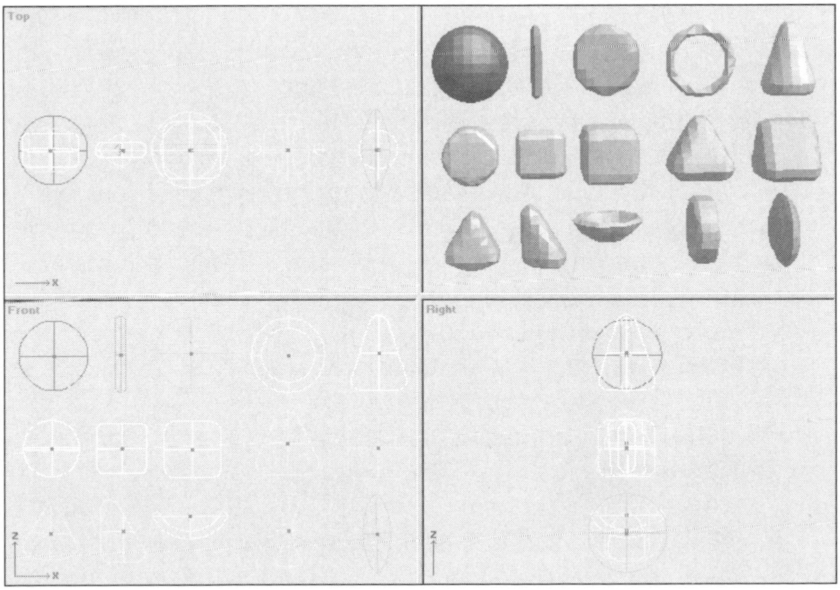

FIGURE 4.24 *More metashape examples*

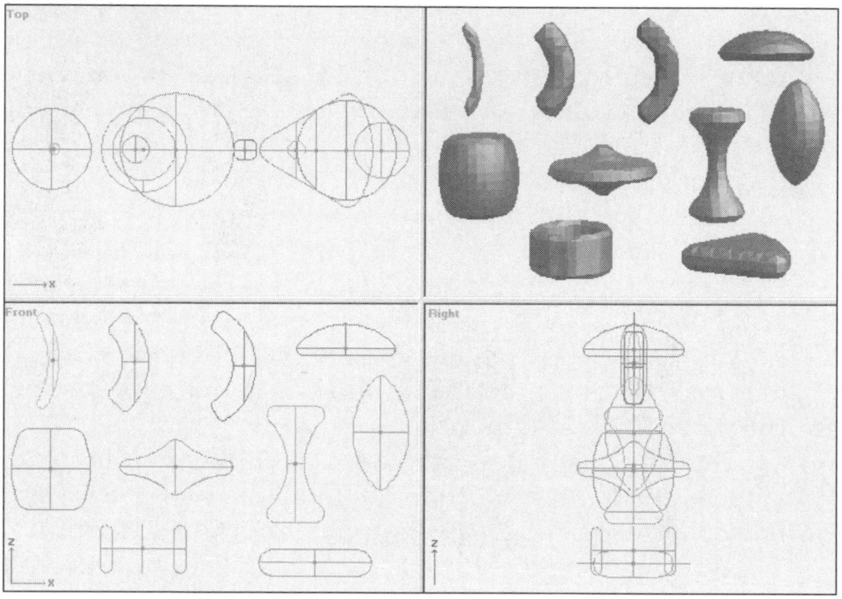

saving you time because it could take dozens of metaballs to create one simple metashape. In fact, let's take a look at a few metashapes and their metaball equivalents. In Figure 4.25 you see a metashape bent cylinder and the metaball equivalent.

As you can see, it takes six metaballs to create the single metashape, and it's not as clean. The metaball shape has the trademark bubble appearance while the metashape is perfectly smooth. Now let's examine a more complicated metashape shown in Figure 4.26.

Here we have bowl metashape and the metaball counterpart. While the shape is easily created with metaballs, it's rather useless because the negative metaball creating the depression will affect the metaballs around it, pushing them out of shape. The metashape will not affect the surrounding metashapes in a negative manner. This particular metashape is a real time-saver because it allows you to create very cool details such as eyelids, which would be very difficult with metaballs.

OK, one last comparison and we'll be on our way. Take a look at the torus in Figure 4.27.

This is a perfect example of why metashapes are so much better than metaballs. It takes 28 metaballs to create the same shape, and it's not as clean. If you were to create an insect body with these metaball tori, you'd have 28 times more objects in your model, making it virtually impossible

FIGURE 4.25 *A metashape/metaball comparison*

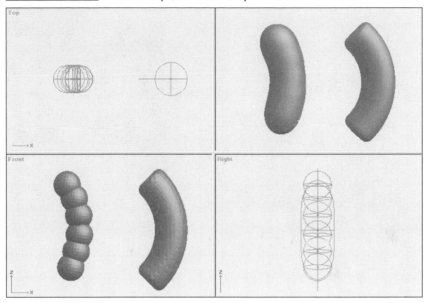

FIGURE 4.26 *Another metashape/metaball comparison*

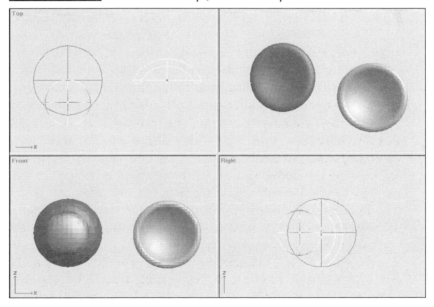

FIGURE 4.27   *A metashape torus*

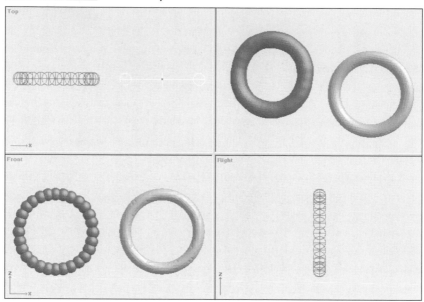

to edit and opening the way for countless errors. And, of course, don't forget the lumpy mesh you'd have.

It's easy to see that metashapes are significantly more flexible and functional than metaballs. Of course, we've only seen metashapes in their singular form. How about a model? Well, take a look at Figure 4.28.

This is a metashape model of a human torso. It has an amazing amount of surface detail, yet it only took a few hours to create. Notice the variety of metashapes in the model. It's this diversity that makes rapid modeling possible. Creating the same object with metaballs would take more than ten times as long and it probably wouldn't be nearly as smooth. Let's take a close look at the model so we can see the effect of the metashapes. Figures 4.29 and 4.30 show a close-up of the torso.

Figure 4.29 shows the metashapes that make up the torso, and Figure 4.30 shows the resulting skinned mesh. Take a few moments to examine the two images and get a feel for how the metashapes really improve the metaball modeling process. Notice that there aren't that many shapes, yet the skinned mesh is flowing and free of the lumpy look you get with metaballs. Metashapes definitely have their advantages.

Before we move on the pros and cons of metashape modeling, let's take a moment to look at one last metashape object. Figure 4.31 shows an insect creature I modeled based on work done by another Organica artist.

FIGURE 4.28   *A metashape model*

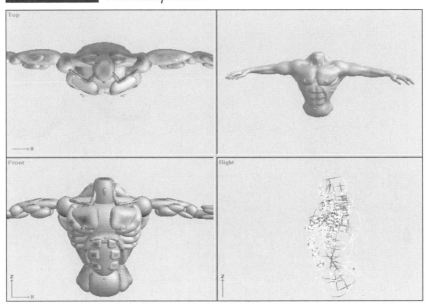

FIGURE 4.29   *The metashape torso*

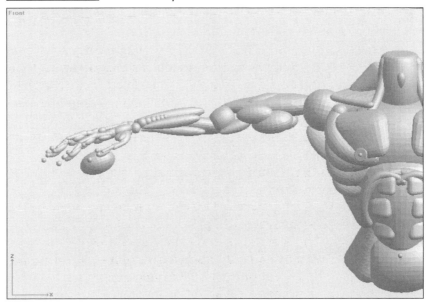

FIGURE 4.30 *The skinned metashape torso*

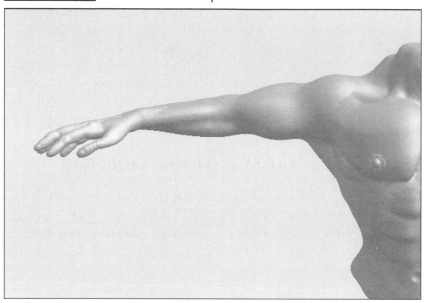

FIGURE 4.31 *A very complex metashape creature*

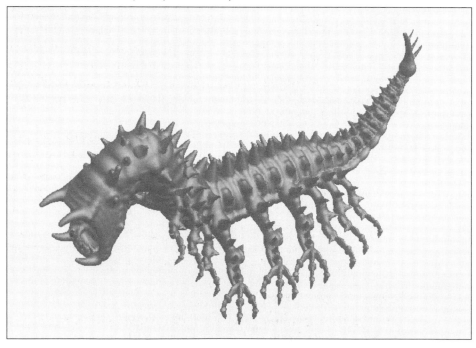

This creature took a little over two hours to complete, starting from scratch. That's not bad for a creature that would blow the minds of Hollywood effects professionals. There is an abundance of organic detail on this creature, yet it's made entirely of simple objects that have been rotated, sized, twisted, and tapered. There is just no end to the amazing objects you can create with metashapes. Of course, there are some things to consider before you dive into metashape modeling. Let's take a look at the pros and cons of metashapes.

The Pros and Cons of Metashape Modeling

The pros and cons of metashape modeling are nearly the same as those of metaballs, since metashapes are actually just variations of metaballs. Of course, the wide variety of shapes gives you greater possibilities than metaballs, but this method of modeling does come with a few problems. Let's take a look.

Metashape Pros

- **Complex Organics:** The main advantage of metashape modeling is that you can create very complex organic objects without much effort. Metashapes can be better than metaballs because you have a wider variety of shapes to deal with. Creating a humanoid with metaballs would take thousands of metaballs, but it would only take a few hundred metashapes. This can be quite a positive asset when you consider the massive difference in resources needed for thousands of metaballs and only a couple of hundred metashapes. You could spend quite a while waiting for that many metaballs to refresh on your screen after each editing change.

- **Rapid Modeling:** Metashapes are the fastest modeling method available. You can very quickly generate highly complex objects without a great deal of effort. Creating the same detail with metaballs would take five times as long, and polygons would take ten times longer. Of course, it would be impossible with splines and NURBS.

- **Animation:** Just as with metaballs, animation with metashapes is incredible—even more so than with metaballs, because you have fewer objects to animate and a wider variety of shapes.

Metashape Cons

- **Model Visualization:** One of the difficulties with metashape modeling is trying to determine the placement of the metashapes. It can be even more confusing than metaballs because you have a wider variety of possibilities with the shapes. As with metaballs, you often need to place the metashapes apart from one another to produce the proper effect. It takes a bit of experimentation to find just the right placement, size, and rotation of the metashapes, not to mention bend, twist, and taper. It can be a bit challenging until you get the feel for it. Even then you'll still need to experiment.

- **Mesh Quality:** This is a bigger problem with metashapes than with metaballs, because you have more shapes, which dramatically increases the chance of errors and pinches in the mesh. It can take some tweaking to reduce the errors.

- **Fine Details:** Small details are easier with metashapes than with metaballs, but they are still a challenge. It's much easier to create small details with polygons. In fact, it's often a good idea to create the basic mesh with metaballs and add the details with basic polygon editing and tools such as Sweep and Smooth Shift.

You can see that the pros and cons of metashapes are more extreme than those of metaballs. Metashapes are typically a better choice than metaballs, but not always a better choice than polygons or splines. It's all a matter of knowing the strengths and weaknesses of each modeling method.

OK, now let's take a look at where and when to use metashapes.

Where and When to Use Metashapes

Metashapes are a very flexible organic modeling technique. This means they're perfect for organic objects, but fall short of being desirable for linear objects. Let's take a look at where and when you should use metashapes.

When to Use Metashapes

- **Detailed Creatures and Characters:** This is the perfect place to use metashapes. You'd be surprised at how quickly your creature will take shape.

- **Natural Organics:** Need to create a dead tree with lots of branches? Metashapes is the modeling method of choice. In fact, it's actually perfect, since it will likely give you polygon errors in the mesh, which happen to work well with a tree. You can quickly model just about any natural organic object with metashapes. Yes, leaves are possible, but you'll want to avoid objects that are relatively flat since that is not a strong point in metashape modeling.

- **When Time is Short:** Under the gun to finish a model? Well, metashapes are the answer. Nothing is faster. Metaballs are close, but they still don't match the speed of metashapes. It's very simple to get a detailed model going with metashapes. Well, it is after you've had a chance to get used to them.

When Not to Use Metashapes

- **Linear Models:** It's very tough to achieve a straight line with metashapes. They are meant for more organic shapes. They are perfect for objects that require plenty of flowing lines, but a bad choice for objects such as furniture, high-tech equipment, or anything else with mainly flat surfaces. It's best to use polygon modeling for flat surfaces.

- **Mechanical Organics:** When it comes to precision, metashapes are your last choice. Actually, metaballs are your last choice, but metashapes are right behind them. There is no accuracy to metashapes. It's pure chaos, which is great for creature modeling but lousy for mechanical modeling.

- **Models That Require Close-ups:** Just like metaballs, metashapes are not the choice for models that require close-ups. You'll want to use a spline or NURBS modeling method since those have infinite curve resolution. Metashapes are best used on models that won't be viewed closely.

You can see how metashapes have several advantages over metaballs, but still have the same shortcomings. They are consistently a better choice than metaballs, but not as readily available. Metashapes are only available in a few 3D programs while metaballs are in nearly every one of them, including the popular freeware programs.

Now let's take a look at how the metashape modeling process differs from that for metaballs.

A Metashape Walk-through

This section illustrates the process of metashape modeling, not as a tutorial, but rather as a walk-through. I'll be building a model and explaining briefly how and why the modifications were made so you can see how the process of metaball modeling works.

The modeling method used in this walk-through can be used in such 3D programs as Organica and 3D Studio Max. Metashapes haven't been widely accepted in the 3D industry because they are, quite frankly, a pain in the butt to program. It's unfortunate, because they are truly an exciting modeling method. In the future we will likely see more programs adopting metashapes and also a marked improvement in the mesh quality.

Without further ado, let's take a look at how these wacky metashapes work.

Modeling Chuckie's Leg

Chuckie's leg is a highly organic shape just like the arm, making metashapes a great method for modeling it. The leg has a bit more detail than the arm, but it requires no more work because metashapes are more efficient.

The leg is started the same way as the arm. Basic shapes are laid down to create the general form of the leg, as shown in Figure 4.32.

There are four metashapes that form the foundation of the leg. There are two squashed spheres for the thigh, a squashed sphere for the calf, and a cylinder for the lower leg. This is the base that will be built upon to create the detailed leg. The next step in the process is to fill out the knee and the hip joint, which are shown in Figure 4.33.

A few spheres were added to fill in the knee area and add a rounded joint to the top of the thigh. Even though we're exploring metashapes, there are many uses for the classic metaball. Now it's time to add some depth and flesh to the knee area. A young child has flabby skin, so the leg needs to have some extra skin tissue over the bony areas. Figure 4.34 shows the metashapes that were used to wrinkle the knee.

FIGURE 4.32   *The start of the leg*

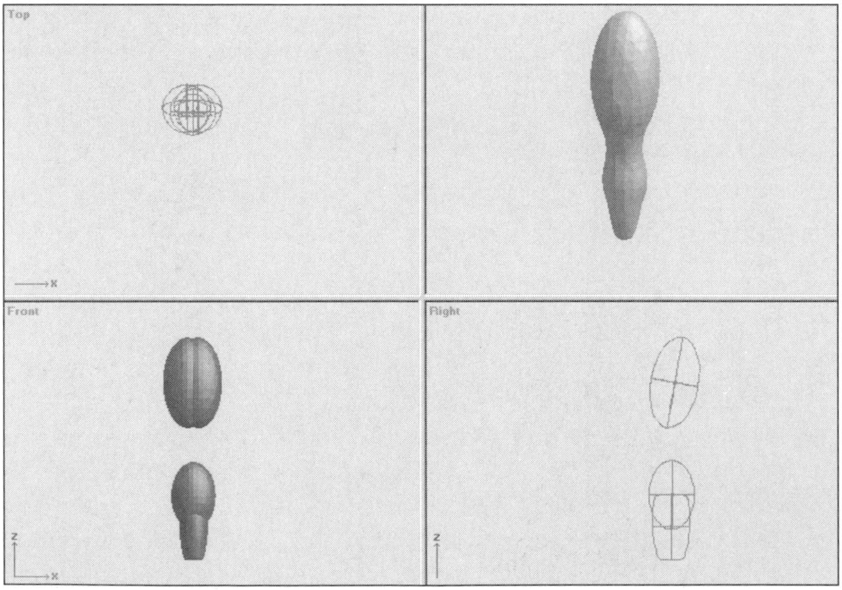

FIGURE 4.33 *The knee and hip*

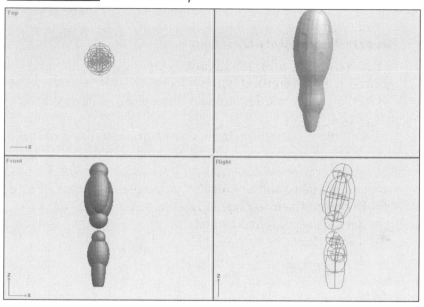

FIGURE 4.34 *The knee wrinkles*

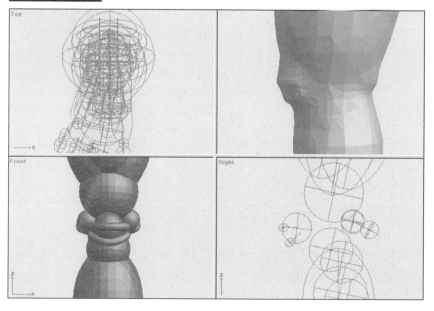

This is a case where metashapes come in handy. The knee was first started by adding a metaball. Then curved tube metashapes were added to create two folds of skin. You can see how the metashapes have greatly expedited the process of adding details. The back of the knee was also modified with a curved tube. A metaball was added to either end of the tube to facilitate blending into the back of the leg. To finish off the knee, depressions need to be added to either side of the knee. This is easily accomplished by adding a negative metaball on either side of the knee as shown in Figure 4.35.

The negative metaballs are moved away from the knee so the depressions aren't exaggerated. You'll find that negative metaballs have a severe reaction on the mesh, so you need to move them away from the other metaballs to soften the effect.

Now it's time to move down the leg and complete the ankle. The ankle is created with another cylinder metaball and one that hasn't been used yet, a tube. Figure 4.36 shows how the ankle was created.

Notice how the tube creates a very nice tendon on the back of the leg. That's the beauty of metashapes. They come in such a wide variety that you can solve most modeling problems with a single shape.

FIGURE 4.35 *Creating the knee depressions*

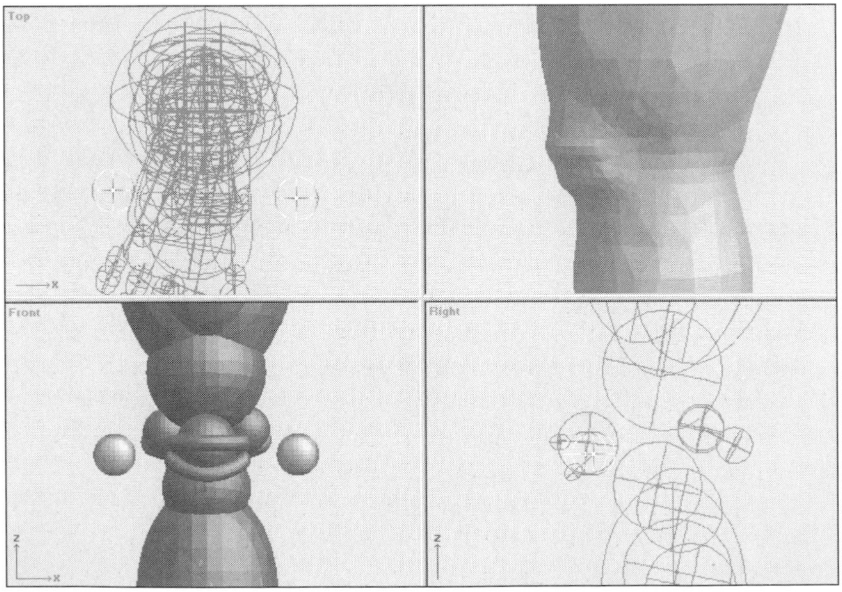

FIGURE 4.36 *Creating the ankle*

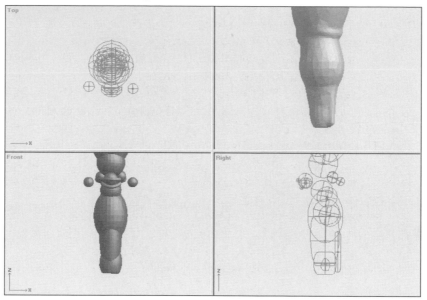

OK, that does it for the basic leg shape. Now it's time to finish this leg up with a nice, detailed foot. Objects such as feet and hands can be very challenging, because choosing the wrong shapes can cost you a lot of time trying to create the right details. Proper shape selection is paramount. Of course, determining the proper shapes takes a bit of experimenting.

The foot was started by placing several squashed spheres at the front of the ankle as shown in Figure 4.37.

The upper sphere is a unique detail. It will form a thick fold of skin just above the foot. The other spheres are placed to create the contours on either side of the ankle. Once the base for the foot is created, the basic foot bones are added. This is a particular instance where proper shape selection is important. There are many shapes that could have been used, but a squashed and bent tube was the best because it creates the flowing lines of the foot bones as shown in Figure 4.38.

To create the other bones in the foot, this shape is cloned three times, then scaled and placed as shown in Figure 4.39.

Now the foot is starting to take shape. It's almost ready for the toes, but before those are added the ball at the end of the foot needs to be created. It basically serves as the socket for the toes as shown in Figure 4.40.

FIGURE 4.37   *Starting the foot*

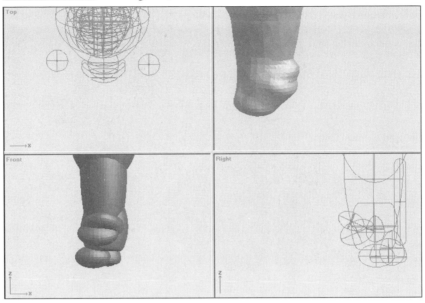

FIGURE 4.38   *The foot bone metashape*

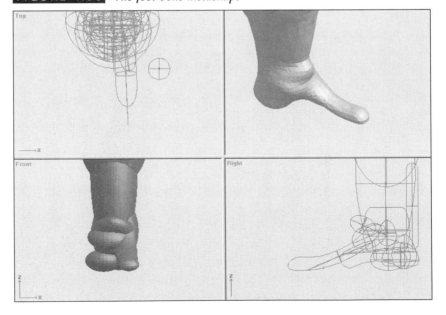

FIGURE 4.39   *The completed foot bones*

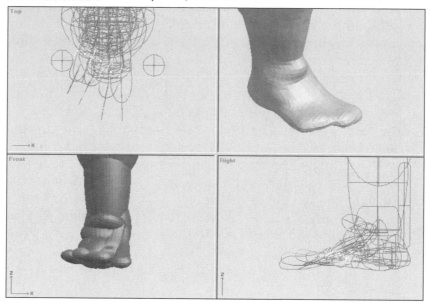

FIGURE 4.40   *The ball of the foot*

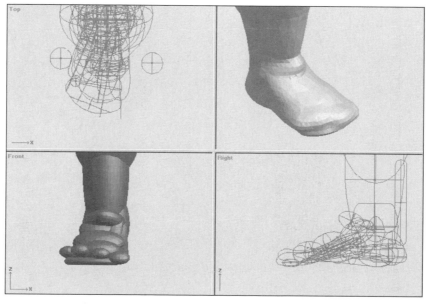

The foot now looks as if Chuckie is wearing a sock. We're just about done with the foot now. The only thing left are the toes. They are actually quite simple to create. First a metaball is added to the end of the foot to create the joint where the toe attaches. Then a squashed tube is added to create the first bone. Now the tube is copied and scaled to create the toe as shown in Figure 4.41.

It looks pretty convincing, doesn't it? Well, it's not that difficult to create awesome details if you just take the time to experiment. Completing the foot is a snap. The three metashapes that make up the big toe are copied and scaled to create the other four toes as shown in Figure 4.42.

Now the foot is complete, and it looks great. There is one thing to be aware of, though. When you create small details that are close together like the toes, you can run into blending problems between them. To eliminate the problem you'll need to tweak the objects, scaling and moving them until the problem is resolved. It can be frustrating, but it doesn't take too much effort.

Well, we now have a completed leg for Chuckie, which is shown in Figure 4.43.

As you can see, metashapes were instrumental in creating a highly detailed and realistic child's leg. You'd be surprised at how quickly you'll

FIGURE 4.41   *The completed big toe*

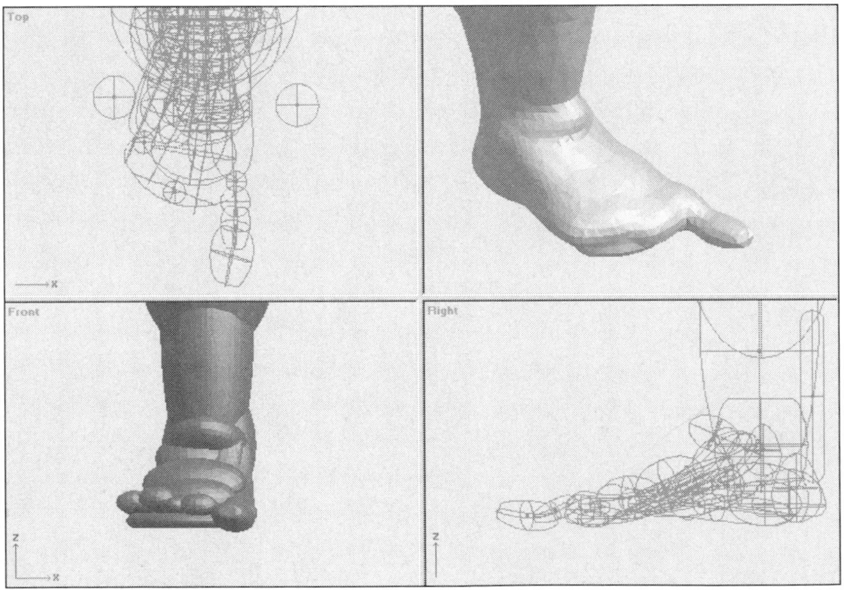

FIGURE 4.42   *Completing the toes*

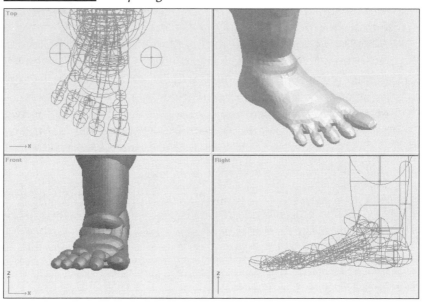

FIGURE 4.43   *The completed metashape leg*

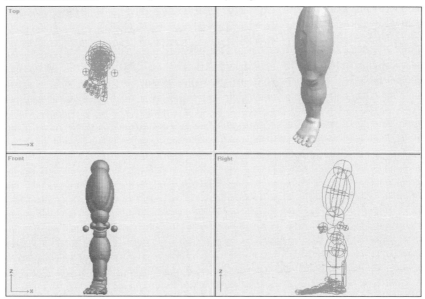

create objects with metashapes. Of course, there is a price to be paid. If you look close you'll see some polygon errors in the leg. This is the by-product of metashape modeling.

This problem can be resolved by increasing the resolution of the mesh before you save the object. It can also be corrected in another modeling program by merging the points with an absolute value. The exact value depends on the model but doesn't take too much effort to determine. Merging the points with an absolute value will eliminate the points that are close together. It's these points that are causing the majority of the pinching in the mesh. It's a quick fix that works very well.

Wrap-up

It's now clear that metaballs and metashapes are a unique and productive modeling method, not to mention a lot of fun. It's a blast to just start dropping shapes on the screen and see what unfolds. I admit that it's my personal favorite when it comes to killing time. I've created some rather strange objects as the result of playing around with metaballs and meta-shapes.

Well, we're done with all of the popular polygon-related modeling methods. You can see that there are a number of ways to model with polygons. This is because they are the oldest modeling method. Developers have been working for thirteen years to perfect the polygon modeling process, and they're just about there. There are probably a few more innovations coming in the near future, but you can be assured that anything you imagine can be created with the current polygon modeling tools.

Speaking of new developments, it's now time to take a look at a recent development in the 3D modeling world—splines and NURBS.

CHAPTER 5

Splines, Patches, and NURBS

In this chapter we'll be taking a look at one of the newer modeling methods—splines. There are some similarities between splines and polygons, and without a doubt, some major differences. We'll explore these issues as we progress in our discussion.

3D developers are constantly searching for the next modeling wonder tool. This search has led many of them to the development of splines and NURBS, both of which are very powerful modeling techniques with their pros and cons.

We're going to be taking a look at each of these modeling methods in detail so you can make an informed decision about them. We'll start by taking a look at splines.

Splines

What is a spline? Simply put, a spline is a curve, but a little more complex. To get a better grip on what this difference is, let's take a very brief look at spline history.

In the days before computers, drafting designs for airplanes or ships had to be done by hand using tools you're probably already familiar with: compasses, straightedges, protractors, and T-squares. With these tools the draftsman could accurately describe any line or curve. If it wasn't possible to describe the necessary curves with these tools, he could always eyeball it with sufficient accuracy. There were, however, times when life-size templates had to be drawn to assist in the building of ships and planes. What could he do then? Imagine trying to accurately draw a curve 30 feet long just by eyeballing it.

The solution was quite creative. The draftsmen would bend flexible strips of metal or wood into the shape of the curve, and hold them in place with heavy pins called "ducks." Around these ducks the strips, called splines, would reach a point of minimal strain, thus flowing very smoothly. The shape of the curve would vary depending on the placement of the ducks. Computer splines are very much the same. Basically, a spline is a curve running through a set of points.

The use of splines in design has become much more common since they were described mathematically. If you haven't been designing Concordes or Stealth bombers on your PC, one place you may have encountered splines is in a vector graphics program such as Adobe Illustrator or a bitmap program such as Adobe Photoshop, which use splines to create paths. These programs use a specific type of spline called a Bezier spline, with handles you can use to adjust its curvature. Bezier splines are the most common spline in the 3D modeling world. Figure 5.1 illustrates the elements of a spline.

As you can see, it's not overly complex. The representation of a spline you see on your screen is actually like a simple interface for the curves you create, consisting of several major tools:

(A) Control Points (or Anchor Points, or Control Vertices): These are the points you lay down to create the curves. They are used to control their general form and position. They are the shipbuilder's "ducks."

(B) Handle (or Tangent) Points: The handle has two functions. First, rotating the handle alters the curvature of the spline as it passes through the control point. In addition, the handle can be pulled in and out adjusts the *weight* of the control point, or its *influence* over the curve. The greater the influence, the more the curve is attracted to that control point.

(C) Linear Spline: This is actually a spline rather than a tool. It's a spline with zero curvature, used for constructing hard edges in models.

A great deal of research has gone into finding better methods of creating splines. Thus, there are a great number of spline types. However, the names are far less important than an individual program's implementation

FIGURE 5.1 *A common spline*

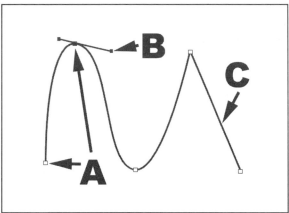

of splines. Their actual use is almost the same from one program to the next, with the exception of NURBS, which we'll discuss later in the chapter.

In this book we're only going to focus on basic splines and NURBS. Ultimately, aside from any technical discussion of the different types of splines, you will develop an intuitive feel for the particular spline technology you are using, which is what matters most.

OK, so we know what a spline looks like and something about how it works—but how do we build models using splines? Let's take a look.

Building Models with Splines

You build a spline model by creating a spline mesh, also called a cage. The process is known as spline-patching, which means creating contour splines and connecting them into patches that can be rendered. Figure 5.2 shows an example of a spline cage.

Here we have a spline cage for a human nose. Let's take a look at the specific elements of this spline cage.

(A) Contour Splines: These are the curves that make up the model. The curves themselves don't actually render. To render the object you need to create a surface known as a patch.

(B) A Patch: This is the actual surface that is rendered. A patch is defined by four intersecting splines.

Patches are actually defined by crisscrossing contour splines. They look similar to a polygon mesh, but there are distinct differences. Figure 5.3 shows a polygon-mesh version of the same nose.

FIGURE 5.2 *A spline cage*

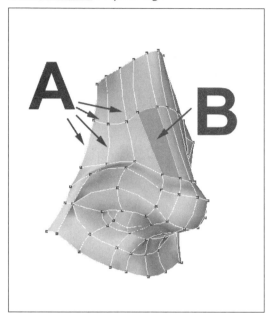

FIGURE 5.3 *A polygon mesh*

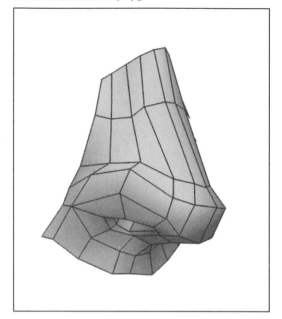

Notice that the polygon mesh doesn't look extremely different from the spline cage. The only noticeable difference is that each patch (the analogue of a *polygon*) has curved edges instead of the straight edges on the polygon mesh.

Usually a spline cage is converted into polygons before rendering, since rendering engines can only render polygons. This process is called *tessellation*. In some packages tessellation is handled automatically at render time. In others, you convert the spline cage to polygons by hand. Figure 5.4 shows a spline cage and its tessellation.

The tessellated version obviously has a far greater number of lines running through it. In fact, the polygons are so dense that it's actually black in some places! Typically you can control the density of polygons when you tessellate a spline object. The polygon nose in Figure 5.3 was tessellated at one polygon per patch, which is why it looks so much like the spline object.

OK, now that we have some idea of what splines are and how they are used, let's take a look at *why* we might want to use them—in other words, their pros and cons.

FIGURE 5.4   *A spline cage and its tessellation*

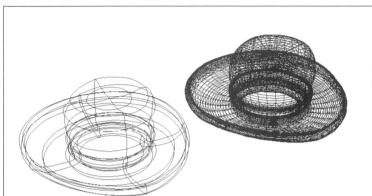

The Pros and Cons of Using Splines

Splines can be a very productive modeling tool, but you need to know exactly where and when to use them. The last thing you want to do is start modeling something that can be created faster and better with another modeling tool. Let's take a look at spline pros and cons.

Spline Pros

- **Infinite Resolution:** One of the advantages a spline model has over a polygon model is that a curved edge has infinite resolution, whereas in a polygonal model it does not. This means you can move your camera in as close to a curved surface edge as you like, and you will still see a smooth curve as shown in Figure 5.5.

  On the other hand, do the same with a curved edge constructed out of polygons, and you'll soon see that it is made up of straight edges as seen in Figure 5.6.

  What does this mean for the modeler? Well, it depends. If you're modeling precise objects that will be reproduced in the real world, such as bicycle seats or automobiles, it means a great deal. You need your edges to have infinite resolution, not facets. Otherwise the machined part will be too rough on the edges.

- **Curves:** Generating accurate and easily editable curves is a major benefit of modeling with splines. Figure 5.7 shows a spline curve that has

FIGURE 5.5   *A spline-patch sphere shows no faceting*

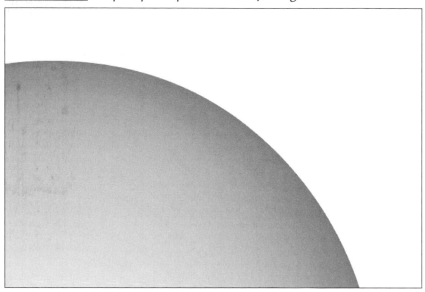

FIGURE 5.6   *A polygonal sphere shows straight edges*

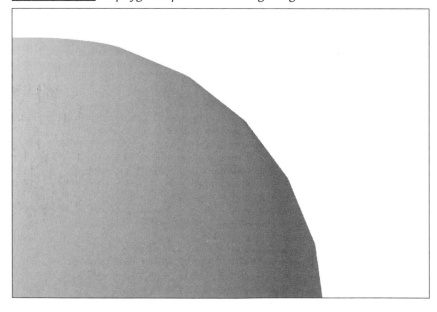

FIGURE 5.7 *A spline curve and a polygon-edge curve*

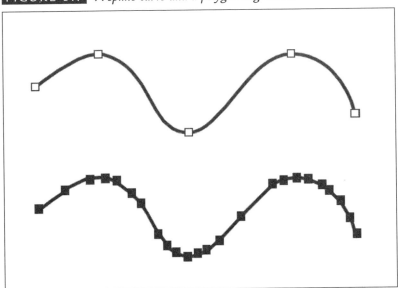

five control points (top), and a similar curve constructed out of polygon edges containing twenty-four points (bottom).

Which will be more accurate and easier to edit? Well, the spline version can be manipulated very easily, while maintaining smooth curvature. The polygon model is far more difficult to manipulate, since you need to manually tweak each point in an effort to create a smooth curve.

Spline Cons

- **Minute Detail:** A major problem with spline modeling is the difficulty of modeling details such as bumps, divots, detail branching, and small wrinkles—in other words, anything that juts out or sinks into the smooth surface of the patches. Figure 5.8 shows a moderate detail spline model, and Figure 5.9 shows a polygon equivalent.

  This old guy is named Grumps. Notice that the polygon model in Figure 5.9 has a great deal more detail. This detail only took a few minutes to create. Trying to do the same thing with splines will make you old and ornery like Grumps.

- **Closed Splines in Regular Patches:** Complex features such as holes or branches cause problems because we need to place a closed spline amidst the regular grid of patches. Figure 5.10 illustrates this problem.

FIGURE 5.8   *A spline model showing moderate detail*

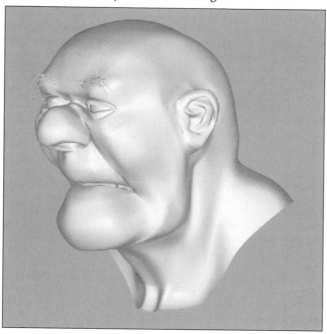

FIGURE 5.9   *A polygonal model showing great detail*

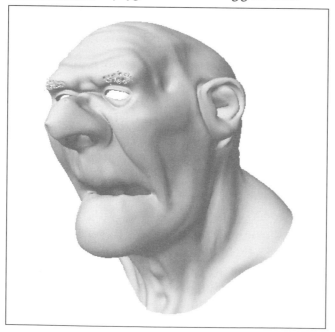

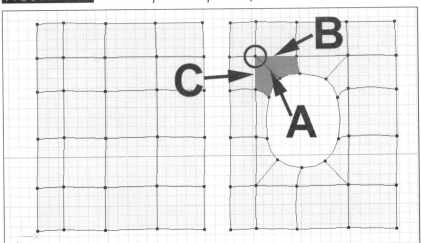

FIGURE 5.10   *A closed spline in a spline surface*

On the left we see the regular grid. The splines flow from top to bottom and left to right without stopping anywhere (except at the outer edges, of course). On the right we have a closed spline placed among a grid of rectangular patches. Curve A is continuous with neither curve B nor curve C; it simply stops at their intersection. Because of this, the software has no way to know how to blend the two patches that are partly defined by spline A (darkened in the figure) into those adjacent to it, creating the artifacts shown in Figure 5.11.

This is definitely an unsightly error that is simply unacceptable if we want to create smooth models.

- **Subdivision:** If your spline surface has creases and artifacts such as those you see in Figure 5.11, you have no choice but to fix it through directly manipulating the splines. If there is no way to solve the crease, you either have to find a way to hide it or give up. On the other hand, with polygons you can perform subdivision, which removes the creases and the associated artifacts.

One common misconception is that polygon models are more difficult to manage than spline models because they have more visible data. Well, this just isn't true. When working with polygons you edit a low-resolution mesh, and just before animation you subdivide it to smooth the mesh. The polygon mesh you edit is virtually identical to the spline mesh and refreshes much more quickly because you don't have to wait for the curves to be computed.

FIGURE 5.11   *Rendering artifacts*

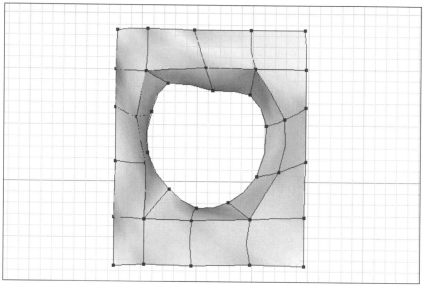

OK, those are the pros and cons of spline modeling. To get a better idea of how these affect your modeling efforts, let's take a look at where and when splines should be used.

Where and When to Use Splines

You can see that splines do have some benefits over polygons in modeling, but have their limitations as well. Let's take a look at exactly where you should use splines.

When to Use Splines

- **Exacting Curves:** When you need exacting curves to describe a physical surface, such as in the automobile model you see in Figure 5.12, splines are a good choice.

    This doesn't necessarily mean that splines are only to be utilized when the product is going to be recreated in the real world. If you were building objects for a commercial or even a feature film, exacting curves would be unnecessary—but the ease of editing them does make them desirable.

- **Prototyping Low-Detail Models:** Splines are a good choice when you don't need a great deal of detail in the model or when you wish to rapidly prototype an object with many organic curves. Figure 5.13 shows an example of a low-detail model created quickly with splines.

FIGURE 5.12 *A good use for splines*

FIGURE 5.13 *Two bottles requiring organic curves but minimal surface detail*

The curves of this bottle are very organic and flowing, but the object itself doesn't have many minute details. Another good use for splines is starting a creature or character model. Often it's a good idea to use splines to create the basic form, and then export it as a polygon model so you can add the fine details with polygon tools.

When Not to Use Splines

• **Minute Detail:** When you need to model a great deal of minute detail, as in the fish in Figure 5.14, splines are not a good choice.

The overall shape of the fish is not the problem. However, if you look closely you'll see that most of the detail has actually been *modeled*, not simply applied via surface maps. This sort of thing is rather easy using polygon modeling tools, but extremely time-consuming using splines. You'd spend days doing something that could be accomplished in minutes using polygons.

• **Protrusions:** Modeling a large number of protrusions just can't be done with spline. Well, it can be done, but it's not a wise choice, since it would take infinitely longer than using polygons. Figure 5.15 show an example of a model that would be nearly impossible to do with splines.

Details such as the spikes on his back or the little pimple-like lumps on his fins are not something you want to model using splines.

FIGURE 5.14   *Complex surface details in a polygon model*

FIGURE 5.15 *A polygon model with a great number of protrusions*

As you can see, splines do have their advantages, but not necessarily the ones people in the 3D industry might lead you to believe. Splines are a great way to model, but only for jobs that require low detail and precision curves. Anything else and you're better off using polygons.

OK, now that we have a handle on splines, let's take a look at how a model is created with them.

Spline Modeling Walk-throughs

As with polygon modeling, there are a number of different methods of building models with splines. Some depend on the software, and some depend on the user's choice. Some programs will let you patch splines together by hand, building a network of curves spline-by-spline, while others will allow you to loft in various ways along one or more curves or skin between them to build your surface. With some programs the process of tessellation will be transparent to the user; in others the user will create a polygon surface from each patch by hand. There are many ways in which programs have implemented spline modeling.

Of course, you really just need to grasp the spline modeling method in one program and you should be able to repeat the same effort in any other program that uses splines. If you can model well using Hash's Animation:Master, the road is not exceedingly long to developing fluency in another spline methodology, such as the LightWave spline-patching technique, or the standardized NURBS in Rhino, Softimage, or Maya. One thing you do have to decide is whether a particular spline technique, or splines themselves, are right for your project.

In this walk-through we will be exploring two methods of spline modeling to give you an idea of some of the many possibilities. We'll start with a spline patch walk-through.

A Spline Patching Walk-through

In this walk-through we'll be creating a cartoon couch for Chuckie to sit on while watching television. It's a cartoon model, but the technique could easily be applied to building a realistic couch, or any other basic form. Let's get started.

We're going to save time by creating one half of the couch, then mirroring it to create the other half. There is no sense in modeling the same thing twice. The starting spline is created as shown in Figure 5.16.

FIGURE 5.16   *The first spline*

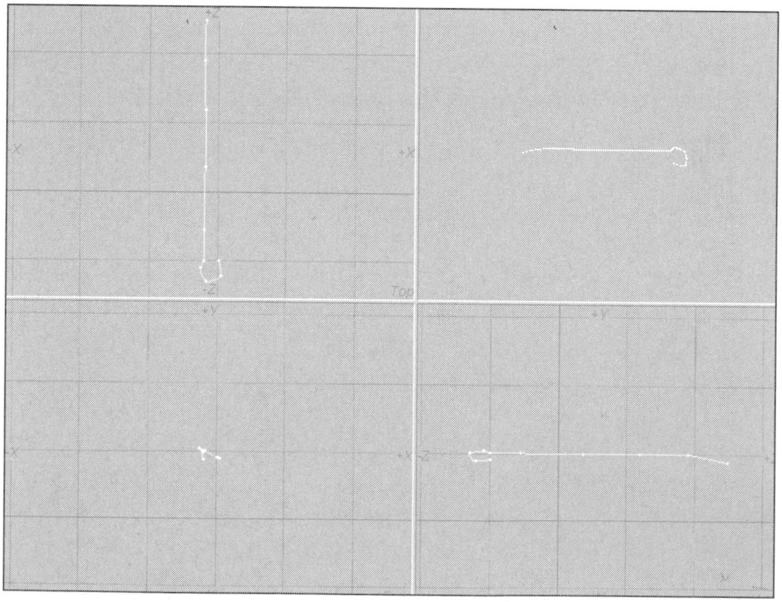

The spline is then cloned six times and placed in an archlike formation to define the shape of the armrest, as shown in Figure 5.17.

We now have the foundation for the spline cage. These splines need to be divided into spline patches so we can create the polygon patches later. We don't want to create the polygon patches until we have completed all of the splines for the couch. Since a patch consists of four intersecting splines, splines are created that intersect our current splines, as shown in Figure 5.18.

The cross-sectional splines were created by picking one point from each existing spline and creating a new spline with them. The key is to do this so you end up with patches consisting of four intersecting splines.

Now the armrest splines are complete. The next step is to create the splines for the body of the couch as seen in Figure 5.19.

Three splines were created to define the seat, and three to define the side. The endpoints of these splines already existed on the armrest splines. To complete the back and seat, the contour splines shown in Figure 5.20 were created.

You can see how more splines have been added to create the contour for the top of the chair and the side. Splines in the existing armrest cage were continued up to points along the newly created back spline. The couch is now starting to take shape. The next step is to create a spline on the center of the couch, shown in Figure 5.21.

FIGURE 5.17   *The spline cloned and positioned*

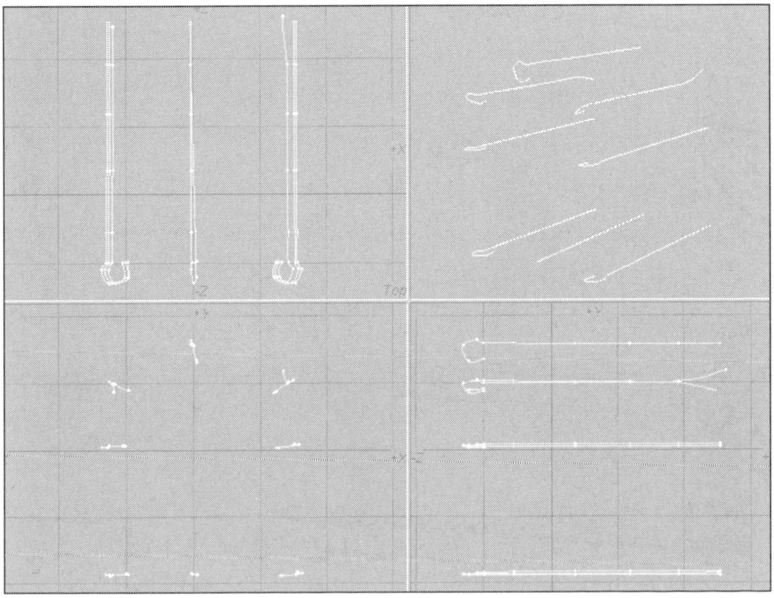

FIGURE 5.18 *Cross-section splines created out of existing points*

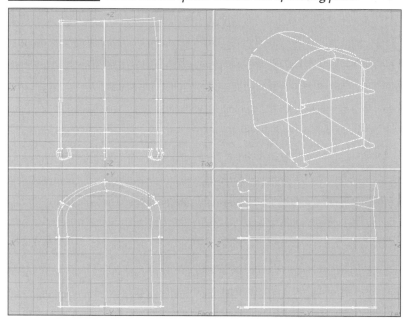

FIGURE 5.19 *Additional splines to define the side and seat of the couch*

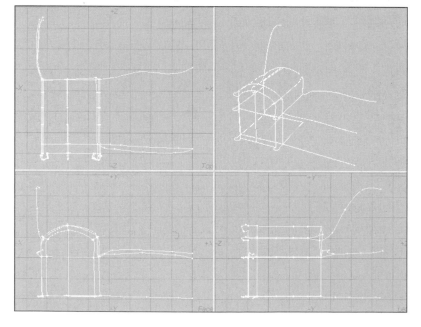

FIGURE 5.20 *Contour splines for the top of the couch*

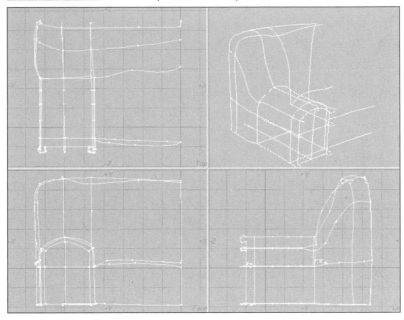

FIGURE 5.21 *A contour for the center*

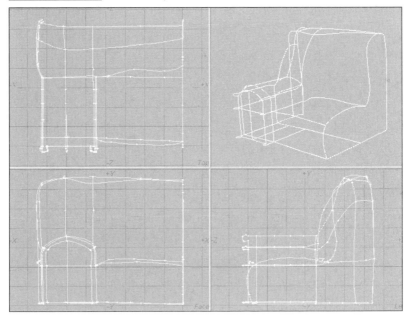

You can see that the center has not been closed, since the couch will be mirrored later in this walk-through. Finally, the spline cage is completed by running splines along the back and filling in any missing splines on the bottom, as shown in Figure 5.22.

You can see it's a bit of work to create the splines. It helps if your software is able to render a real-time preview of your spline cage, so you can spin your model around to inspect the relationship of the splines and visualize how the surface will appear after you patch it. Speaking of patching, that's the last step in modeling the couch.

Creating patches will differ slightly depending on your software package. For example, in 3D Studio Max you would create a flat patch for each intersection of four splines and mold this patch to the shape of the splines; the spline cage basically acts as a guide. On the other hand, in LightWave you select the four splines, hit a button, and the polygon patch is automatically generated for you.

Once all the polygon patches are created, the polygon mesh is mirrored and points are merged to remove those that occupy the same space. Figure 5.23 shows the finished couch model. Well, half of it, anyway.

The model of the couch is complete and ready for Chuckie to cover in gooey stuff. OK, now let's take a look at another method of spline modeling.

FIGURE 5.22 *Completing the spline cage*

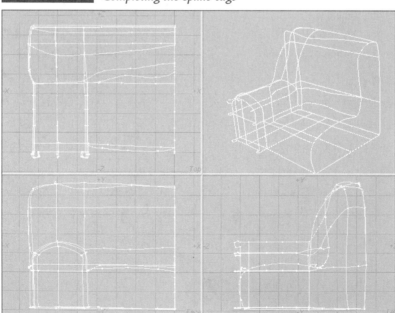

FIGURE 5.23   *The spline cage converted to polygon patches*

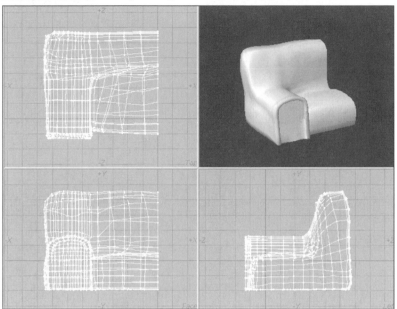

A Hash Patch Modeling Walk-through

In this walk-through we're going to create a cartoon television using Hash-type spline patches. We have to keep Chuckie occupied, or he will wreak havoc on the house. This spline modeling method can be accomplished using Animation:Master, 3D Studio Max's SurfaceTools plug-in, or Mike Clifton's freeware "Spatch" program.

The first step is to create a closed spline that outlines the screen itself. Of course, this isn't the only possible place to start. It could be started anywhere, but the screen is a logical place to begin since it defines the television's shape. Figure 5.24 shows the screen spline.

A spline by itself won't render. It needs to be turned into a surface by extruding it. The screen is extruded and scaled down twice as shown in Figure 5.25.

Notice the closed spline in the center. The area within this spline will not render in many programs because any closed spline is defined as a hole. This is actually a very useful property, as it allows you to create holes. However, in the case of our television screen we don't want a hole in the center, so the hole needs to be closed with four-point patches as shown in Figure 5.26.

FIGURE 5.24 *A closed spline*

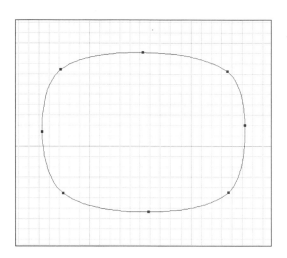

FIGURE 5.25 *The first spline extruded and scaled down*

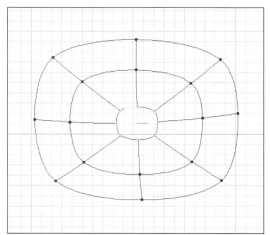

FIGURE 5.26 *The closed spline filled in with patches*

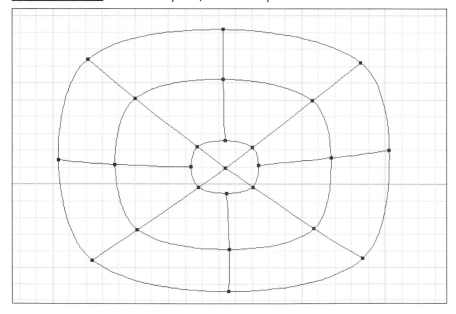

The two corners of the open patch were connected diagonally, creating four patches with a single control point in the middle. To create the metal rim around the TV, the outer spline is selected and extruded four times. Each time it is scaled and moved as shown in Figure 5.27.

With the new outer edge still selected, it's extruded once more and scaled up to create the front panel of the television as shown in Figure 5.28.

Notice that the outer edge of the front panel is rather round—probably a little more than we want. The tools for adjusting the curvature of a spline will vary depending on the software you're using. In the case of Animation:Master we can turn on the Bias Handles and simply adjust it visually. Alternately we can type values into the Properties Panel. Figure 5.29 shows the outer edge with the curvature adjusted.

To complete the main body of the television, the top, side, and bottom edges are extruded and moved back as you see in Figure 5.30.

The right side was left open in the previous step so a recessed edge between the main body and the control panel can be created. To do so, a new spline is inserted as shown in Figure 5.31.

This step is repeated on the bottom half to create a new edge, which is extruded and scaled three times as shown in Figure 5.32 to create the recessed edge.

The main body and the recessed edge are now complete. The next step is to create the control panel.

FIGURE 5.27 *The television-screen rim extruded out*

FIGURE 5.28 *The front panel extruded out*

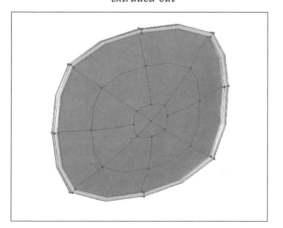

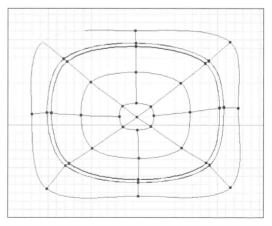

FIGURE 5.29 *The curvature of the corners adjusted*

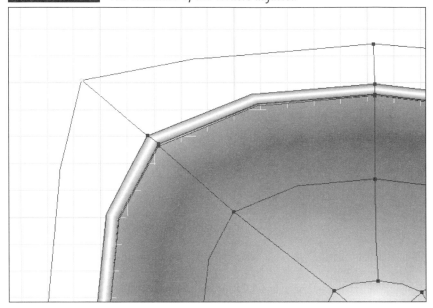

FIGURE 5.30 *The top, side and bottom extruded back*

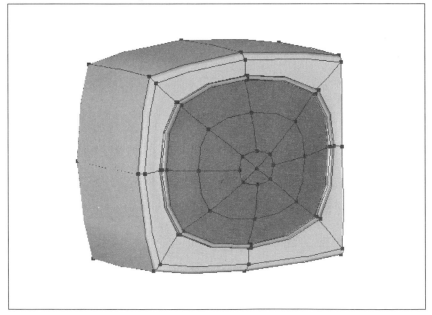

FIGURE 5.31 *Two splines on the right side of the television*

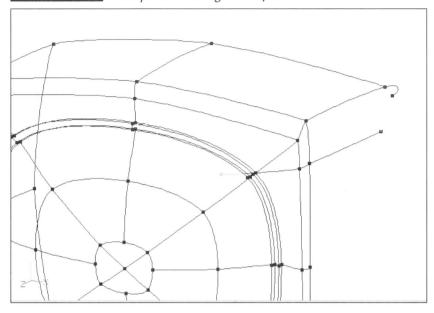

FIGURE 5.32 *The recessed edge*

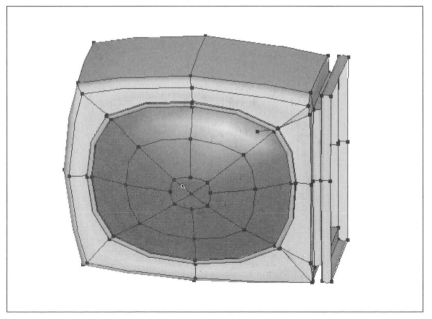

Closed splines usually cause the most difficulty in creating a patch network, so the control panel is started by creating two holes for the channel dial sockets. Figure 5.33 shows one possible solution to the problem of placing a hole within a rectangular mesh.

It's a bit sloppy, and if the surface were curved, the three-point patches indicated by the letter A would cause undesirable artifacts in the render. However, it is a flat surface, so there won't be a problem. But what if the surface were curved? Well, another option would have been to continue the splines, pointed out by letter B in Figure 5.33, through the whole model instead of terminating them. Of course, this would be a real headache because of the number of splines we'd have to edit.

An additional solution would be a five-point patch. This allows us to select a patch consisting of five points, which would normally not render, and define it as a renderable patch—meaning we can avoid the use of three-point patches, not to mention those pesky terminating splines.

OK, back to our walk-through. Once the holes have been connected to the TV, the remainder of the control panel is completed by extruding the bottom edge downward and connecting it to the rest of the mesh as you see in Figure 5.34.

Now the top, side, and bottom of the control panel are extruded back and connected to the main mesh as shown in Figure 5.35.

FIGURE 5.33   *The control panel with two holes*

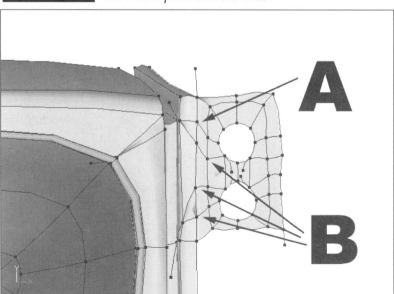

FIGURE 5.34 *The control panel extruded and connected to the bottom splines*

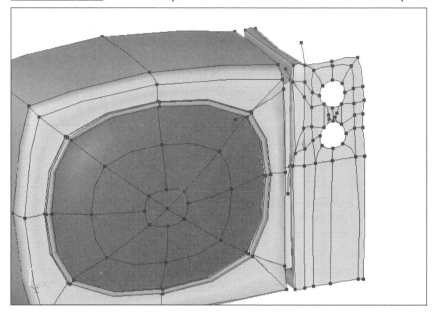

FIGURE 5.35 *The side of the television*

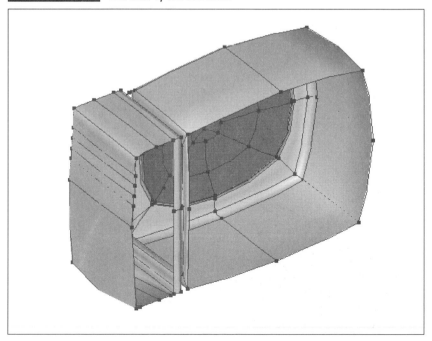

We almost have a complete surface now. All that's left is to create is the back of our TV. First the outer rim of the main box is extruded inward in the same way the front of the TV was constructed. This is shown in Figure 5.36.

Then the back is extruded out and closed in the same manner as the hole in the middle of the screen. The result is shown in Figure 5.37.

To finish up the main mesh, the back of the control panel is closed in the same manner as before—by extruding, then patching the final hole as shown in Figure 5.38.

If we rendered the TV now, we would see that our surface is *infinitely* thin around the circumference of the control-panel holes. These holes are extruded into the TV and then closed to give the illusion the object is solid. This is shown in Figure 5.39.

The last element of the TV is the dials. After all, what if Chuckie lost his remote and needed to switch from *Sesame Street* to *Story Hour?* Creating the dials is relatively simple: A spline outlining the contour of the dial body is created and then lathed, as shown in Figure 5.40.

The handle is then constructed with a simple extruded spline, then connected to the dial as shown in Figure 5.41.

FIGURE 5.36   *The back surface of the television*

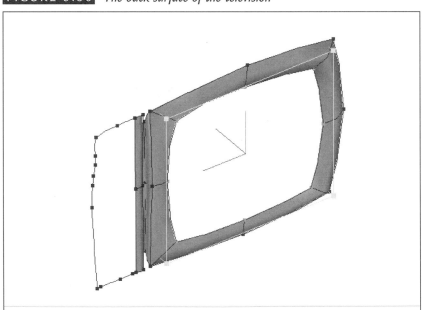

FIGURE 5.37 *The back panel extruded*

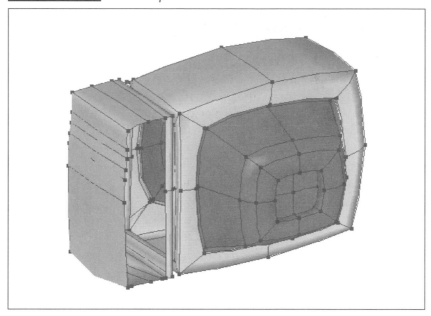

FIGURE 5.38 *The back panel closed up*

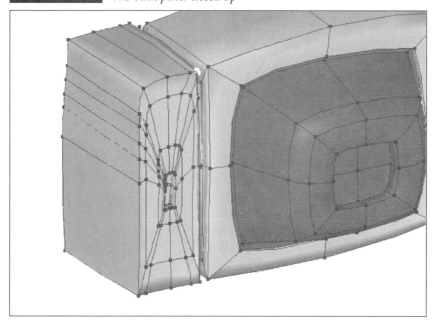

FIGURE 5.39 *The dial sockets extruded back*

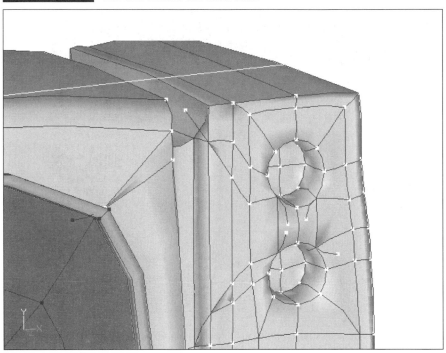

FIGURE 5.40 *The dial lathe*

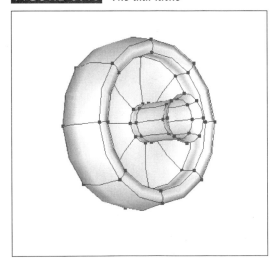

FIGURE 5.41 *The dial handle*

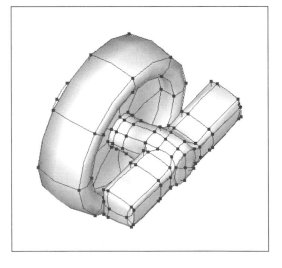

FIGURE 5.42   *The television*

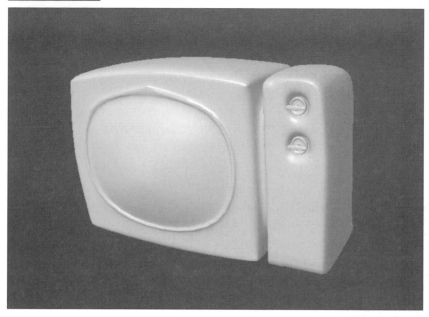

Now the TV is ready to go, and it's about time, too. Chuckie has been dying to watch his favorite show, *Space Goon*. The completed cartoon-television is shown in Figure 5.42.

As you can see, creating the TV with splines wasn't all that bad. It's just a matter of understanding the possibilities as well as the limitations of the tools.

This wraps up our television walk-through. As you can see, spline modeling has its problems, but there is no questioning its power and flexibility. Of course, just about any other object can be modeled with splines, from animals and creatures to skyscrapers and airplanes.

OK, now we're ready to take a look at the latest incarnation of splines—NURBS.

NURBS Modeling

NURBS stands for "NonUniform Rational B-splines." The name itself is wrapped in technical mystery, but don't let that fool you. We won't be going into their mathematical basis, but rather their application in 3D modeling. What the term NURBS actually *means* is of far less importance to us than their use in building objects. Even so, there are a few terms that we should get out of the way first, as we'll probably be mentioning them often while working with NURBS.

The first thing we should know is that NURBS are splines, not all that different from the other spline types we explored in the previous section. They have points that control the shape of the curve just like the other spline types. However, a difference (since NURBS are based on B-splines) is that the shape of a NURBS curve is defined by two types of points: control points (control vertices) and edit points. Let's take a look at the differences between these points. Figure 5.43 illustrates control points.

- **Control Points:** Control points are positioned off the curve and influence its general shape. Often they are connected together by "hulls" (otherwise known as "control polygons"), as shown in Figure 5.43. The large boxes are the control points, and the dotted lines running between them are the "hulls." Now let's take a look at edit points, shown in Figure 5.44.

- **Edit Points:** Edit points, or knots, sit directly on the spline. They are not only points that allow you to adjust the curve, but part of the very description of the curve. Edit points define how many spans (sections of curves smoothed together) will define the curve as a whole.

FIGURE 5.43 *Control points*

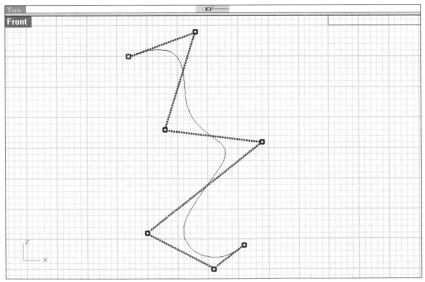

FIGURE 5.44 *Edit points*

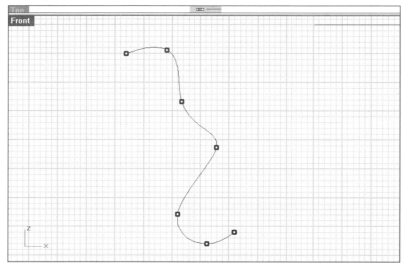

Edit points have a more obvious relationship with the curve, but once surfaces are made from the curves, we are faced with manipulating those surfaces with control points alone. Speaking of surfaces, let's take a look at NURBS surfaces.

A NURBS surface is made up of UV coordinates defining a flowing shape between four boundary curves, or isoparms. Yes, it's a bit technical, so we'll take a close look at these new terms:

- **UV Parametric Space:** UV is a coordinate system for curves and surfaces. A location on a curve has a single value "U," which is a number (usually between 0 and 1) indicating the location on the curve. You can think of this value as meaning 0 to 100% of the curve length. Thus, a value of 0.5 (50%) is the midpoint of the curve.

  A location on a surface has a value UV. In other words, to specify any location on the surface we need only specify a UV value (two numbers, usually between 0 and 1—for example, 0.5, 0.2). In the simplified case of a sphere, you can think of U and V as latitude and longitude.

- **Isoparms or Isoparameters:** A surface is made up of crisscrossing lines called isoparms, which are a visual display of UV coordinates on the surface. The isoparms are usually drawn at locations corresponding to the control points on the surface's edge curves. The spaces between isoparms are the patches.

Well, that was certainly a load of technical mumbo-jumbo. To be perfectly honest, these terms mean absolutely nothing in regard to modeling. They are covered here so you know what they are when you are bombarded with them by your program.

Now that we know probably 'way too much about NURBS, let's take a look the advantages and disadvantages of modeling with them.

NURBS Pros

- **Precise Circles:** NURBS are capable of defining precise circles. Polygons can't even come close, since they are made of straight lines. Most other spline representations can only come close, because they have no means for mathematically defining a circle. This is obviously important asset in manufacturing, though much less in artistic endeavors where precision isn't a factor.

- **Infinite Resolution:** As with other spline types, NURBS have curves of infinite resolution. We can zoom in as close as we want to a surface edge and it will never break up into any sort of component parts.

- **Easily Editable Curves:** Generating accurate and easily editable curves is a major benefit of modeling with NURBS.

- **Added Control Points:** NURBS allow you to add points to a curve without altering its shape. For example, let's say you've built a model of a head. In constructing the ear, you find you need additional control points to attach it to the head. You must run a number of additional splines through the front of the face to accomplish this. As you add control points to the existing splines, they change shape. See where I'm going with this? It can be a constant hassle to have to readjust the curvature of a large number of splines as you add points to them. This isn't a problem with NURBS.

NURBS Cons

- **Detail:** As with most other spline-modeling technologies, creating minute details is extremely difficult.

- **Workflow:** There are often a great number of steps between constructing a curve network and actually getting the visual feedback of a renderable object. In many cases that work needs to be done over and over, such as selecting a series of curves for a loft. It can be a very time-consuming process.

- **Holes and Branching:** Holes and branching objects are problematic as we discussed in the spline section of this chapter. There are certain so-

FIGURE 5.45 *Problems with blending*

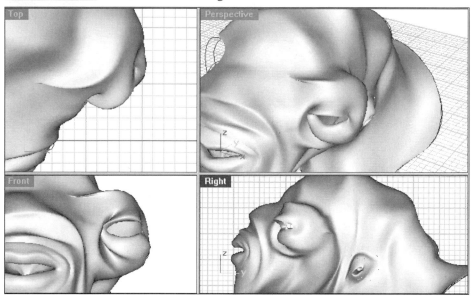

lutions, such as trimming and blending, but these are complicated. For one thing, they can be difficult to control, as you can see in Figure 5.45.

Although the creases might look somewhat cool, they weren't intended. We want our modeling to be predictable so we can make assumptions. Another issue is modifying a surface with blends. If you deform a surface connected by a blend, the continuity between it and the blend surface can be lost, as you can see by the tears in the surface in Figure 5.46.

A few programs work around this by using a "construction history" to deform the surface and blend it using the curves the surfaces were originally constructed with.

• **Floating Control Points:** This is a problem from a practical modeling perspective, since the control point doesn't always have an immediately apparent relationship to the curve, as shown in Figure 5.47. It can be extremely difficult to see which control point will deform which curve while you're deforming a surface.

OK, those are the pros and cons of modeling with NURBS. As you can see, there are several things to consider before you begin modeling with NURBS. In fact, let's take this time to explore when you should use NURBS.

FIGURE 5.46   *A seam in the blended surface*

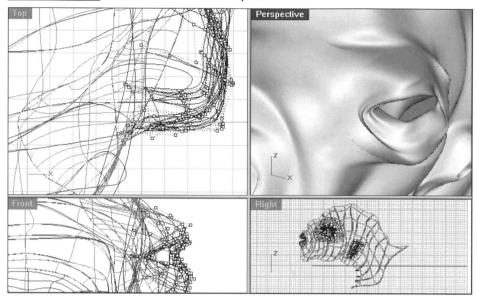

FIGURE 5.47   *A tangle of control points*

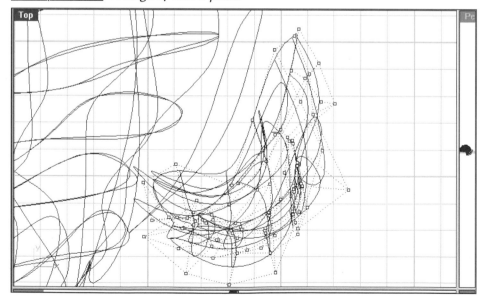

Where and When to Use NURBS

NURBS can be used in many of the same applications as splines, though there are some major differences that pertain to engineering applications. Let's take a look at these differences.

When to Use NURBS

- **Exacting Curves:** As with splines, use NURBS when you need exacting curves to describe a physical surface, such as an automobile model. As a matter of fact, NURBS are even more capable of defining precise mathematical curves.

- **A Starting Point for Polygonal Modeling:** NURBS can be used as a beginning point to polygonal modeling. You build the general form using splines and/or NURBS, tessellate it, and then add all your details with standard polygonal modeling tools. Polygons rule the detail world.

When Not to Use NURBS

- **Minute Detail:** When you need to model a great deal of minute detail such as the model we looked at in Figure 5.14, NURBS are not the best choice. However, as we just mentioned, you can begin with NURBS and add your detail in a polygonal modeler.

- **Protrusions:** When your model contains a good number of protrusions that can't be modeled with bump maps, NURBS is definitely not the way to go.

Again, it is up to you as the modeler to decide which method is best suited to your needs. NURBS are a necessity when you need accurate curves to describe real-world, man-made organic objects. They can also be used for building natural organics such as creatures and characters, though not nearly as effectively as polygons or metashapes.

Speaking of polygons, let's take a look at how NURBS and polygons can work together to create a complex model.

A NURBS Modeling Walk-through

In this walk-through we'll explore the making of a creature head. This is a creature that haunted Chuckie's dreams for a month or so after he sneaked into the den one night and turned the television on, only to be visually assaulted by scenes from a B-movie called *Creature from the Twelfth Planet*. He looked only briefly, but the image stuck with him, occasionally invading an otherwise pleasant dream.

Well, that's enough background. Let's get started with the walk-through. Since we'll be beginning with his mouth, the first tool we'll explore is the lathe or revolve tool. This is often a good starting point for building a head with a NURBS modeling program, especially if it doesn't allow for easily creating a surface by welding smaller patches together into a larger structure, which is the technique we saw in the spline patch walk-through earlier.

The NURBS modeling process involves the software automatically generating regular grids of patches from a few splines provided by the user, and later joining them together into a single surface, unlike the spline patch technique, where the user often builds a model spline by spline, patch by patch.

The creature head begins with a single spline defining the outline of the creature's mouth, as shown in Figure 5.48.

This spline is then lathed or revolved to create the vaselike shape in Figure 5.49.

OK, so that doesn't look very much like a mouth. It will have to be worked over a bit to sculpt something more reasonable. To do so, control points are turned on and the sides are dragged out as you see in Figure 5.50.

FIGURE 5.48   *The outline of the creature's mouth*

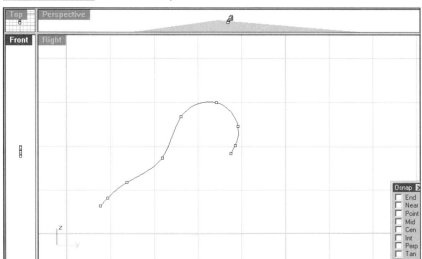

FIGURE 5.49   *The lathed spline*

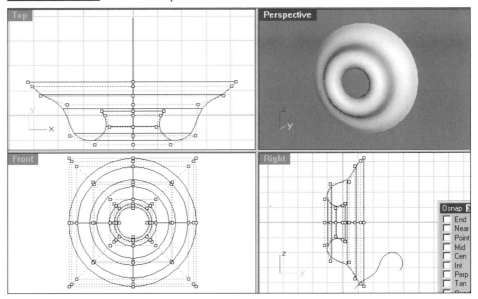

FIGURE 5.50   *Shaping the mouth surface*

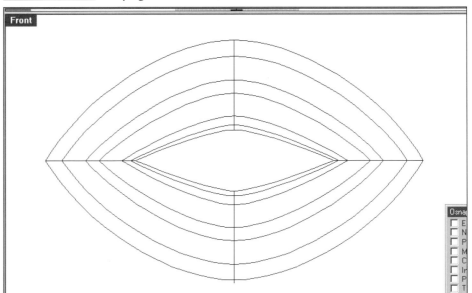

It's beginning to look a little better, but since there are only four isoparms running in the V-direction, it will be difficult to sculpt the necessary shape. So additional knots are inserted, running out from the center of the mouth, as you can see in Figure 5.51.

That's more like it. Now there are enough control points to work with. With so many it can be difficult to figure out which control point will affect which spline, but if you work at it a while, it will get easier. Figure 5.52 shows the mouth after a few minutes of pulling points.

It definitely looks more like a mouth. The next step is to create the throat and tongue. To accomplish this a handful of closed splines will be lofted, starting with the inner spline of the mouth just created. That way the surface will match up perfectly at that point. Figure 5.53 shows the series of splines used.

One closed spline was copied thirteen times and modified, which helps to keep the same number of edit points on each spline. Now to loft these, they have to be selected in the correct order, as shown in Figure 5.54.

This is important because if they are selected out of order, the loft will build the skin across the wrong splines. Figure 5.55 shows the correctly lofted surface.

FIGURE 5.51 *Inserting additional control points*

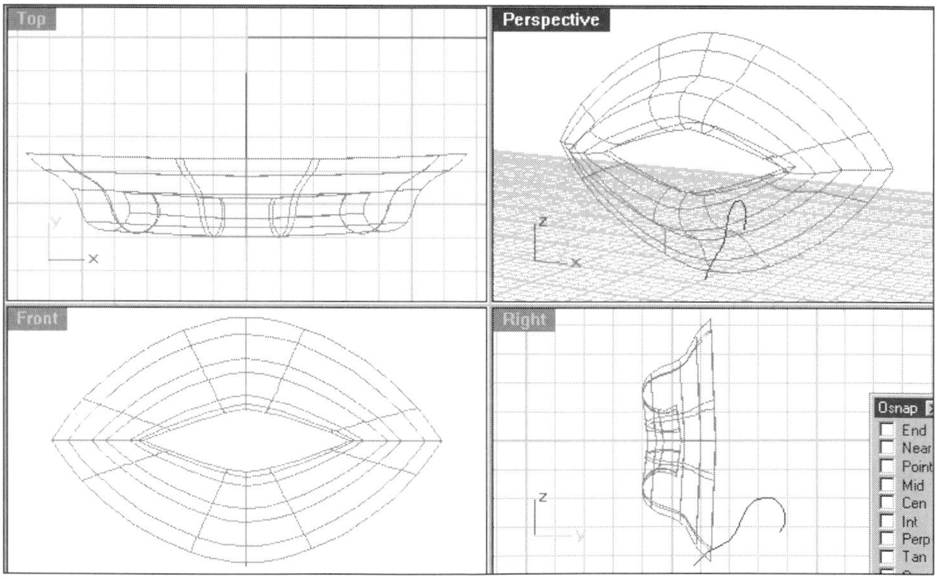

FIGURE 5.52 *The creature's mouth*

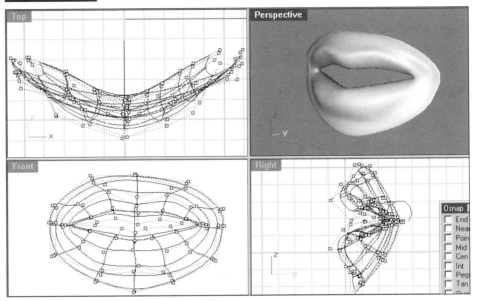

FIGURE 5.53 *The splines defining the inner mouth*

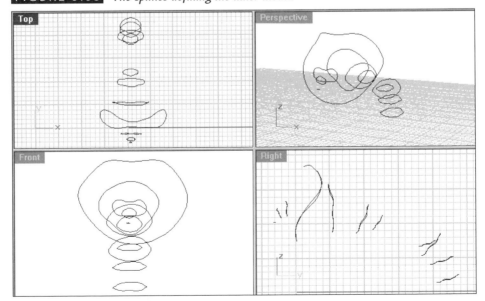

FIGURE 5.54 *The order of selection for lofting*

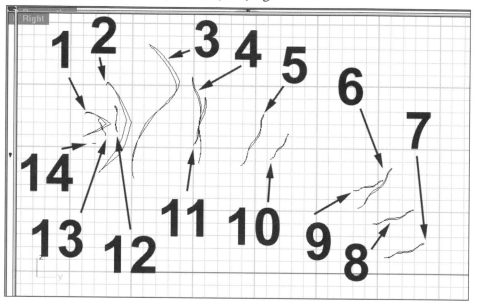

FIGURE 5.55 *The throat splines lofted*

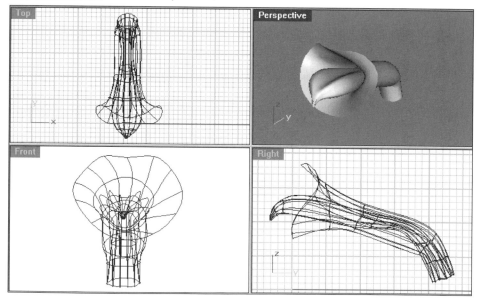

159

You may find you prefer working on the surface rather than the spline, or vice versa. The benefit of working directly with the lofted surface is that you get immediate feedback from your modifications in the render window. The drawback is that the control points will always float off the surface, making it difficult to modify the shape exactly. When working with the splines alone, however, you can work with edit points that directly intersect the splines. It really doesn't take very long to select the splines, loft them, and then inspect them.

Now the main head surface will be constructed following exactly the same procedure. Figure 5.56 shows the head splines.

The first spline in this series is the outside edge of the mouth. The order of selection from there is simply in order down to the neck. Figure 5.57 shows the loft of these splines.

That completes the head. Next, little amphibian-like alien ears are added to the side of the neck. The first step is to create a series of lofting splines, as you see in Figure 5.58.

Only splines 1, 2, and 3 will be lofted. Spline 4 will be used to project onto the surface of the head as a cutting tool, which we'll get to shortly. Figure 5.59 shows the first three splines lofted.

FIGURE 5.56 *The loft splines for the head*

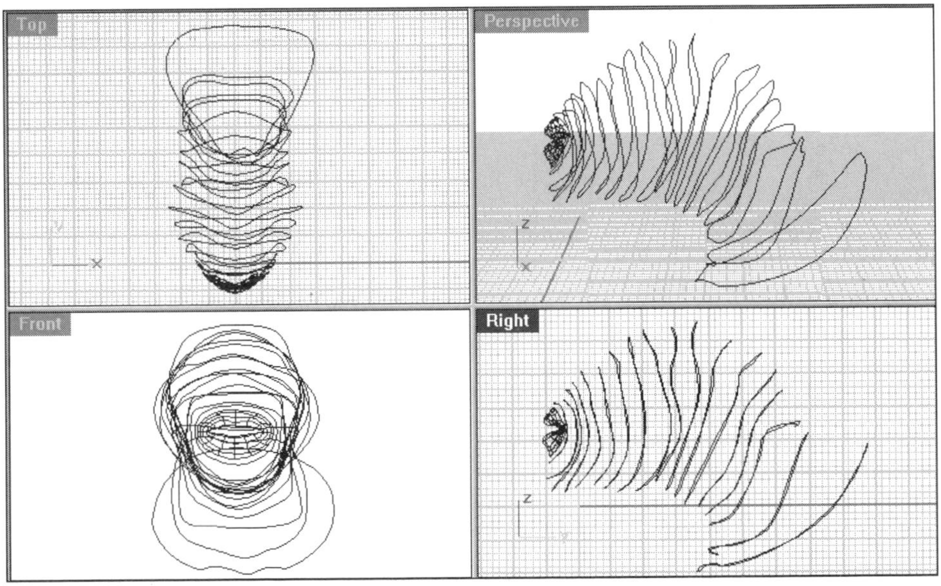

FIGURE 5.57   *The head splines lofted*

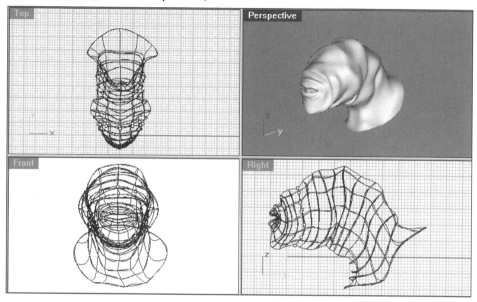

FIGURE 5.58   *Lofting splines for the ear*

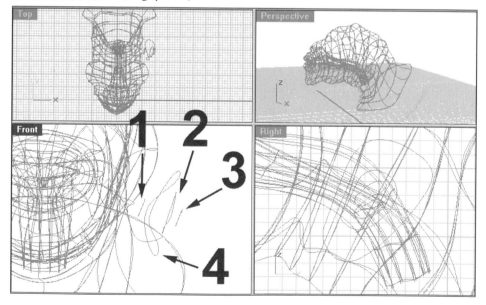

FIGURE 5.59 *The lofted ear*

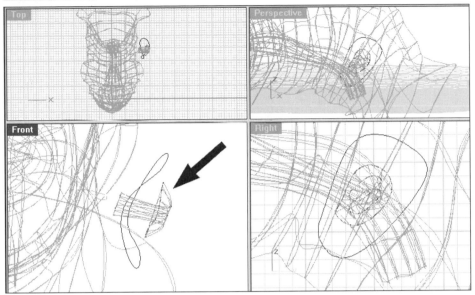

The next step is to project the fourth spline onto the head surface. The Project Spline (Curve) command is selected, and in the side viewport, the fourth spline is selected as the spline to project and the head as the surface to project onto. This creates two new splines: one conforming exactly to the contours of the head on the right side, and one doing the same on the left, as you can see in Figure 5.60.

There are now two new splines, one on each side of the head. "Split" is selected; then the head surface is chosen as the object to split, and the two new curves are selected as the cutting objects. This doesn't exactly act as a boolean operation; nothing is actually added or removed. It simply "splits" one portion of a surface from the rest. These separated portions are simply selected and deleted, as you can see has been done in Figure 5.61.

Now the ear surface is "blended" to the head surface, which means generating a transitional surface between the two. This is an automatic function in most NURBS modelers. Figure 5.62 shows the blend on the right side.

The surface render is not smooth because the three surfaces haven't been joined into one surface yet. Once they have been joined, it won't be a problem. To complete the other ear, the process of splitting and blending is repeated on the opposite side of the head.

FIGURE 5.60   *The ear spline projected onto the head*

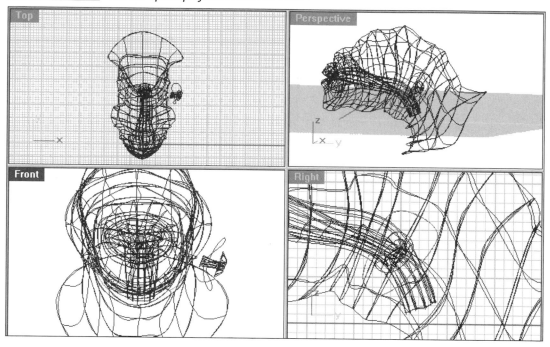

FIGURE 5.61   *The trimmed head surface*

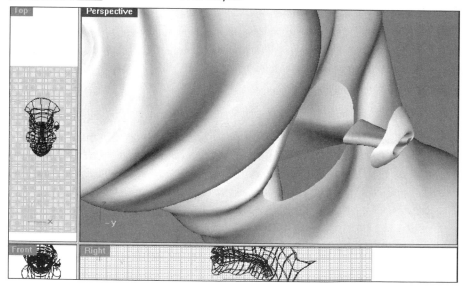

FIGURE 5.62 *The ear blended to the head*

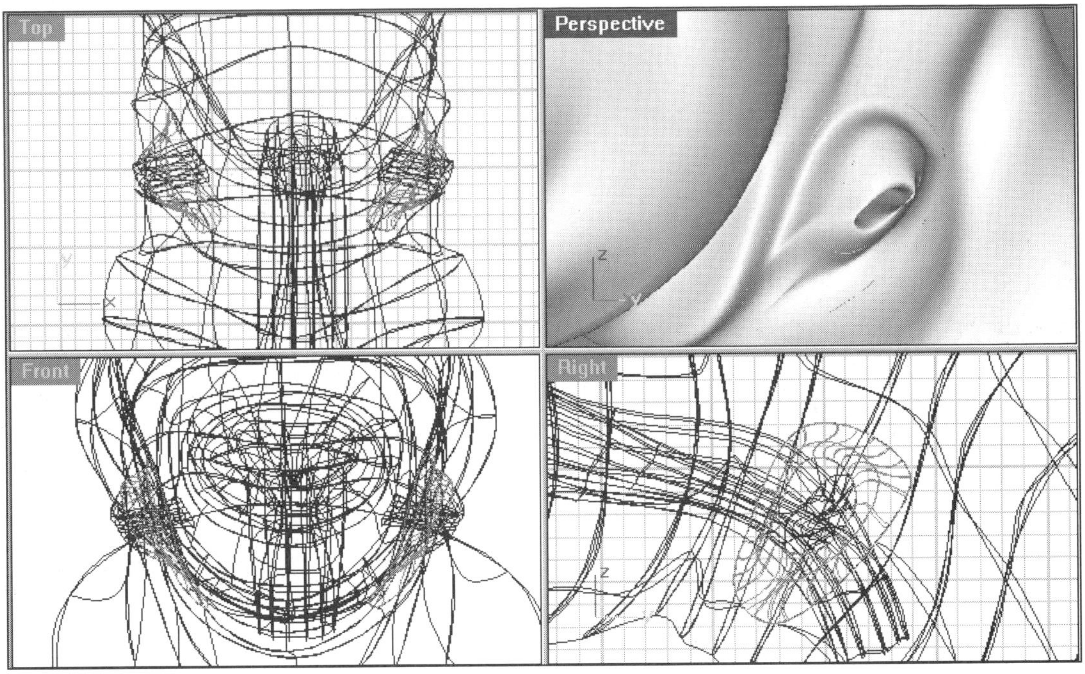

Now the eyes will be constructed following the same process: create lofting splines, loft these, project the last spline onto the head surface, trim the surface, and create a blend between the eye and the head. Figure 5.63 shows the lofting curves for the eye.

Once those splines have been lofted and blended to the head, the last step is to 'join' all the separate pieces into one surface, which allows them to be rendered as a single object instead of a number of separate objects butted up against each other. The joined head is shown in Figure 5.64.

All the pieces are still there, but the tessellation ignores the fact and assumes the model is all one surface. Otherwise, it would create separate polygonal models to render, which of course would show seams.

Well, that does it for our NURBS modeling walk-through. We certainly haven't used all the tools available to the NURBS modeler, but we have explored the technique well enough that you should be able to pick up the tools and begin creating your own models—not to mention deciding if you should pick them up at all.

FIGURE 5.63   *Lofting curves for the eye*

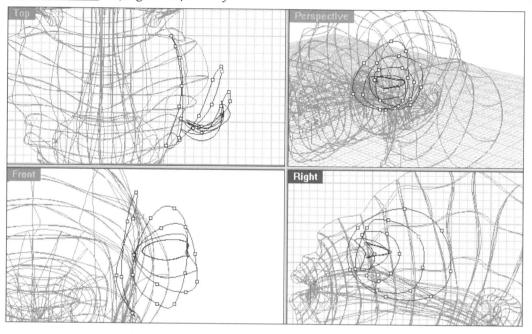

FIGURE 5.64   *The joined head*

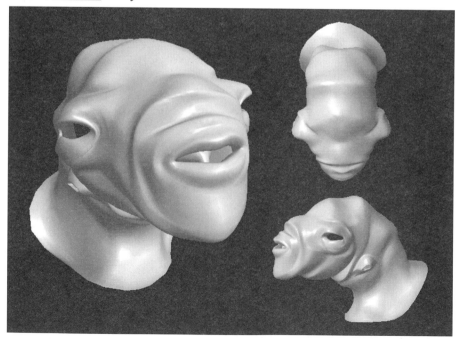

Wrap-up

There you have it. We've seen that spline modeling originated in engineering field. We've also seen that there are some applications for spline modeling in the artistic realm, though those applications are by no means free of problems. You should be better able now to decide whether or not to use splines for a given modeling project, and to do so with some confidence.

This concludes our look at modeling methods. In Part II, Modeling Tools, we will explore the most productive modeling tools at your disposal.

PART III

Modeling Tools

N ow that we have a handle on the different modeling methods, it's time to explore the popular modeling tools. Having a good set of modeling tools can make all the difference in your modeling efforts. Knowing how to use them can save you countless headaches. It's one thing to know which modeling method to use, but then you also need to know how to apply the modeling tools.

There are several modeling tools that are common to nearly every 3D program:

- Bevels
- Boolean operations
- Lathe
- Extrude, Sweep and Smooth Shift
- Path manipulation
- Cloning

Although there are many more modeling tools, these seven are the most powerful and useful when creating your 3D worlds. In this part we will cover each of these modeling tools and how they are used to create 3D wonders. At the end of each chapter we'll explore the application of the tool with a modeling walk-through.

The first tool we'll examine is Bevel. Let's take a look at how the Bevel tool is used to create detailed object surfaces.

CHAPTER 6

Working with Bevels

Bevels are a wonderful addition to 3D models. They really help to add realism. OK, so what is a bevel? Well, it's the buffered edge you find on most manufactured products. They are created to smooth the harsh 90-degree angle on the edges of objects. This is done for both aesthetics and safety. Those hard edges can be like the blade of a knife. Recently homebuilders have started rounding and beveling the edges of walls because children keep running into them. You can imagine the mess a hard edge would create. Let's take a look at a typical bevel, shown in Figure 6.1.

Here we have a 3D model of a PDA (Personal Digital Assistant) handheld computer. A PDA is handled quite a bit, so all of the edges are beveled for safety. It also tends to look better than hard edges. If you look at the front edge of the case, you'll see a smooth edge that runs around the lower half of the case. The same applies for the upper half of the case. Now let's get in a little closer and take a look at the buttons, shown in Figure 6.2.

Notice how the top edges of all the buttons are rounded with a bevel. These keys get thousands of strokes a day, so they need to be very smooth to prevent injury. All of the bevels on this object were created using a bevel tool. Bevels are an important feature in 3D objects that simulate manufactured objects. What this means is any 3D object that is simulating a man-made object needs to incorporate bevels. Bevels serve three purposes on an object.

FIGURE 6.1 *A typical bevel*

FIGURE 6.2 *A closer look at the PDA model*

1. **Safety:** A hard edge is dangerous, so manufactured objects have smooth, beveled edges. If we are going to simulate real-world objects in our 3D worlds, we need to incorporate bevels. Obviously, safety isn't a concern for us, but think about the 3D characters in your world. I'm sure they'd appreciate it. Figure 6.3 shown a 3D telephone that makes liberal use of bevels to soften the edges of buttons that are frequently pressed.

   Although the surfacing of the model has a great deal to do with its realism, the beveled edges have solidified the deal by reflecting the attributes we are accustomed to seeing in real-world objects.

2. **Aesthetics:** Hard edges look terrible on objects. It also makes them look artificial. We're accustomed to seeing beveled edges in reality, so a 3D model without them will look odd and out of place. Besides, beveled edges make the object more appealing. Figure 6.4 shows a fine example of bevels being used to make a 3D object more aesthetically appealing.

   As you can see, the object looks very realistic and appealing. It has smooth flowing lines with soft edges. Aesthetics are important. Just take a look at how well foreign cars sell in the United States. They do

FIGURE 6.3 *Bevels used for safety*

very well because they're aesthetically pleasing to the eye. Until recently, American cars have been like boxes with wheels, which isn't very appealing. 3D objects look far better with smooth edges.

3. **Specularity:** Dull objects look artificial and boring. Specularity is simply the light source reflected on the surface. It's those white spots you see on shiny objects. Hard edges won't show specularity, which makes the object dull in appearance. This poses two problems. The first is that we're used to seeing specular highlights on surfaces. If they're absent, the object looks artificial. The second is more of a technical problem. If you have dark surfaces with plenty of detail such as the PDA, you'll need specularity to separate the details. Without specularity, the details will blend together and literally become invisible. To better illustrate this problem, let's take a look at Figure 6.5.

This is the same PDA we saw earlier, but now it has been surfaced. Notice that you can see plenty of highlights on all of the beveled edges. This brings out the details in the object. In fact, if you take a close look you'll see a tiny specular highlight along the front of the lower case. This is the seam where the two manufactured parts come together. It's a small seam that would be completely invisible if not for the tiny beveled edge.

FIGURE 6.4 *Bevel aesthetics*

FIGURE 6.5 *Bevel specularity*

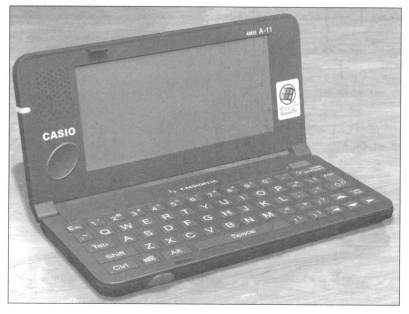

As you can see, bevels are a necessity if you intend your manufactured 3D objects to be believable and catch the viewer's eye. Of course, bevels don't make sense for every model. They are really only important when you're simulating a manufactured object. You wouldn't want to bevel the edges of a natural object, since natural objects aren't manufactured. While they do have smooth edges, they aren't beveled. A bevel would appear far too manufactured on natural organics.

OK, so now that we know the benefits of bevels, let's take a look at how they are applied to 3D models.

Applying Bevels

3D programs such as LightWave and 3D Studio Max have tools for creating bevels, although they don't necessarily work equally well. LightWave has probably the best Bevel tool on the market. It's very intuitive and does a great job. The 3D Studio Max Bevel tool doesn't do nearly as well. The unfortunate thing about 3D programs is that the quality of the tools and feature will vary dramatically from one program to another. To make life more interesting, there is no 3D program that has the best of all tools. They all have several good ones and several bad. It can be very frustrating.

To avoid the problems of poor tools, many 3D artists use at least two 3D programs so they have an opportunity to use better tools. It's not a perfect solution, but it does work.

OK, so how do we apply bevels? Well, a bevel is very much like a sweep. It takes the selected polygons and moves them outward, creating additional polygons to join them to the object. Figure 6.6 shows a simple bevel.

When you use a Bevel tool you are given a few options for shaping and positioning the new polygons. Let's take a look.

• **Inset:** This determines the scaling of the new polygons. A positive inset value makes the polygons smaller, and a negative value makes them larger. This sounds backwards, but an inset is a negative operation, so a positive value will move the outer edge of the polygons inward. Figure 6.7 shows the difference between a positive and negative inset.

   The top polygon on both cubes has been beveled. The cube on the left has a positive inset value, while the cube on the right has a negative inset value.

• **Shift:** This determines the distance the new polygons are moved away from the object. A positive shift value will move the polygons away

FIGURE 6.6   *A beveled edge*

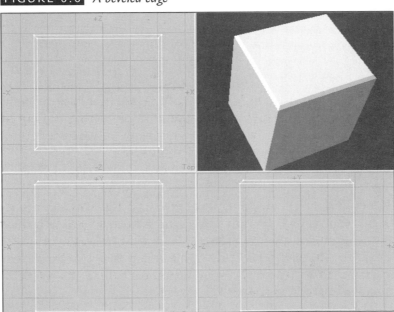

FIGURE 6.7   *A positive and negative inset*

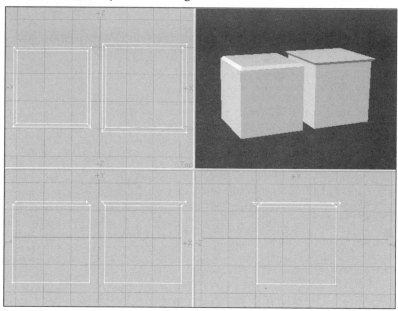

from the object and a negative value moves them into the object. Figure 6.8 shows the difference between a positive and negative shift.

The cube on the left has a positive shift value, while the cube on the right has a negative shift value.

The Bevel tool is relatively simple, but the results can be very complex. It's all about how you utilize it. Of course, there are a few things to consider before you actually apply the bevel. Planning is a big part of modeling, but it's crucial when you are creating bevels. The first thing to consider is the difference between a bevel and a sweep.

A sweep shifts a group of polygons as a single unit, while a bevel will shift each individual polygon. Figure 6.9 illustrates this difference.

On the left is the result of a sweep. As you can see, the sweep has created a new, joined group of polygons, while the bevel on the right has created a group of separate polygons. This isn't always the desired effect, but it can be very useful for creating complex effects on high-tech objects such as space ships. In fact, let's take a look at how the Bevel tool can be used to create a segmented spaceship canopy.

In Figure 6.10 you'll see the basic shape of a spaceship canopy.

FIGURE 6.8   *A positive and negative shift*

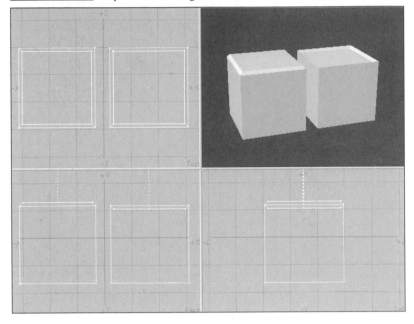

FIGURE 6.9   *Comparing a sweep to a bevel*

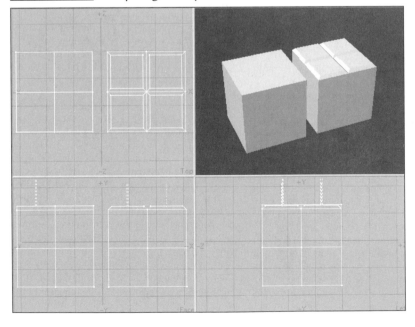

FIGURE 6.10   *A spaceship canopy*

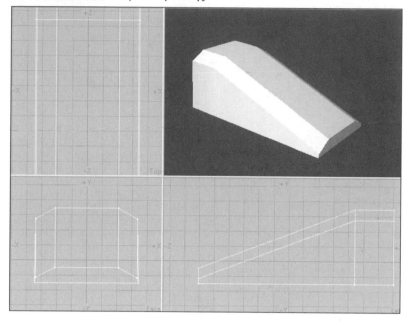

Although this object has the proper shape and proportions, it lacks the detail we've come to expect from high-tech objects. What it needs is multiple segments. Fortunately, this is a simple press of the mouse button away. You simply select the polygons on the outside of the canopy and bevel them. The result is the multisegment canopy shown in Figure 6.11.

As you can see, it took only a second to transform a simple object into something rather complex. That's one strong point of bevels. Of course, while the effect is definitely interesting, and useful in many high-tech objects, it does limit what bevels can do. If you wanted to bevel the polygons on the top of the cube to resemble a sweep, you would need to merge the polygons into a single polygon, then bevel it. Then you'd have a singular beveled surface as shown in Figure 6.12.

Of course, you no longer have the four polygons at the top, but this shouldn't be a problem, since beveling is usually the last step in the modeling process. This brings me to the second consideration with bevels—timing. Choosing the proper time to bevel your surface is extremely important. If you do it too soon, you can destroy several hours of modeling effort. Let me illustrate what I mean.

FIGURE 6.11   *The beveled canopy*

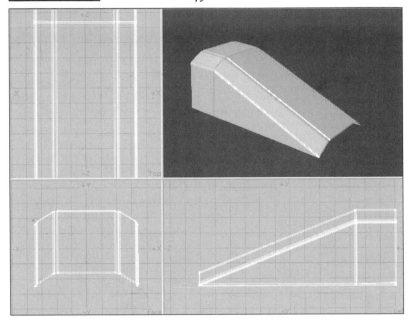

FIGURE 6.12   *Creating a bevel with multiple polygons*

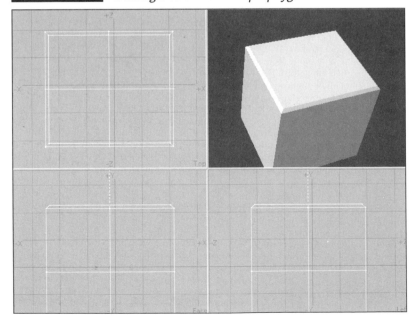

Let's assume we are going to build a keypad for a piece of high-tech equipment. We would want to bevel the top of the keypad so the edges are clean, and the holes where the keys are will be softened. OK, this is a simple process, but it's the order in which you do things that's important. If you bevel the top of the keypad before you cut the keyholes, you won't have a bevel around the keyholes. You need to cut the holes first, then bevel the surface. This will create a small bevel around each keyhole.

Proper planning is crucial. If you got ahead of yourself and beveled too soon, you might find yourself rebuilding the keypad, which is not only a waste of time, but downright aggravating.

Of course, you don't need a Bevel tool to create bevels. There is a technique you can use to bevel your surface if no Bevel tool is available. It actually involves using the Sweep or Smooth Shift tool. Let's take a look at how this technique is applied.

Creating a Manual Bevel

If your 3D program doesn't have a Bevel tool, and many don't, you'll need to manually bevel your surfaces. The effect is the same, but it requires a bit more work. What you need to do is select the polygons to be beveled and sweep them. Once they're swept, you'll need to manually size and scale them to create the bevel. It's a simple solution and the result is no different from a bevel. In fact, it can be more advantageous in some circumstances. For example, if you have a curved surface that needs a bevel, you really won't be able to merge the polygons and bevel them because polygons can't be bent. Instead, you can select the polygons and sweep them. You can sweep along any curve, so in some cases the manual method is superior to the Bevel tool. You need to be creative when 3D modeling. There are many solutions to any common problem—you just need to take a step back and look at it from a different angle.

OK, we've talked about bevels as a finishing tool, but they are also a powerful modeling tool. I know it sounds odd, but they can be used to create a number of complex objects. Let's take a look at how this is accomplished.

Modeling with Bevels

You can build some very cool objects with bevels. A good example is the spaceship shown in Figure 6.13.

It's a very complex object, but when you break it down to each individual part, it's really not that complicated. The bevel modeling process is a

FIGURE 6.13 *A model created primarily with bevels*

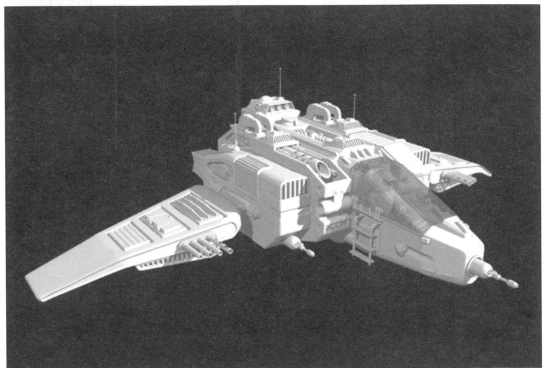

very quick and efficient method of creating high-tech objects. You start with the basic shape and start making bevels to create the details. In fact, let's take a moment to see the bevel modeling process works. In Figure 6.14 we have a simple tube, which is the foundation of a fuselage.

With only 10 bevels, the tube was transformed into the complex fuselage you see in Figure 6.15.

You could keep adding details like these all day long with the bevel tool. There are infinite combinations you can create by using bevels and a bit of ingenuity. For example, the recessed panel at the top of the fuselage was created by merging several polygons and beveling them. Don't limit yourself to beveling only the single polygons—group them so you can create more interesting details.

You can see how easily complex objects can be created with the bevel tool. In fact, since we're on the subject of modeling with the Bevel tool, let's take a look at the modeling process in action.

FIGURE 6.14 *The basic shape of a fuselage*

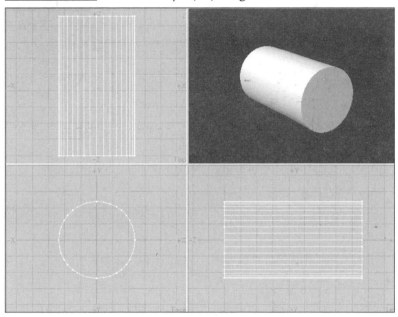

FIGURE 6.15 *The beveled fuselage*

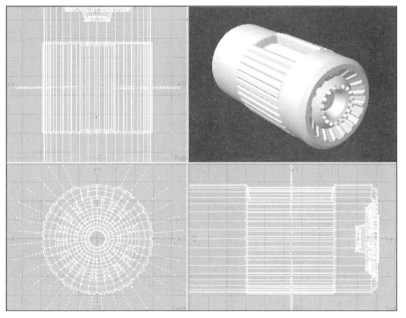

A Bevel Walk-through

In this walk-through, we're going to be creating a toy block for Chuckie. You know: the kind with the letters of the alphabet on them. Creating the block is actually an extremely simple process using the Bevel tool. It's a matter of only five steps. To begin, the block is started with a simple cube like the one shown in Figure 6.16.

The next step is to bevel all of the sides with a small inset and a shift so all of the edges on the block are beveled as shown in Figure 6.17.

Now there are no rough edges on the block, so Chuckie won't hurt himself. Well, he probably will anyway, but it will be no fault of ours. OK, now it's time to add some detail to the sides of the blocks. A simple beveled cube just isn't interesting enough. It needs a little more detail and depth. The first thing to do is bevel all six sides with a small inset like the original bevel, but this time the shift is set to zero so the polygons don't move away from the block. The result is something like the object in Figure 6.18.

FIGURE 6.16   *The foundation of the block*

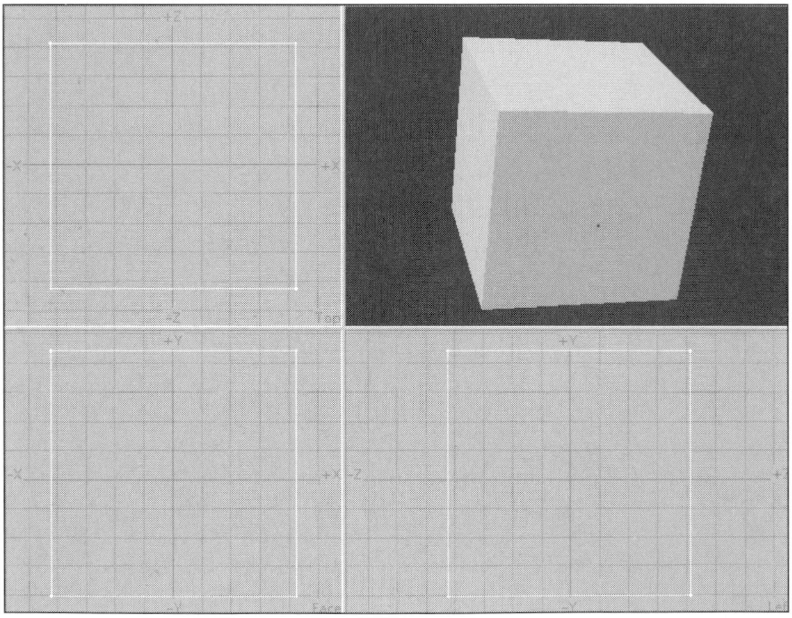

FIGURE 6.17 *Beveling the hard edges*

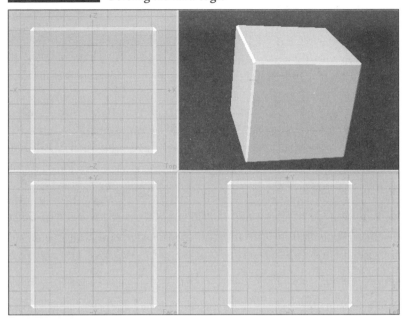

FIGURE 6.18 *Another bevel*

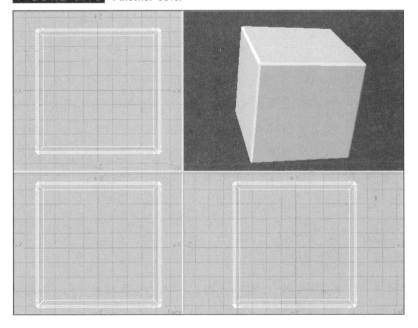

The object looks the same in the OpenGL preview, but now there is a thin border along the outside edge. This is the start of a ridge around the sides of the block. This ridge gives the block character and something for Chuckie's little hands to get a grip on. The actual ridge is created by beveling the outside polygons with a small inset and a small, negative shift. The shift is negative so the polygons move inside the block to create the ridge shown in Figure 6.19.

Now we have a nice ridge around the sides of the block so Chuckie can get a grip on it. Of course, to make gripping a bit easier, the ridge should be given more depth. This is easily accomplished by beveling the selected polygons with an inset of zero and a small negative shift. The zero setting for the inset prevents the polygons from being scaled, and the negative shift moves them inward. The result is the finished block shown in Figure 6.20.

Now that is much better. You see how simple it is to create objects with the Bevel tool. This block would have taken more than four times as any steps with any other method. Once again, selecting the right tool is paramount. Bevels can be a great asset as long as you properly plan the model and use them efficiently.

FIGURE 6.19 *The completed ridge*

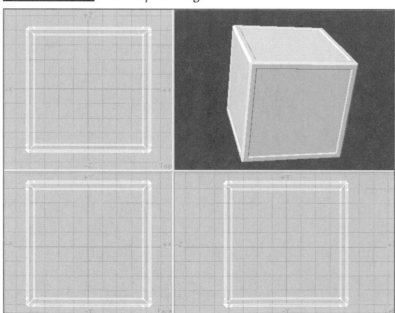

FIGURE 6.20 *The completed block*

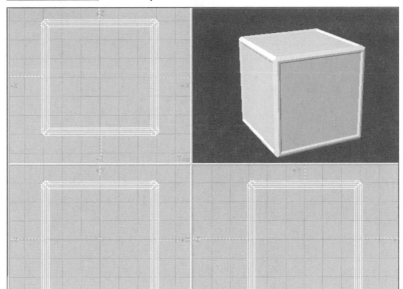

Wrap-up

It's easy to see how the Bevel tool is a significant addition to your 3D modeling toolbox. It can be both a finishing tool and a modeling tool. There are endless applications for bevels; you just need to be creative in your thinking. Most 3D artists fail to take full advantage of bevels. They tend to make objects with harsh edges and opt for taking much longer to model something that could have been created with bevels in minutes. Knowing your tools is just as important as knowing the modeling methods.

The next tools we'll be exploring are boolean operations. These are some great tools for creating killer objects. In fact, they are the tools I will use to add the letters to Chuckie's block in the boolean walk-through. Why don't we jump on over to the next chapter and get started?

CHAPTER 7

Boolean Operations

Boolean operations are used to either add or subtract details from a model. The name "boolean" refers to the mathematical operation performed. It's really of no consequence unless you're a mathematics enthusiast. I'm sure most of you remember the fun you had in algebra class. Actually, fun isn't exactly the word for it, but I'll bet you never thought you'd need to learn algebra to get by in life. Well, you were right. Your 3D program does all the math for you!

The important thing to know about boolean operations isn't how they're computed, but rather the types that are available, and when you should use them. A boolean operation is rather simple. You start with an object that you want to modify. Then you create another object that becomes the modifier. Figure 7.1 shows an example of a boolean modifier.

The cube in the image is the object and the tube is the modifier. The modifier object is used to either add or subtract information from your original object. Boolean operations are most often used to create holes in objects, but they're also handy for merging objects to reduce polygon counts. The tube penetrates the cube so it can be either added or subtracted from it. Let's take a moment to explore each of the four types of boolean operations and see how this cube would be affected.

- **Subtract:** This boolean operation subtracts the volume of one object from another. If you wanted to create holes in your object, you would model an object in the shape of the desired hole and use it as the modifier object to perform a boolean subtract operation on the original object. Figure 7.2 shows the effect of a boolean subtract operation.

As you can see, the cube now has a hole in the shape of the modifier tube object. Of course, this is a very simple example, but we'll be taking a look at more complicated examples after we cover all four types of boolean operations.

- **Add:** This boolean operation is the opposite of subtract. It simply adds the volume of the modifier object to the original object, as shown in Figure 7.3.

  One important thing to note about the boolean add operation is that it doesn't blend the objects, removing the unseen portion. It merely adds the two objects together. If you want to remove the unseen data, you'll need to use the boolean union operation.

- **Union:** A boolean union operation adds the volume to the modifier to your object and removes the unseen data, as shown in Figure 7.4.

  This can be a great benefit because it reduces the polygon count by removing the excess polygons that won't be seen. So why not use boolean union instead of boolean add? Well, not all 3D programs have

FIGURE 7.1 *A boolean modifier*

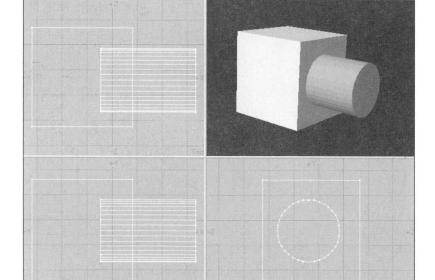

FIGURE 7.2 *A boolean subtract operation*

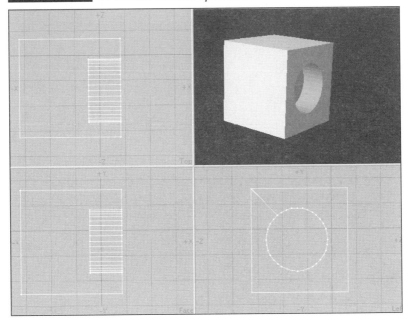

FIGURE 7.3 *A boolean add operation*

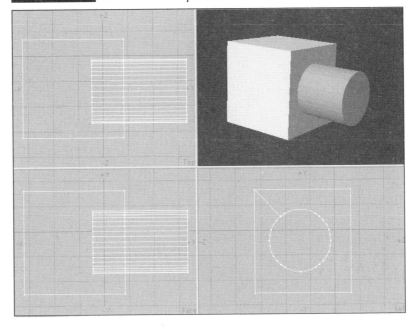

both union and add, so you may be forced to use boolean add on your objects.

OK, now let's take a look at the last boolean operation—intersect.

• **Intersect:** The boolean intersect operation is a very useful tool that performs the opposite action of a boolean union. Instead of removing the polygons where the objects overlap, it removes everything *but* the area where they overlap, as shown in Figure 7.5.

As you can see, the only thing we have left is the volume where the two objects overlapped.

So why is this boolean intersect a useful tool? Well, let's take a look at a good example of when to use boolean intersect.

Let's assume that you are trying to create a seam in your model so it looks manufactured, as if it's two pieces assembled. You may not want to actually create the two pieces, because your model may be a little too complicated and it would take too long. The solution is to boolean out the seam. Figure 7.6 shows a rather bizarre but complicated manufactured model that needs a seam.

The first thing you want to do, before you create the seam, is to make a copy of the object and hide it. We will need this copy for our boolean intersect operation later. Most 3D program allow you to hide objects so

FIGURE 7.4   *A boolean union operation*

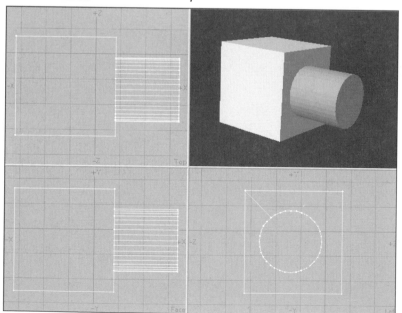

FIGURE 7.5   *A boolean intersect operation*

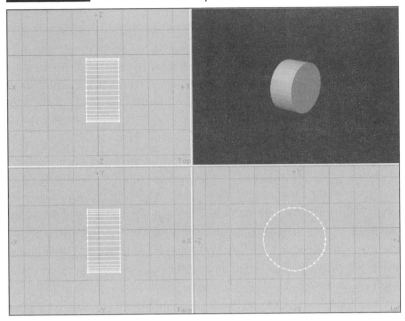

FIGURE 7.6   *A manufactured model requiring a seam*

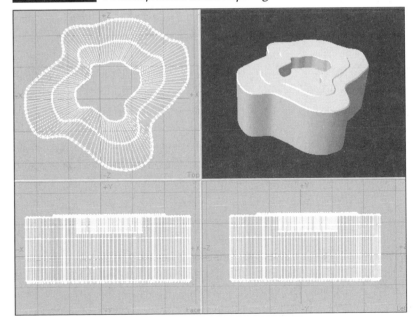

you can see what you are doing and also keep more objects on the screen. Another solution to the crowding problem is layers. A few programs such as LightWave and Rhino have layers so you can keep objects organized. Layers are a much better solution, but they aren't widely available in 3D programs.

OK, to create the seam, a thin modifier plane is created like the one shown in Figure 7.7.

This plane is used with a boolean subtract operation to create the thin gap seen in Figure 7.8.

Now the small segment in the middle of the seam needs to be created so we don't have a hole. This is where the boolean intersect operation comes in handy. To create the seam filler, we could just model another piece, but that would take too long. Instead we use the same modifier object to perform a boolean intersect on the copy of our object, which creates the thin slice shown in Figure 7.9.

This new object will be used as a modifier object to fill in the seam. First, it's scaled down so it's slightly smaller than the object; then it's stretched vertically so it extends into the object, as shown in Figure 7.10.

The last step is to use the new modifier to perform a boolean union operation on the object, which combines their volumes and deletes the unseen portion as shown in Figure 7.11.

FIGURE 7.7   *The modifier plane*

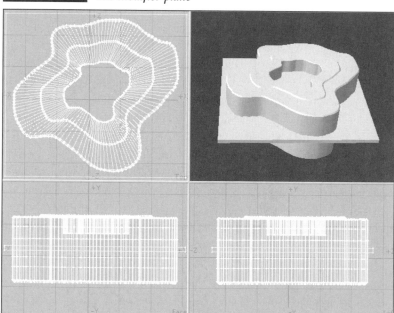

FIGURE 7.8 *The result of the boolean subtract operation*

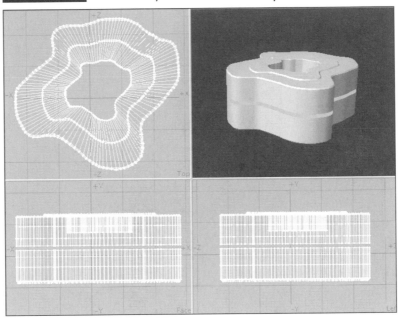

FIGURE 7.9 *The result of the boolean intersect operation*

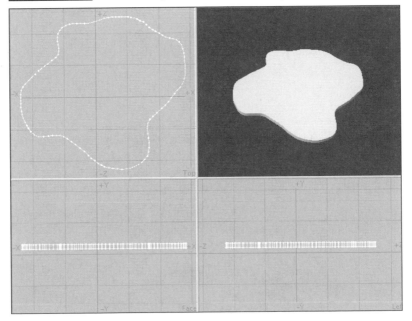

FIGURE 7.10 *Editing the new modifier*

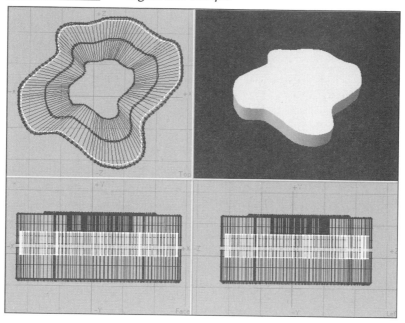

FIGURE 7.11 *The completed seam*

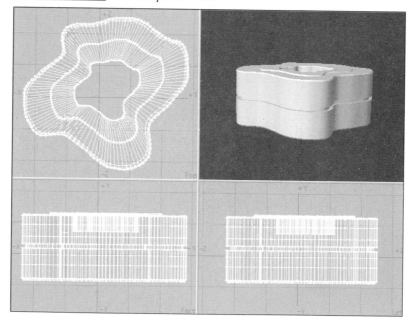

We now have a nice manufactured seam around the object. You can see how the boolean intersect tool saved us a great deal of time we might have spent creating the new modifier object. Boolean operations are very productive tools, which you'll use frequently in your modeling efforts. It's easy to see that the combination of all four provides us with some very powerful modeling tools. In fact, let's take a look at an example of a model that made liberal use of boolean operations.

A Boolean Operation Case Study

Remember the PDA we explored in Chapter 6? It had some very high detail, which was the result of boolean operations. Let's take a look at some of the areas where boolean operations were used on the object.

In Figure 7.12 you'll see an image of the PDA with some booleans indicated.

(A) The locking tab was created by using a boolean union operation to attach the tab object to the lid of the PDA.

(B) The thumb rest was created by using a boolean add operation.

(C) The hole for the pen was created using a boolean subtract operation.

These are just some of the many places where boolean operations were used to create the PDA. Figure 7.13 shows many of the places where the Boolean Subtract tool was used to add details.

FIGURE 7.12   *Examples of boolean operations*

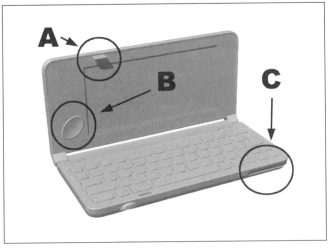

FIGURE 7.13   *Examples of boolean subtract operation*

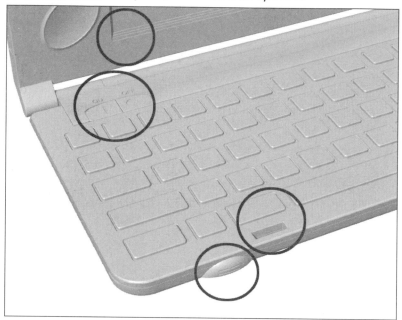

As you can see, the Boolean tool was instrumental in creating the PDA. Of course, most of the details were created with the Boolean Subtract tool.

- All of the buttonholes were created with boolean subtract.
- The grooves in the button that pops open the lid used boolean subtract.
- The layered ridges around the screen were created using multiple boolean subtract operations.
- Lastly, the hole for the locking tab was created with a boolean subtract.

You'll find that boolean subtract is the most common boolean operation you'll use in your modeling efforts. Before we move on to the boolean walk-through, let's take one more look at how boolean operations are applied. We'll use the PDA for our example.

Figure 7.14 shows the base of the PDA, ready for the holes to be cut for the keys.

To create the keyhole, a modifier object is created that shares the shape of the keys. In fact, you can even use the modifier as the keys once the boolean operations are complete. Figure 7.15 shows the modifier object for the keyholes.

FIGURE 7.14 *The PDA ready for a boolean operation*

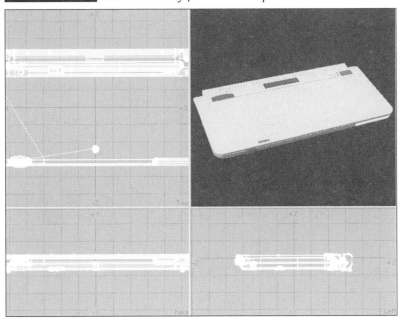

FIGURE 7.15 *The keyhole modifier*

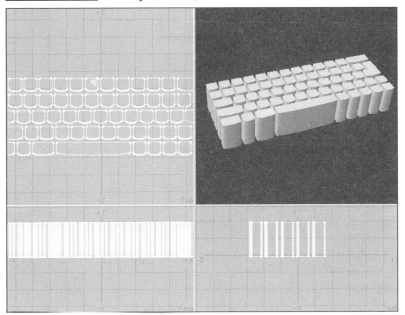

FIGURE 7.16   *The booleaned keyholes*

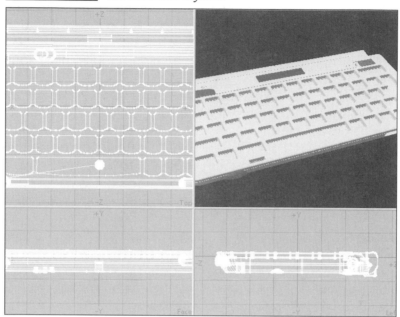

Now, the modifier is applied to the PDA base with a boolean subtract operation, creating the keyholes seen in Figure 7.16.

Now the PDA is ready for the keys to be added. As you've probably noticed, boolean operations are frequently used on high-tech objects, because of their manufactured appearance. You won't find boolean operations being used on too many natural objects, since those tend to be highly organic. Of course, not all boolean operations are performed on high-tech objects. There are some great applications for them in the low-tech world, as we will see in the boolean walk-through.

A Boolean Walk-through

We've seen a number of short examples of the boolean operation process, but in this segment we'll take a much closer look at how a complete model is made with boolean operations.

In this walk-through we'll be seeing how a Duplo play piece is created with boolean operations. A Duplo play piece is the toddler's equivalent of a Lego piece—both are made by Lego, Inc. Since Chuckie is only a year old, we can't give him Legos just yet.

The Duplo piece is a simple object at first glance, but it requires proper planning. There are a number of steps required to create the Duplo play piece, and the majority of them involve boolean operations. Let's get started with the boolean walk-through.

The Duplo play piece begins with a simple cube like the one shown in Figure 7.17.

The next step is to cut out the holes on the bottom of the cube so it can be attached to another Duplo play piece. To create the holes, four small blocks are created in an array like the one shown in Figure 7.18.

This is the first modifier object that will be created for the Duplo play piece. It's applied to the lower portion of the cube with a boolean subtract operation to create the holes seen in Figure 7.19.

Now it's time to turn our attention to the top of the cube. Before the locking cylinders are added, the Duplo play piece needs to have a subtle sign of the manufacturing process. Typically you'll find a little cylindrical dent on the top of the piece, where it was attached in the molding process. This dent is created by making a small cylinder like the one in Figure 7.20, and using it as a boolean subtract modifier to create the hole at the top of the cube, seen in Figure 7.21.

FIGURE 7.17 *The foundation of the Duplo play piece*

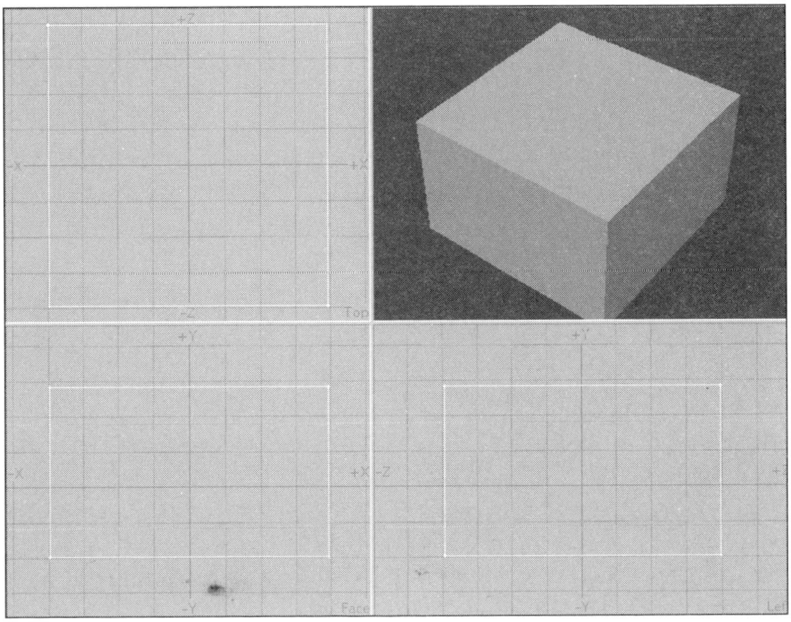

FIGURE 7.18 *The first modifier object*

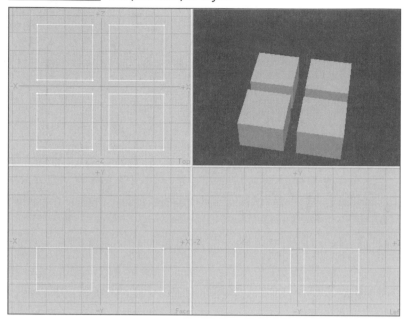

FIGURE 7.19 *The boolean subtract holes*

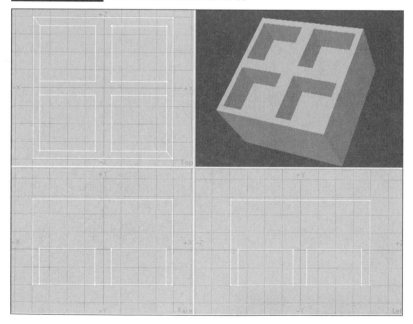

FIGURE 7.20   *The boolean modifier for the dent*

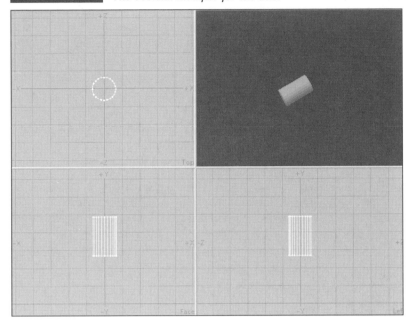

FIGURE 7.21   *The boolean hole*

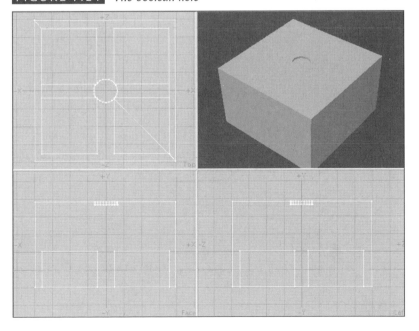

OK, now it's time to utilize some proper planning. Since the Duplo play piece is for a child, the object needs to have beveled edges. The bevels need to be added before the locking cylinders are attached so a bevel isn't created around the locking cylinders. We only want the outside edges of the cube to be beveled. Now is the time to bevel all of the outside edges of the cube, which creates the soft edges seen in Figure 7.22.

Now the locking cylinders can be created. You can see how planning is an essential part of the modeling process. If we saved the bevel until the end, we would have to remodel the object so we could bevel it properly. Always think your models through before you begin working on them.

OK, the locking cylinders are created by making two simple tubes, one slightly larger than the other, as shown in Figure 7.23.

The larger tube is the actual locking cylinder, and the smaller one is the modifier, which is now applied with a boolean subtract operation to create the hollow tube seen in Figure 7.24.

The last touch on the locking tube is to bevel the top edge so Chuckie doesn't hurt himself. Once the locking cylinder is beveled, it's cloned to create the array seen in Figure 7.25.

These locking cylinders are then used as a boolean union modifier to attach them to the top of the cube as shown in Figure 7.26.

FIGURE 7.22 *Beveling the edges of the cube*

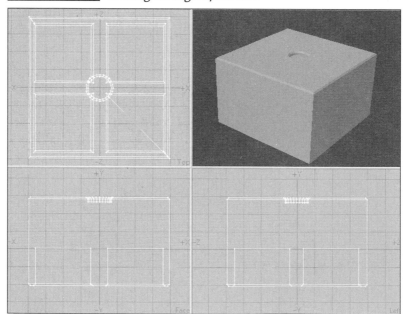

FIGURE 7.23   *Creating the locking cylinder*

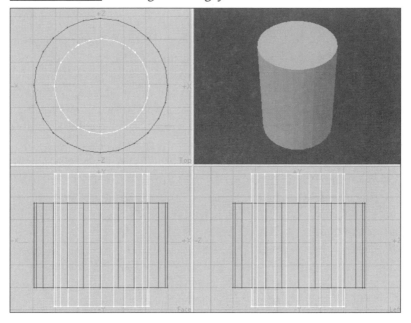

FIGURE 7.24   *A hollow tube created by the boolean subtract operation*

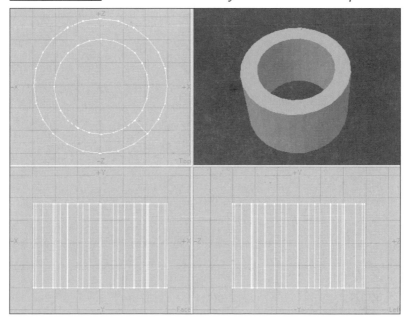

FIGURE 7.25   *The array of locking cylinders*

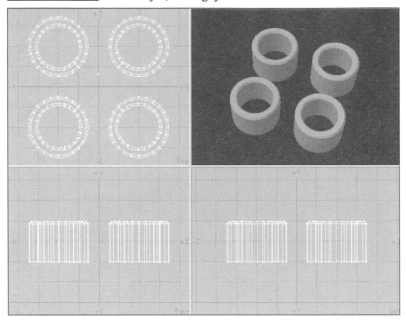

FIGURE 7.26   *The completed Duplo play piece*

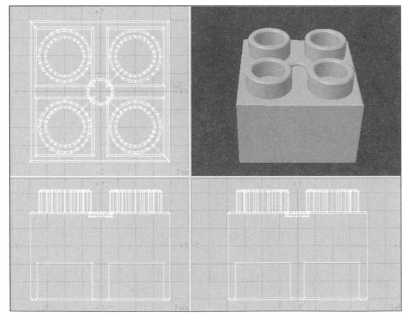

Well, there you have it: an authentic Duplo play piece ready for Chuckie to play with. Of course, he could use a few more, but that's just a matter of copying the object and changing the color.

You can see how boolean operations have made this modeling process very fast and simple. They do some amazing things if you plan your modeling process properly. Just remember, if you plan to use bevels in conjunction with boolean operations, timing is everything. When creating holes with boolean subtract, you'll want to bevel the surface after the holes are created, as I did with the holes on the bottom of the Duplo play piece. On the other hand, if you plan to add details to an object with boolean union or boolean add, you'll need to perform the bevel before the boolean operation, as you saw with the locking cylinders.

Before you embark on your boolean modeling adventure, be sure to draw a map! You won't want to take a wrong turn and end up back where you started.

Wrap-up

Boolean operations are just another of the useful tools in your 3D modeling toolbox. They can be a real timesaver when you're modeling complicated objects. There are ways to create the same effects without booleans, but they're time-consuming and not at all practical. Nothing beats a boolean operation for creating holes or attaching objects.

OK, now it's time to take a look at another common modeling tool—Lathe. This is a great tool for creating complex objects that are cylindrical in shape. Let's move on over to Chapter 8 and check it out.

CHAPTER 8

The Lathe Tool

The Lathe tool is a fabulous asset when making cylindrical objects. If you've ever taken wood shop in school, you'll recognize the tool. A Lathe tool does exactly the same thing a wood lathe does. Well, not exactly the same thing. A wood lathe simply spins the wood while you carve it. On the other hand, a 3D Lathe tool spins the model after you create it. OK, so this sounds a bit confusing. Let's take a look at how a typical lathe operation works.

The Lathe Tool

In Figure 8.1 you'll see a cutaway object that will create a classic spinning top when lathed.

As you can see, it looks just like a top that has been cut in half. When this object is lathed it will create the top shown in Figure 8.2.

Well, after the push of one button we've turned the cutaway into a very detailed top. Creating objects with the lathe tool can be very fast. There are many objects that can only be created with the lathe tool. This top would have taken hours to model with any other method.

We'll be taking a closer look at how the details of the top were created, but first let's take a look at the settings that accompany the lathe tool. To demonstrate the effects created by the settings, we'll be working with a simple disc, offset from the center axis as shown in Figure 8.3.

FIGURE 8.1   *A lathe cutaway*

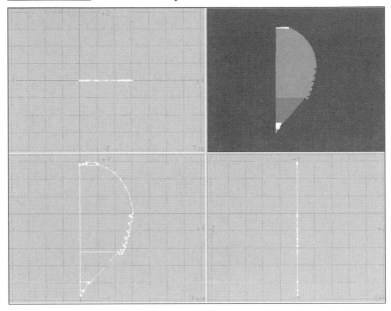

FIGURE 8.2   *The lathed top*

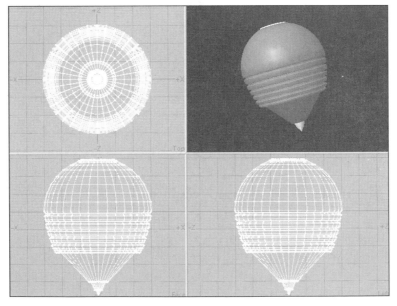

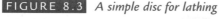

FIGURE 8.3   *A simple disc for lathing*

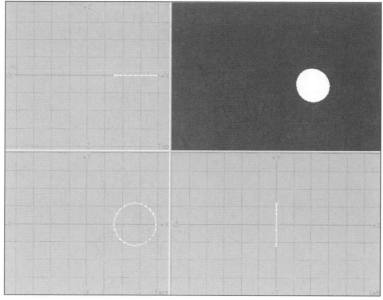

Offsetting the object will give us a more interesting effect, since it won't be a solid object. Let's take a look at the settings and what they accomplish.

- **Start Angle:** This is where the lathe rotation begins. You will typically want to set this value to zero so you have more control of the rotation. It's always a good idea to create your lathed objects at the zero point on the X axis. This will make it easier to position the center of the lathe effect. It's also a great idea to line your center points up with the Y axis at zero so you can simply lathe around that axis. When you lathe an object, you will often have the opportunity to enter the coordinates for the lathe center. It's a lot easier to make them all zero so your lathe is accurate.

- **End Angle:** This is where the lathe will terminate. This can be any value from zero to up in the thousands. When you go past 360, your object begins making a second rotation. This is usually undesirable, but it's very handy when working with offset values, which we will discuss in a moment. Figure 8.4 shows an example of a lathe End Angle of 180.

  As you can see, the disc has created half of a torus shape because it stopped after 180 degrees of rotation. If you set the value to 360, you would have a complete torus shape, which would look like a donut.

- **Sides:** This determines how many segments are in the lathed object. Figure 8.5 shows the disc lathed with the Sides set to 12.

FIGURE 8.4   *A lathe end angle of 180*

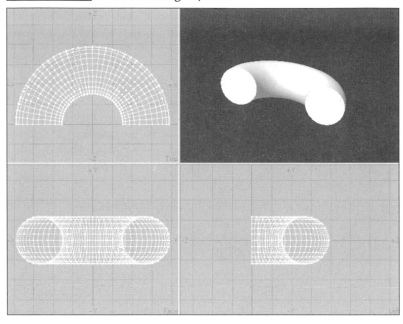

FIGURE 8.5   *Controlling the number of sides*

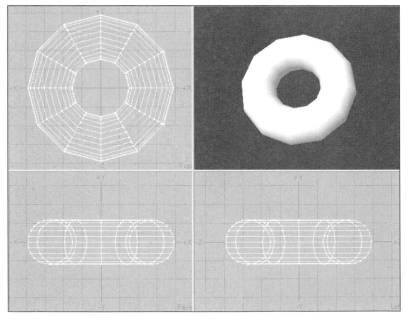

As you can see, a low Sides setting creates a rather rough object. The higher the number of sides, the smoother the object. A typical good setting for Sides would be 36.

• **Offset:** This is a handy feature for creating objects such as tubes. The offset value determines how much the object will shift during the lathe cycle. It will move the object the designated distance along an axis for the duration of the lathe. This means if you set the Offset to 15 inches along the Y axis, the lathe would stop 15 inches above the start point.

When you work with an offset value, you need to increase the end angle as well as the number of sides. For example, take a look at the object in Figure 8.6.

This is the same disc that was lathed earlier, but this time the offset was given a value of 15 inches, an end angle of 1800, and 200 sides. The end angle set at 1800 determines the number of times the object will rotate during the lathe. This is an example of when you'll need an end angle greater than 360. Of course, if you increase the end angle, you also need to increase the sides, or the object will be very rough.

The offset value is a great asset when creating objects such as springs, which require a large number of rotations along an axis. Speaking of the axis, let's take a look at that setting.

FIGURE 8.6 *An object lathed with an offset value*

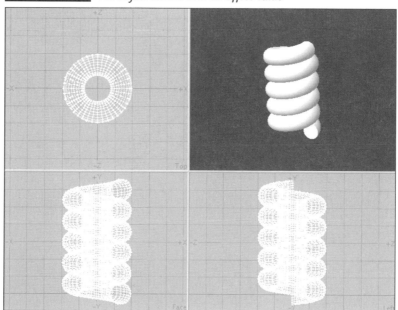

- **Axis:** This is the location that will be the center of the lathe. It can be placed anywhere you want, but it's best to use the 0,0,0 axis in the center of the screen to keep from getting errors. If you lathe on the wrong axis, you can get something like the error in Figure 8.7.

  The axis where the disc was lathed is marked with the X. As you can see, it wasn't aligned with the disc, so the lathing caused the disc to rotate, compressing the torus. This is why it's usually a good idea to model the object to be lathed along the center axis of your modeling program so you can avoid errors by setting the axis to a value of 0,0,0.

Well, those are the lathe settings and the effects they create. With just these few settings, you can create some spectacular models. Speaking of spectacular, let's now take a closer look at how all that detail was added to the top we discussed earlier. When creating the initial object to be lathed, you need to consider the details. Thinking of the starting shape as a cutaway of the final object is the best approach. When creating the top I basically mentally cut away the top. Let's take a closer look at some of the details on the top and how they were created.

Figure 8.8 shows the very tip of the top and the portion of the original lathe object that represents the tip.

The arrow shows the same region on both objects. You can see the inset where the metal tip meets the plastic body. This is a small detail that would be very difficult to create with any other modeling tool, but it was as easy as pulling two points back into the model when working with a Lathe tool. Small details are very easy to create when using lathes to create your model.

Figure 8.9 shows a comparison of the gripping ridges between the lathe object and the final top.

Take a look at the lathe object on the right and you'll see that the ridges were easily created by adding an indent to the original lathe object. When this object is lathed, it creates a groove around the top. You could try to boolean these grooves, but they would end up with very sharp edges, and we know that wouldn't be safe for Chuckie. You can't bevel the groove with a bevel tool, but you can easily drag a single point inward on the edges of the grooves to create the bevel. Within seconds you have a detail that would take you infinitely longer to create by any other means.

OK, one last look at the top and then we'll move on. Take a look at Figure 8.10.

You can see there are grooves around the top of the top, creating individual segments. This is actually the mechanism part of the top. Underneath is where the little ball for the centrifugal force is located so the top spins for a long time. To create the mechanical top, a couple of indents

FIGURE 8.7 *The disc lathed on the wrong axis*

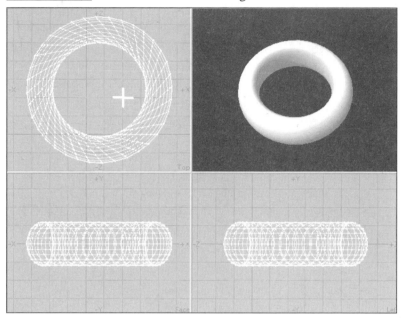

FIGURE 8.8 *The tip of the top*

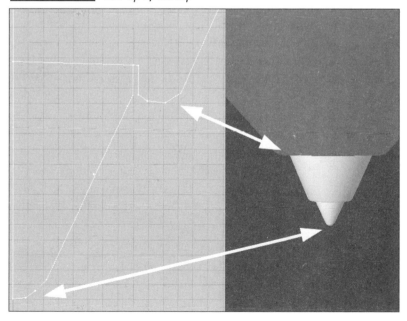

FIGURE 8.9   *A comparison of the gripping ridges*

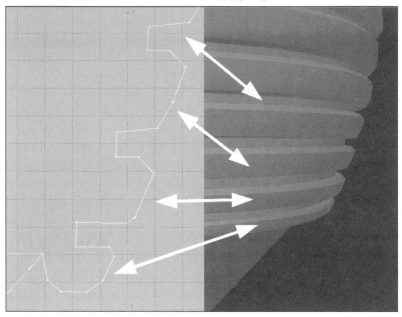

FIGURE 8.10   *The top of the top*

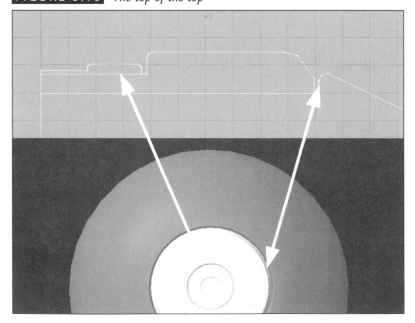

were added to the lathe object as seen in the figure. These simple indents added a great deal of detail to the top and took a few seconds to create.

There you have it. Creating detailed objects with the Lathe tool is simply a matter of adding minor details to your lathe object. Well, it also involves a great deal of planning. You need to think about the shape of the object before you perform the lathe. Fortunately, a lathe can be undone with a push of a button, so it makes for easy tweaking.

Another thing to consider when using the lathe tool is the surfaces you'll want to assign. You can create a lathe object that is a single surface and assign them after the lathe, or you can do it before the lathe, which is the best idea. It can be very difficult to assign the surfacing after the lathe when details overlap. Breaking the object into several surfaces before you lathe saves you plenty of headaches down the road.

Using the Lathe Tool on Square Objects

While the lathe tool is perfect for cylindrical objects, that's not the only use for it. It can also be used to create some very nice details on angular objects. For example, let's suppose you want to create a tabletop with a nicely detailed edge—you know, the kind with the classic detailing along the outside. This would be a bit of a challenge with typical modeling tools, though you could build it with bevels. Fortunately, the lathe tools makes this job a snap. You simply build one half of the tabletop from a cutaway view, as shown in Figure 8.11.

FIGURE 8.11 *The tabletop cutaway*

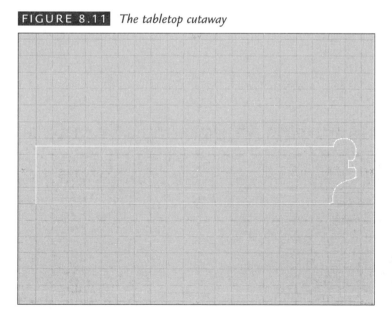

FIGURE 8.12   *The completed tabletop*

Then you lathe it with four segments and 360 degrees of rotation. This creates a great four-sided tabletop with an incredibly detailed edge that would take you hours with the bevel tool and, well, way too long with any other modeling tools. Figure 8.12 shows the completed tabletop.

Sometimes you need to take a creative approach to solving complex modeling problems. You'd be surprised at how easily things can be accomplished as long as you don't limit your thinking to the accepted practices.

OK, that's enough talk about the Lathe tool. It's time we saw how a model was created using it.

A Lathe Walk-through

We're going to walk through the development of two models using the Lathe tool. There are so many possibilities that I wanted to be sure we covered enough to spark your imagination. The first object we will create is a Weeble. So what is a Weeble? Well, it was one of my favorite toys as a child. Yes, I've always been easily amused. Weebles were introduced by Hasbro in 1972 and were made through the mid-1980s. They are currently being produced once again, although the new line looks nothing like the original egg-shaped ones. Though they were very popular, Hasbro only produced about 50 sets.

The Weeble is made up of two parts: the body and a thin, clear plastic cover for the image that wraps around the Weeble. Both will be modeled in this walk-through, but we'll start with the body first. The body is started by creating a simple lathe object like the one shown in Figure 8.13.

Notice the indent on the right side of the object. This will create an indent around the Weeble when the clear plastic protector goes on. The Weeble is lathed with an end angle of 360 and 36 sides to create the completed body shown in Figure 8.14.

You can see how quickly the Lathe tool creates a fairly complicated object. You could have done the same thing with a boolean operation, but it would take much longer and the edges would be very sharp. Once again, this is a child's toy, so safety is an issue.

Now it's time to create the plastic protector. This object needs to fit into the depression created on the Weeble. It could be created from scratch, but it's a better idea to go back to the Weeble lathe object and use it as the template. Basically, the segment with the depression is cut out and used for the back of the plastic protector, as shown in Figure 8.15.

The points circled on the Weeble lathe object are copied. Then the back row of the copied points is moved outward to create the outline of the plastic protector. They are then made into a polygon to be lathed. The lathed object is shown in Figure 8.16.

Now the only thing left is to combine the objects to complete the Weeble shown in Figure 8.17.

FIGURE 8.13 *The Weeble lathe object*

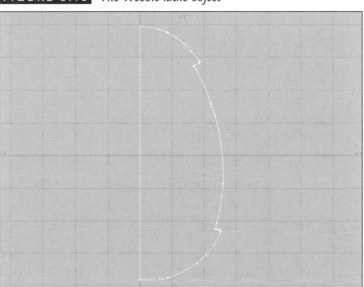

FIGURE 8.14   *The lathed Weeble body*

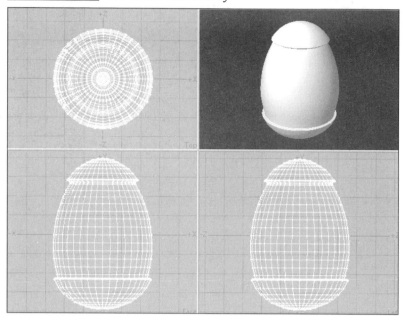

FIGURE 8.15   *Creating the plastic protector lathe object*

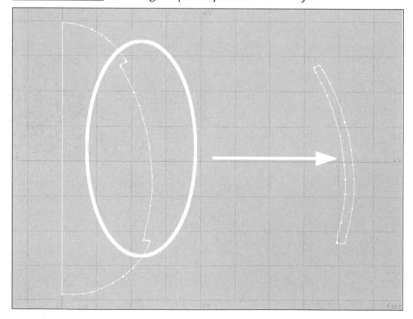

FIGURE 8.16 *The lathed plastic protector*

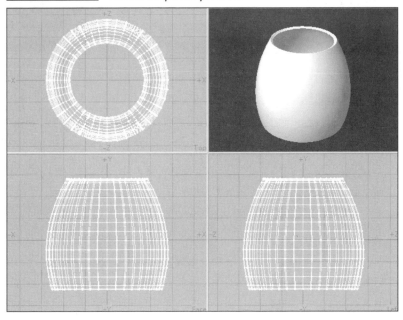

FIGURE 8.17 *The completed Weeble*

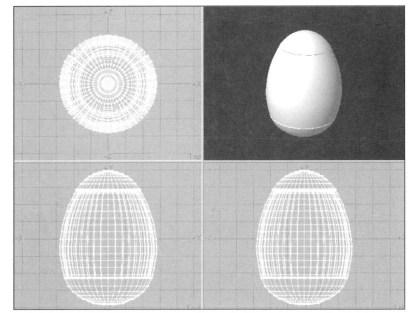

See how simple that was? It takes just minutes to create complex objects with the Lathe tool. This was just one of the numerous ways to use it. Let's take a look at another one.

Many years ago Fisher-Price introduced an amazingly simple line of toys that really took off. They were called Little People. They were little wooden figures—nothing more than tubes, really, yet they were very popular. In the next lathe walk-through we'll see how a Little People toy is created with the lathe tool.

Creating the Little People Toy

Since Little People are nothing more than glorified cylinders, creating them with the Lathe tool is a snap. In this walk-through we'll see how the Little People clown character was created with the Lathe tool. I chose the clown because he has a unique, frilly collar on his shirt that allows me to illustrate another modeling technique. Let's get cracking on this clown.

The first step is to create the basic body lathe object shown in Figure 8.18.

The object is then lathed with a sides value of 36 to create the body shown in Figure 8.19.

We now have the completed body. Simple, wasn't it? Well, that's the beauty of the Lathe tool. Now let's move on to the tricky part of the character. Well, I guess his head should be added first. This is easily created by adding a sphere to the top of the body as shown in Figure 8.20.

Now we're getting somewhere. The next element to create is the frilly collar. This is a relatively complicated-looking object, but it's very simple to create. Once again, you have to be creative in your thinking when modeling complex objects.

The first step in creating the collar is to make the lathe object, using the body and head as a template. Figure 8.21 show how this is accomplished.

Notice how the head and body are used as a template for the collar. This makes it possible to perfectly fit the collar to the body, without its penetrating either the head or body. Once the collar is completed, it is lathed with a sides value of 36 to create the basic collar shape seen in Figure 8.22.

Now for the details. The collar needs to have the frilly look, which can be accomplished easily by selecting every other group of two points around the outside of the collar and pulling them upward as seen in Figure 8.23.

See how easy that was? The completed object looks rather complex, but it was very simple to create. Be sure to take a step back and examine

FIGURE 8.18   *The clown body lathe object*

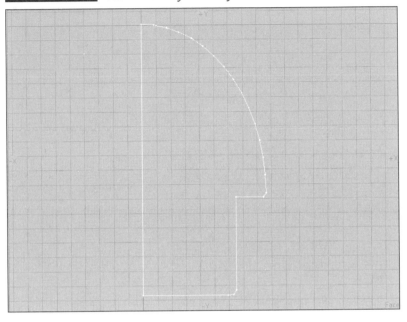

FIGURE 8.19   *The lathed body*

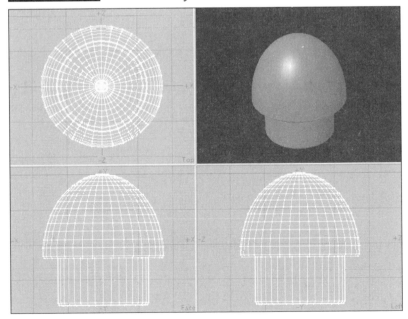

FIGURE 8.20   *Adding the head*

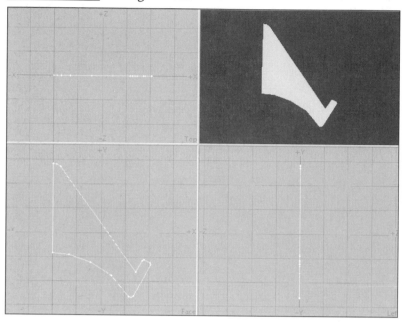

FIGURE 8.21   *Creating the collar lathe object*

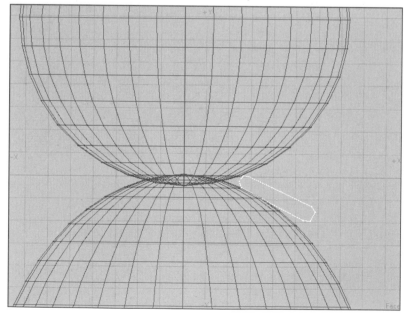

FIGURE 8.22   *The basic collar object*

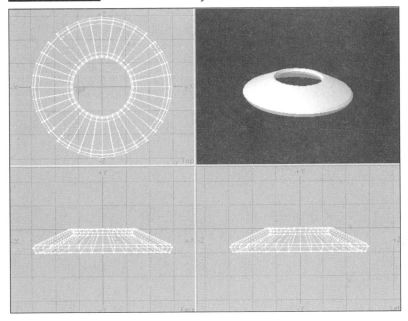

FIGURE 8.23   *Adding frills to the collar*

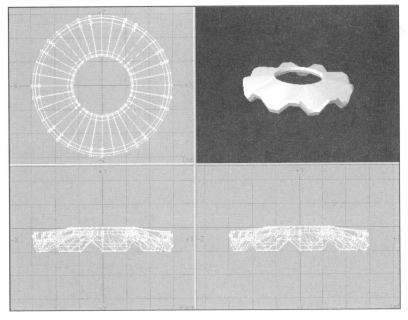

the project before you approach it. It makes it easier to come up with solutions to seemingly difficult tasks.

OK, now for a look at our clown so far.

There is just one element remaining—the hat. Fitting the hat to the head is simple. As we saw with the collar, the head is used as a template for creating the hat lathe object seen in Figure 8.25.

Now the hat is lathed with a side value of 36 to create the basic shape seen in Figure 8.26.

Now for the jagged rim. To create the rim a similar technique to the one used on the collar is used, though the hat is a bit more complicated. It has curved lines between the peaks, so the polygons between the peaks need to be adjusted to smooth the curve. The result is the completed hat you see in Figure 8.27.

It's really not that difficult to create detailed effects if you think with an open mind. Just a few points pulled upward and the hat looks perfect. Why don't we take a look at the total package? Figure 8.28 shows the completed Little People clown character.

Well, there you have it: a classic Little People clown. See how simple that was? The Lathe tool can be a major asset in your modeling tool library. It's essential for a number of applications, such as any object that is somewhat cylindrical in shape and with consistent detail around the object.

FIGURE 8.24   *The clown with collar*

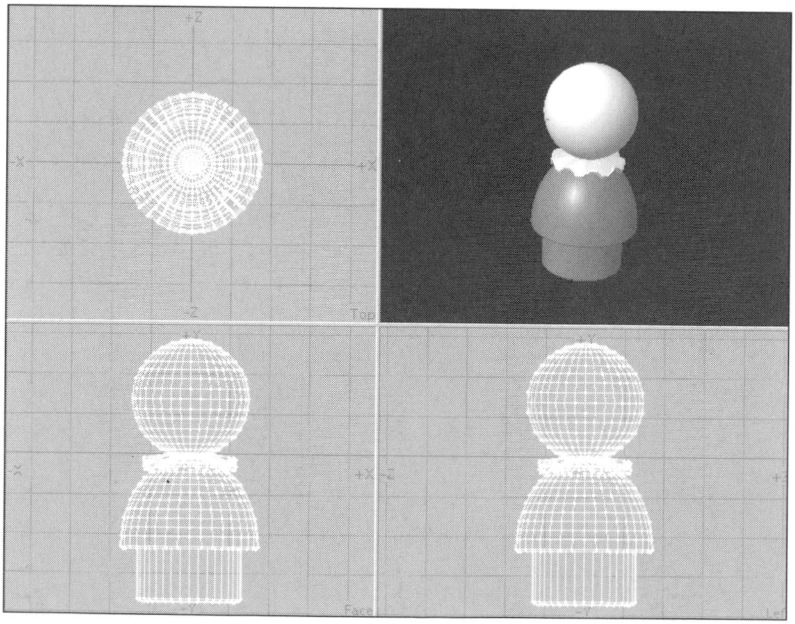

FIGURE 8.25   *The hat lathe object*

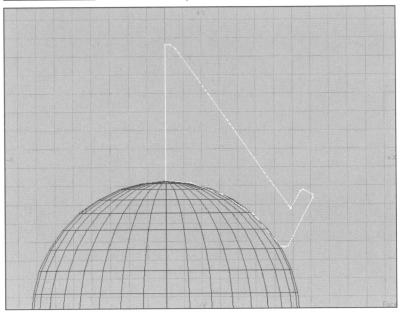

FIGURE 8.26   *The lathed hat*

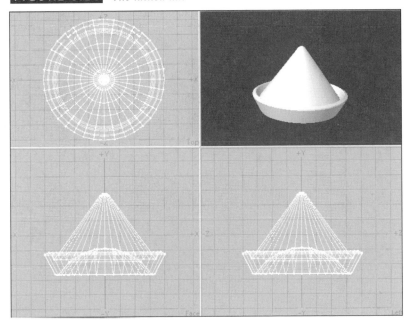

FIGURE 8.27   *The completed hat*

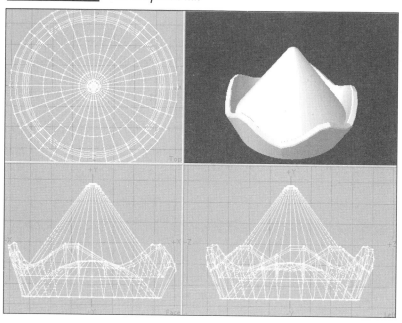

FIGURE 8.28   *The completed Little People clown*

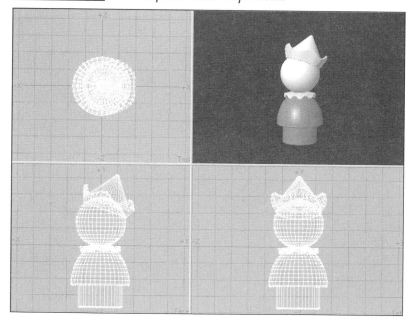

Wrap-up

You've seen several examples that illustrate the power and flexibility of the Lathe tool. It's a real asset when modeling complex cylindrical objects, but it also makes some linear objects, such as tabletops, a great deal easier to create. Don't limit your thinking when using the Lathe tool. There are far more uses than the ones outlined in this chapter. All it takes is a few minutes of experimenting to discover them.

OK, the next stop on our modeling tool journey is Extrude/Sweep and Smooth Shift. You've heard me talk about these in earlier chapters, and now it's time to really get to know them.

CHAPTER 9

Other Useful Modeling Tools

This chapter will focus on several other common and very useful modeling tools, which include the following:

- Extrude
- Sweep/Smooth Shift
- Path Manipulation
- Cloning

These are all very productive tools that are not really used that often—mainly because they're misunderstood. You'd be surprised to find that even the experienced 3D professionals don't fully comprehend the power and utility of most modeling tools. It's not really all that surprising. There are literally thousands of modeling tools out there, with more being created every day. It can be very time-consuming to keep up with them. I've certainly killed my share of hours and days experimenting with these tools to find the best applications for them.

The funny thing is that many of the current tools are completely useless. 3D program developers are all in a feature war, trying to dominate the market by hooking their buyers with new features. The reality is that very few of these "new" features have any value. Most of them are a complete waste of time. You're better off focusing on the classics, like the ones discussed in this book. You can't go wrong with them, and there is absolutely nothing they can't be used to create.

The first tool we'll explore in this section is one of the oldest and most reliable—Extrude. Let's take a look at how the Extrude tool works.

The Extrude Tool

The Extrude tool takes selected polygons and moves them away from the object, spanning new polygons between them. This is easier to illustrate, so why don't we take a look at Figure 9.1?

Here we have a simple plane that has been extruded. The object on the left is the original plane. The object on the right shows the plane extruded back to create a cube. When you extrude something, it creates a copy of the object and moves it to the designated position, creating polygons that connect the new object to the original. It's a very simple tool, but serves as the foundation of the majority of models. Now there are a few settings and other considerations, so let's take a look at them now.

• **Axis:** This is the axis along which the extrusion will take place. You can only extrude along the X, Y, or Z axis. You cannot extrude diagonally, which does limit the application of the Extrude tool.

FIGURE 9.1   *An extruded plane*

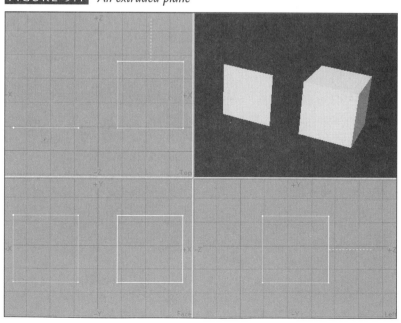

FIGURE 9.2 *Extrusions with different segment settings*

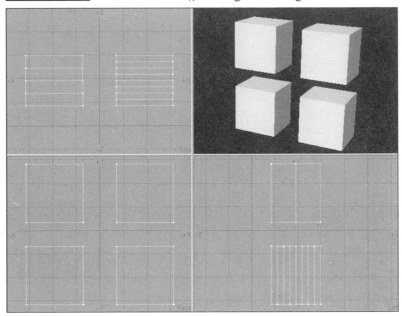

- **Segments:** This determines the number of segments that will be created between the original object and the copy. Figure 9.2 shows several planes that have been extruded with different segment settings.

    Each plane has been extruded to the same distance, but they all have different segment quantities. Sometimes you'll need to have several segments so you can add details to the model. Speaking of distances, let's take a look at the Distance setting.

- **Distance/Position:** This determines how far the extrusion will go.

OK, so those are the settings for Extrude. It's not a complicated tool, but a very necessary one. Most objects start with some form of thickness created by an Extrude operation. It's the backbone of most 3D models. Let's take a moment to follow a brief Extrude walk-through before we move on to Sweep and Smooth Shift.

An Extrude Walk-through

Extrude is a very simple tool, so our walk-through will be relatively brief. What we'll be doing is taking a look at how some of the elements were made on Chuckie's toy train, shown in Figure 9.3.

FIGURE 9.3   *Chuckie's toy train*

The first part we'll examine is the engine block on the front of the train. This object was started with a simple flat shape that represented the engine block from the front. This object is shown in Figure 9.4.

The plane was extruded back twice its width, with a single segment, to create the engine block. A small bevel was then added to both ends and the top to make the toy safe for children. The result is the finished engine block in Figure 9.5.

The next object to be extruded was the cabin on the backside of the engine block. It started with the basic extrusion shape shown in Figure 9.6.

This object was then extruded back a distance slightly less than its width, with a single segment. The result was the basic shape of the cabin shown in Figure 9.7.

To complete the cabin, a modifier object, shown in Figure 9.8, was created to boolean subtract the curve along the back of the cabin.

This shape creates the flowing lines along the back of the cabin. When the modifier object is applied, the cabin takes the shape shown in Figure 9.9.

The cabin has begun to take shape. The last step is to cut out the core of the cabin with another modifier object. For this step, a copy of the original extruded cabin was scaled down and placed in the middle of the cabin as shown in Figure 9.10.

FIGURE 9.4 *The flat engine block plane*

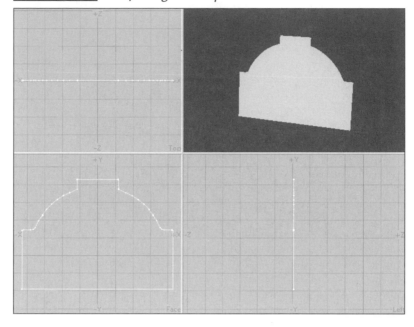

FIGURE 9.5 *The completed engine block*

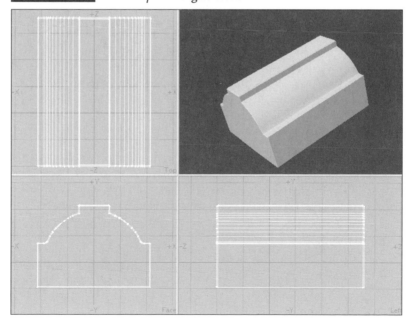

FIGURE 9.6 *The train cabin extrusion object*

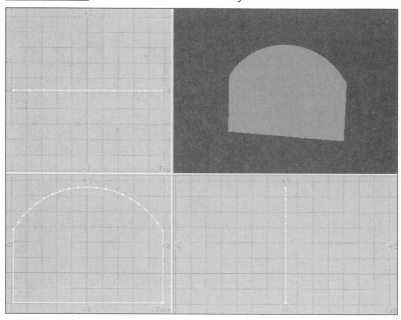

FIGURE 9.7 *The basic cabin shape*

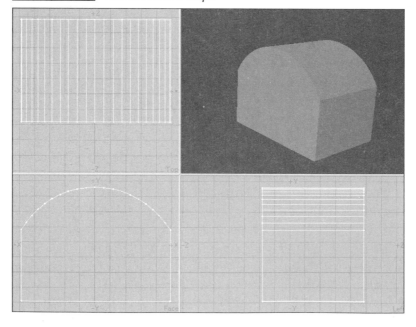

FIGURE 9.8 *The cabin modifier object*

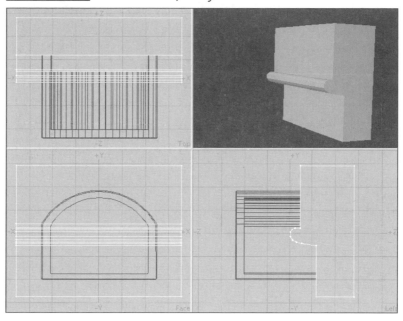

FIGURE 9.9 *The booleaned cabin*

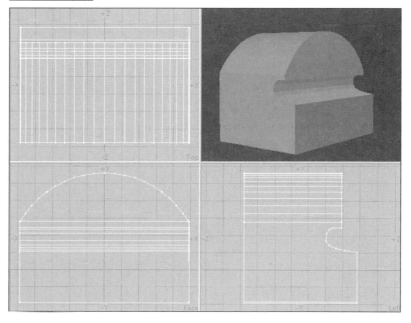

FIGURE 9.10   *The subtractive boolean modifier*

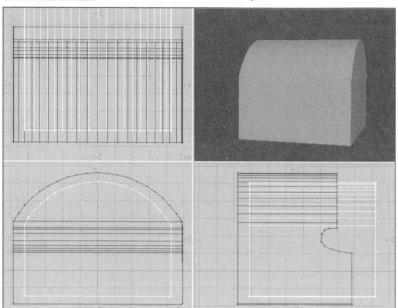

Then a boolean subtract operation was performed, creating a hollowed cabin. The final touch was to bevel the flat edges so the cabin wouldn't be a hazard. The completed cabin is shown in Figure 9.11.

As you can see, the Extrude tool is very handy. It lays the foundation for the other tools to create the details. All of the modifier objects used in the tutorial were extruded from simple flat planes.

The Extrude tool is a valuable addition to any 3D modeling toolbox. Now let's take a look at a similar, but more evolved tool—Sweep.

The Sweep (Smooth Shift) Tool

Sweep and Smooth Shift are the same function. It all depends on the program you are using. Almost every program has a different name for the same tools. It can be very confusing. For the sake of this chapter I'll be referring to the tool as Sweep, since that was the original name.

A Sweep tool performs an Extrude function, but doesn't create a copy of the polygons in the new location. Instead, it physically moves the polygons to the new location. You can also perform a Sweep at any angle; you aren't fixed to the X, Y, or Z axis. You can sweep the polygons anywhere in 3D space. Figure 9.12 shows an example of a sweep action.

FIGURE 9.11   *The completed cabin*

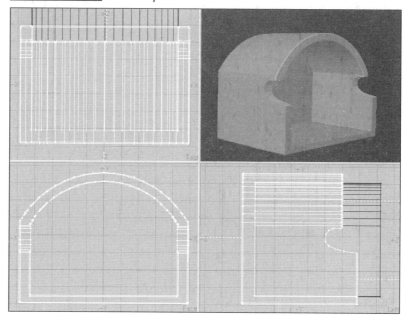

FIGURE 9.12   *A sweep*

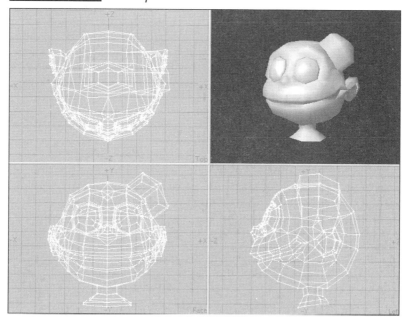

Here we have the head of Herman, Chuckie's playmate. Herman has bumped his head on a table, so several polygons were selected on the side of his head and swept to create a bump. Actually, it's the start of a bump. The same polygons can be swept again and sized to create the bump shown in Figure 9.13.

Notice that the polygons are not parallel to any axis. This is the beauty of the Sweep tool: You can add details without being restricted to an axis. The Sweep tool is commonly used in conjunction with subdivision technology as we discussed in Chapter 3. The low-resolution model is edited with sweeps, and then subdivision is applied to smooth the mesh. Figure 9.14 shows Herman's head with subdivision applied.

Now that's a great-looking model. The Sweep tool laid the foundation for subdivision to smooth the model. Herman definitely has a very smooth cartoon bump on his head. Man, that's got to hurt!

While Sweep is very similar to Extrude, it does have some differences in the settings. Sweep doesn't have an axis or segment setting. The polygons automatically sweep in the direction they're facing, and only for a single segment. There is still a distance setting, though.

The Sweep tool is, hands down, the most valuable of the organic modeling tools. It's absolutely paramount for creating creatures and characters with polygons. Speaking of characters, let's take a look at a Sweep walkthrough where we'll see how the hair was added to Chuckie's head.

FIGURE 9.13 *Herman's completed bump*

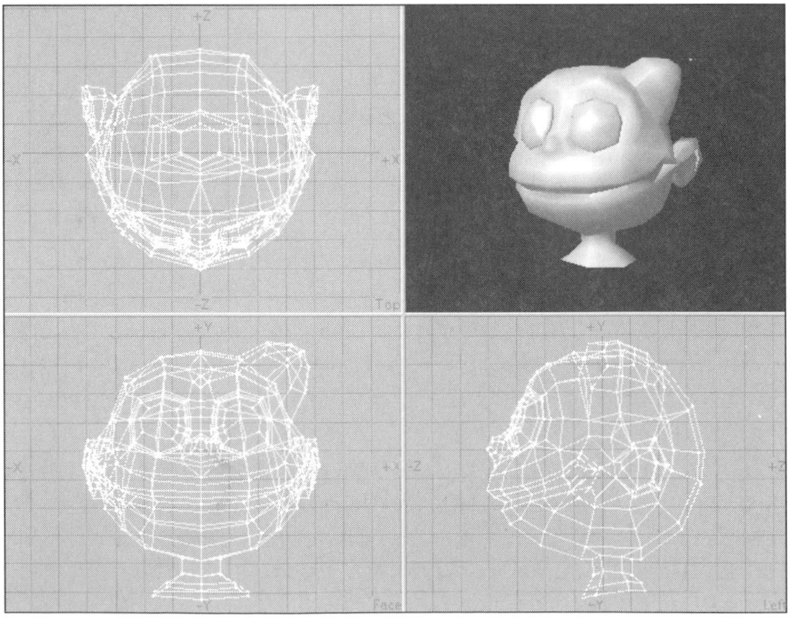

FIGURE 9.14   *Herman's head with subdivision applied*

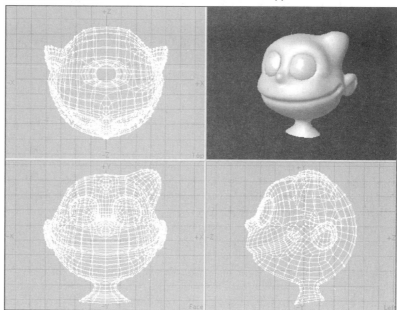

A Sweep Walk-through

The Sweep tool is a staple for creating details on characters and creatures. In this walk-through we'll take a look at how the single hair on the top of Chuckie's head was created.

The first step in adding the hair is to create the hair follicle. We could just drop a hair on top of the head, but that wouldn't look natural. Yes, I know he's a cartoon character, but the details matter no matter what the character is. It's the details that make them interesting.

To create the follicle the four polygons at the top of the head are swept, scaled, and shaped, as shown in Figure 9.15.

Now you might think an Extrude tool would work here, but that's not the case. Yes, the polygons are pretty much aligned to the Y axis, but when you extrude polygons, the tool only creates a copy of the polygons to be placed in the new position. It leaves the original where it was, as shown in Figure 9.16.

The original polygons are selected at the base of the head. You don't want these polygons, since they will only cause errors when you subdivide the object. You can't have polygons in the middle of the object when you subdivide. When working with organic objects you'll need to use the Sweep tool to add details.

FIGURE 9.15   *Starting the hair follicle*

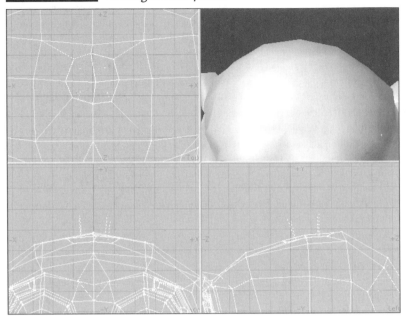

FIGURE 9.16   *The original polygons left by the extrude*

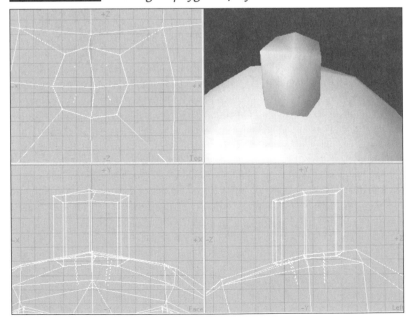

OK, let's get back to our hair follicle. Now that the polygons for the follicle have been shaped, the depth can be added. The first step is to sweep the polygons and scale them down to represent the diameter of the hair follicle as shown in Figure 9.17.

Now the polygons are moved back into the head slightly with another sweep, as shown in Figure 9.18.

The new polygons are scaled down slightly to build a small bevel around the hole. This bevel is created to smooth the edge of the hole when subdivision is applied. Now the polygons are swept and moved deep into the head to create the actual follicle shown in Figure 9.19.

The polygons are given a new surface now so they can be surfaced separately later. The hair is now ready to be developed. This is done by performing a series of sweeps, scaling them down each time to create the hair seen in Figure 9.20.

Now the last step is to select the hair polygons and bend them to create a little personality. Figure 9.21 shows the bent hair.

Finally, the object is subdivided to smooth and shape it. The result is a very cute Chuckie with a single hair on the top of his head, as shown in Figure 9.22.

FIGURE 9.17 *The beginning of the hair follicle*

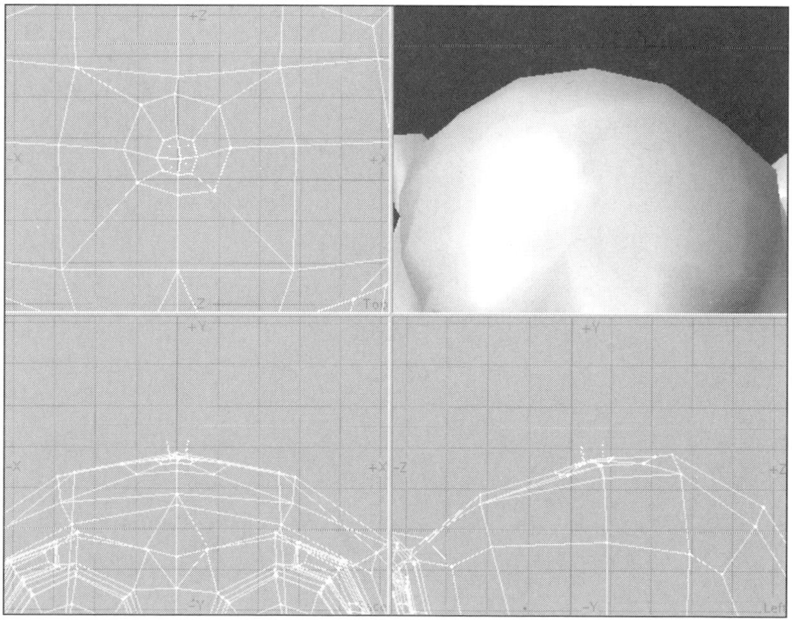

FIGURE 9.18   *Moving the polygons into the head*

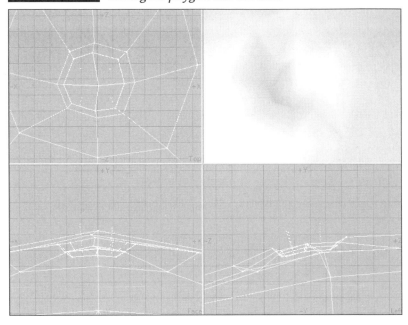

FIGURE 9.19   *The hair follicle*

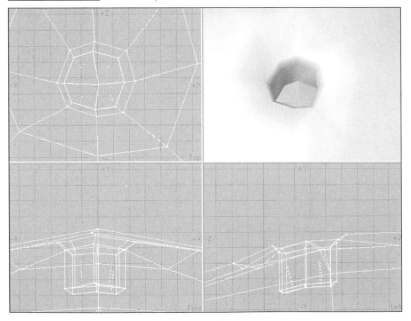

FIGURE 9.20   *The completed hair*

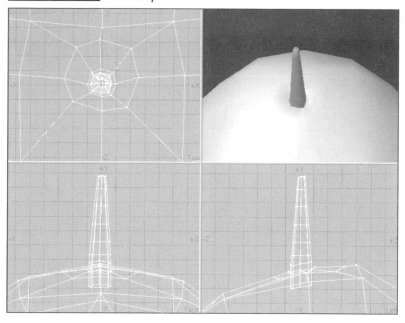

FIGURE 9.21   *The bent hair*

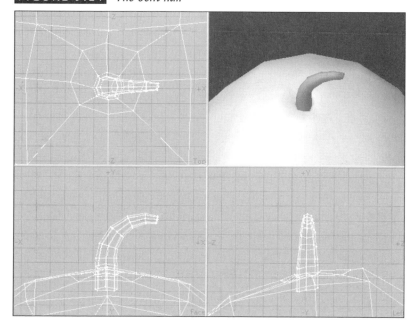

FIGURE 9.22   *The completed head*

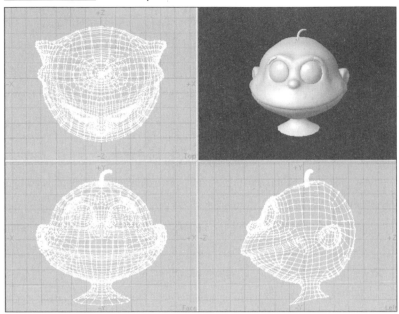

As you can see, the Sweep tool is of real value for creating details for your 3D creatures and characters. Of course, it's not limited to characters alone. The Sweep tool is the backbone of many polygon modeling techniques. You can create just about anything with the Sweep tool. In fact, we used it extensively in Part II where we modeled Chuckie's head, shirt, and diaper.

OK, that does it for the hands-on model building tools. Now it's time to take a look at a few really unusual and automated surface generators, such as Paths.

Working with Paths

There are a number of uses for paths in 3D modeling. They can be used to create very complex effects. OK, so what exactly are paths? Well, they're simply what they sound like. A path is a line you draw to designate the direction something should take. A path is typically a spline object. A spline is used because it creates an infinite-resolution curve, which is necessary for paths. A polygon path would have far too many bumps in the road. Figure 9.23 shows a typical spline path.

FIGURE 9.23 *A spline path*

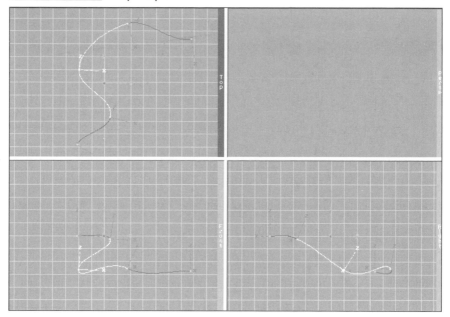

Take a look at the path and you'll see five control points that are used to modify the path. They can be moved and rotated to change the direction of the path. Editing a path is very simple. OK, so now we have a path—what do we do with it? Well, there are two main uses for paths. Let's take a look at each one.

Path Extrusions

This is the same as the normal extrude operation, except that the object is extruded along the path. You first create the path, like the one in Figure 9.23. Then you create an object to be extruded along the path. Figure 9.24 shows an object shaped like a cutaway of a vine.

To extrude the object you must place it at the beginning of the path, which is usually determined by the first control point you created. Figure 9.25 shows the vine cutaway properly positioned at the end of the spline path.

The object needs to be placed with its axis on the center of the path, or the extrusion will not follow the path properly. It also needs to be rotated to be parallel with the start of the path, or it will not extrude properly. The placement of the object is very important if you want to ensure that the effect is accurate.

FIGURE 9.24   *A path extrusion object*

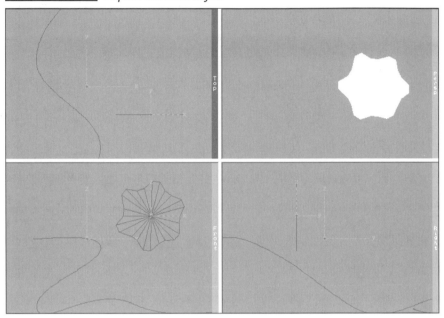

FIGURE 9.25   *Positioning the extrusion object*

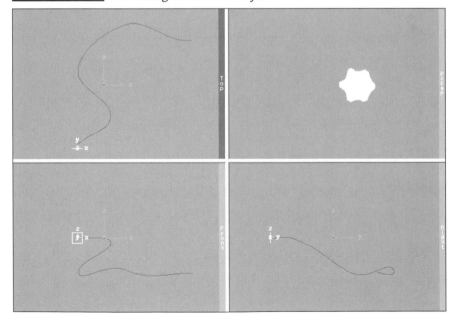

FIGURE 9.26 *The extruded vine cutaway*

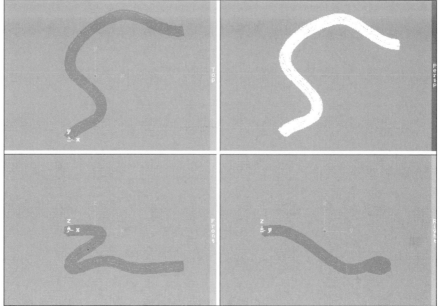

Once the object is in place, you can extrude it along the path as shown in Figure 9.26.

Notice how the object followed the path as it was extruded. This technique can be used to create some fascinating effects. Speaking of effects, let's take a look at the settings for path extrusions to see how they can be manipulated to create some very impressive effects.

- **Number of Sections:** This determines how many segments will be in the extrusion. You'll want to use a fairly high number if you want the object to be smooth. The more sections, the smoother the extrusion.

- **Uniform Lengths:** This feature evenly spaces all segments in the extrusion for a clean object. If you want the polygons to be the same size all the way down, you'll want to use this feature. For example, you may want to manually add some leaves to the vine extrusion. When doing this, you'd want the polygons to be the same size so you can sweep some stems.

- **Uniform Knots:** This is a great feature for building efficient extrusions. What it does is focus the bulk of the segments along the curves for maximum smoothing. A normal extrusion along a path will distribute

the segments evenly or close to it. If you have relatively straight segments in your path, you'll end up wasting a lot of polygons on the
straight zones because of the even spacing. On the other hand, selecting Uniform Knots will reduce the segments on the straight areas and
use them to smooth the curves. Figure 9.27 shows the effect of applying Uniform Knots to the vine extrusion.

Notice how the segments are focused on the curves. These areas are
now smoother than they would have been with a standard extrusion,
and we didn't have to add any segments. This is a very nice tool for re-
ducing the polygon counts of your objects.

• **Align Y to Path:** This ensures that the object follows the path along its
rotation—it's often called Oriented, since the object would be oriented
to the path's axis. If you don't select this attribute, your object will stay
aligned along its own Y axis, which means it won't rotate with the
path. Figure 9.28 shows the result of extruding the object along the
path with no orientation to the path's Y axis.

As you can see, the extrusion is a mess. The object stayed aligned to
its original orientation, which means it did not rotate on its Y axis as it
followed the path. You should always use orientation when extruding
objects along a path.

FIGURE 9.27 *Using Uniform Knots with extrusions along paths*

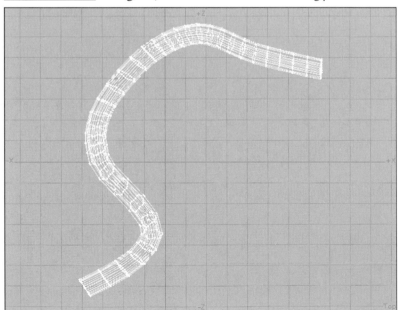

FIGURE 9.28   *A path extrusion with no orientation*

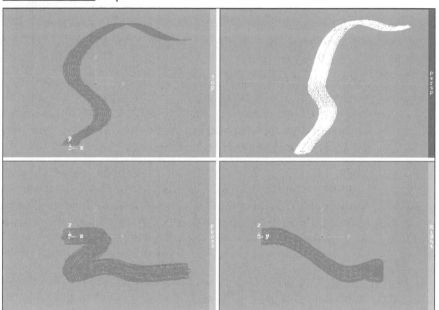

- **Scaling:** Scaling is one of the most powerful features of path extrusions. They allow you to scale the object as it moves along the path. For example, when creating a vine, you'll want it to taper as it approaches the tip. To do this, you'd set the scaling of the vine to something like 10%, which will taper it from 100% at the start to 10% at the tip as shown in Figure 9.29.

    As you can see, the vine looks a lot more realistic with the tapering. The scaling feature will save you countless hours you would otherwise spend manually scaling the segments.

- **Y Rotation:** Now this is a real sweet setting you'll only find in a few programs. This setting rotates the extrusion object along the Y axis as it follows the path. You can set the rotation to any value, which means you can rotate it a number of times. This is a great way to twist an object like the vine we've been exploring. Vines are usually twisted, so this setting becomes a necessity to properly model a vine. Figure 9.30 shows the extruded vine with a Y Rotation of 1000.

Not bad! Now it looks just like a vine. This effect would be a real pain to create by any other means. You could do it manually, rotating the segments by hand, but it would take a very long time to do. In fact, it would

FIGURE 9.29   *Scaling a path extrusion*

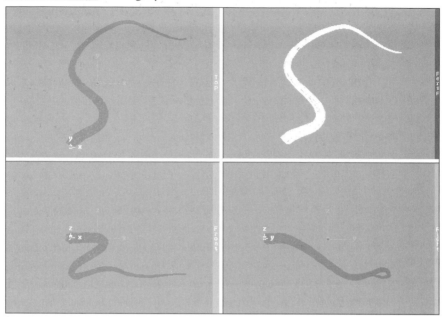

FIGURE 9.30   *The extruded vine with Y Rotation*

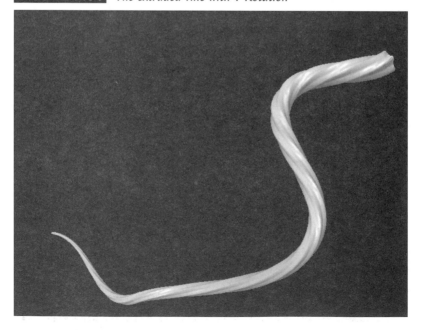

be in multiples of segments—50 segments would take 50 times as long to recreate manually, and they still wouldn't look as good. The bad news is that very few 3D program have this feature. One program that does is Imagine from Impulse, Inc. It has the best path features of any 3D program.

OK, so that's path extrusion. Now let's look at the other use for paths—cloning.

Path Cloning

Path cloning is a great asset. It allows you to clone an object along a path. It operates in the same way as a path extrusion; the difference is that you aren't creating a single object, but rather multiple objects along the path. Cloning is used to create great effects such as leaves on a vine as shown in Figure 9.31.

Notice how the leaves are wrapped around the vine, scaling down as they approach the tip. This is a great effect and it took no more than a second to create. Manually placing the leaves could take 20 minutes, since you need to manually rotate, move, and scale the leaves.

The settings for path cloning are the same as those for path extrude. The only difference is that you are modifying individual objects rather

FIGURE 9.31   *Cloning leaves along a path*

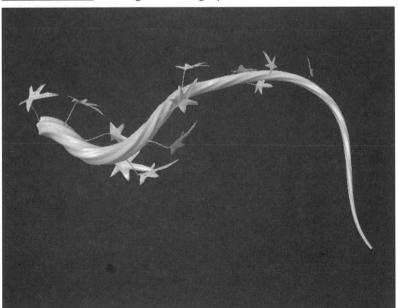

than a single skinned object. Well, there is one additional difference. The Sections setting is now called Copies since we are creating clones of the original object. The following settings were used for the leaves on the vine in Figure 9.31:

- Copies: 20
- Scaling: 10%
- Orientation: Active
- Y Rotation: 1000

You can see that the effect was simple and quick to create using path cloning. Paths can be your best friend when it comes to creating complex objects that follow a path. They are perfect for creating flowing vines, cables, ropes, and even slithering creatures. There are countless uses for paths.

Speaking of uses for paths, let's take a moment to see how paths are used to create complex objects.

A Path Walk-through

In this walk-through we will see how both path extrude and clone were used to create Chuckie's toy train track. It's a great example of how the two can be used together to model complex objects. Let's start with the track railroad ties—the crossbeams that support the rail.

The first step is to create the spline path, which is shown in Figure 9.32.

The little diamond on the path shows the beginning of the spline curve. The path was created to turn the railroad into a square. We can't have Chuckie building the railroad all over the house, can we? OK, now to add the railroad ties. The first step is to create the actual tie, which is a simple rectangle with the top beveled as shown in Figure 9.33.

This object is then scaled and positioned at the beginning of the path as shown in Figure 9.34.

Now for the cool part. The rail is cloned along the path to create the railroad ties. This process takes some experimenting, because you don't want the ties to overlap as they round the corners. After a bit of tweaking, the tie was cloned 84 times to create the foundation for the railroad pictured in Figure 9.35.

As you can see, it's a very cool effect that took minutes to create. Manually placing and rotating the ties could take hours to get them just right.

FIGURE 9.32   *The railroad path*

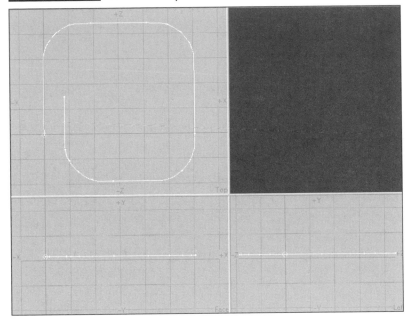

FIGURE 9.33   *The railroad tie*

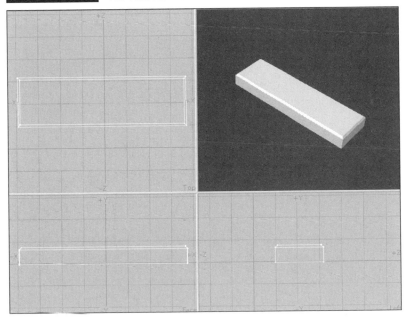

FIGURE 9.34   *Positioning the rail tie*

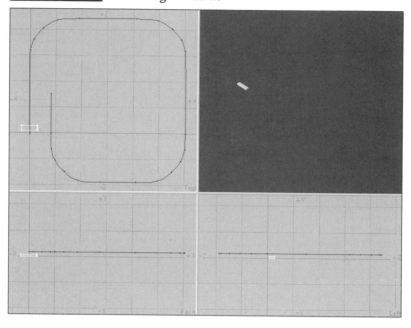

FIGURE 9.35   *The cloned railroad ties*

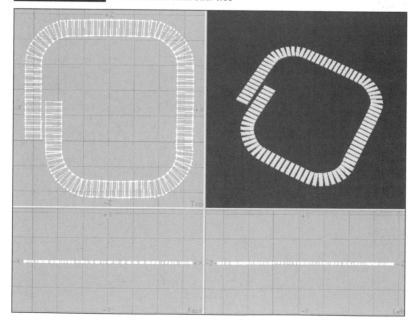

Fortunately, the Path Clone tool does it for us in a second. To complete the railroad we need to add the ties. For this we will use the Path Extrude tool.

The rail is started by creating two rail objects that are sized to match the rail tie. Figure 9.36 shows the rails I created.

These rails are then positioned at the beginning of the path and extruded to create the rails shown in Figure 9.37.

Now that looks great. Within a few seconds we now have two rails that are perfectly formed to the ties. When the rails were extruded, the Uniform Knots setting was used to concentrate the segments along the curves to ensure that they were smooth and to reduce the polygon count. They were also oriented so they would properly follow the path. Let's take a look at the rails and ties combined, shown in Figure 9.38.

Now, doesn't that look awesome? Just a few minutes and we have a highly detailed railroad. It's easy to see that paths can be a real asset in your 3D modeling toolbox. They can save you countless hours of tweaking.

I'm sure by now you've noticed a time-saving trend with these tools. These tools are all about saving you time. All of the effects we've covered in this chapter can be created by other means, but they would take a really long time—and time is money. Who can afford to waste it? I certainly can't. There's nothing wrong with being thrifty when it comes to 3D modeling.

FIGURE 9.36 *The rail extrusion objects*

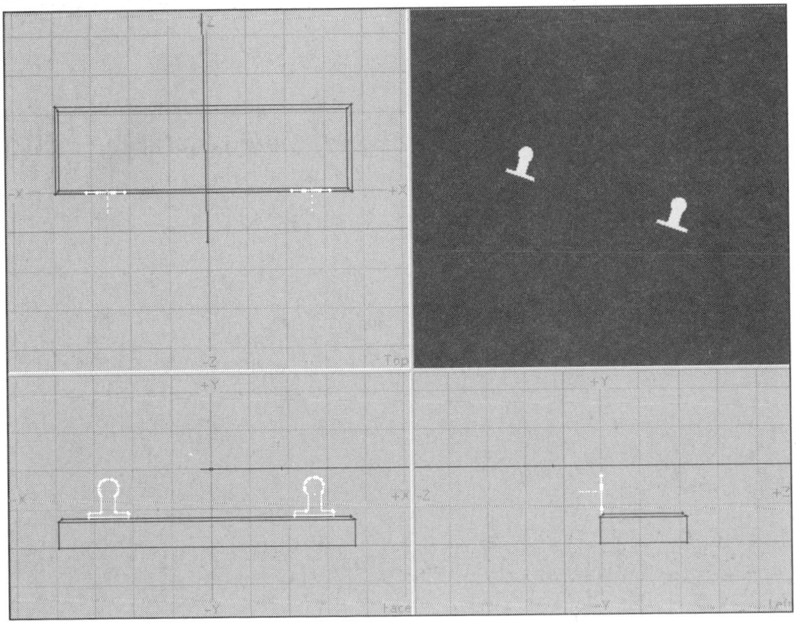

FIGURE 9.37   *The extruded rails*

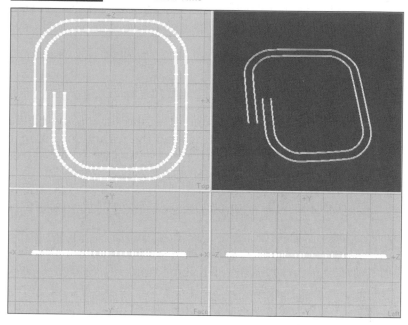

FIGURE 9.38   *The completed railroad*

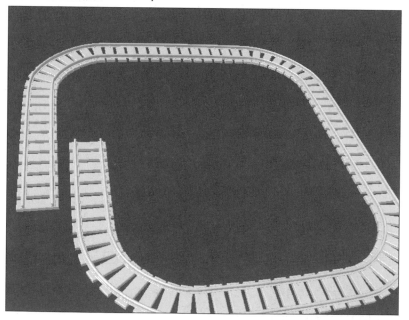

Well, we're coming to the end of the modeling tools. We have just one left to cover—cloning. Let's take a look at how cloning works.

Using Cloning

Cloning is a great time saver. Oops, I said it again. Well, if there ever were a tool dedicated to saving you time, it would have to be the Cloning tool. There is nothing more aggravating than the redundancy of manually recreating objects. The Cloning tool takes the headaches out of creating highly repetitive objects.

Basically, the Cloning tool makes copies of an object you have created. There are a number of settings for the Cloning tool, so let's take a look at them before we continue.

- **Number of Clones:** Well, this one is fairly obvious. It determines the number of copies to make of the object.

- **Offset:** This determines how much the object will be moved along each axis, X, Y, and Z. It's typically represented in actual measurements such as meters or feet.

- **Rotation:** This determines how much the objects will be rotated when it's cloned. This doesn't apply to all of them, but rather individually—meaning, if the rotation is set to 30 degrees on the Y axis the first clone will be rotated 30 degrees. The second clone will be rotated 30 degrees based on the first clone, or 60 degrees from the start object. Figure 9.39 shows a sample of cloning rotation.

  Here we have a spiral staircase created with the cloning tool. Well, the steps, anyway. The object was started with a single step that was cloned with a rotation of 30 degrees on the Y axis, which caused the clones to gradually work their way around in a circle. Of course, they needed to be moved away from each other vertically, which was accomplished by setting an offset value of 1 foot along the Y axis. It's a great effect, which was created in less than a minute.

- **Scale:** This setting scales the clones the same way the rotation setting works. Each subsequent clone will be smaller than the previous one. If you set the scale to 50%, your clones would disappear in only after a couple have been created, because each would be 50% smaller than the one before it.

- **Center:** This determines the axis that the objects will be cloned around or along. Typically you want this set to zero so you have a little more

FIGURE 9.39 *Cloning rotation*

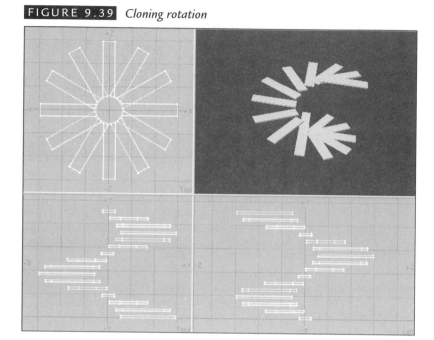

control over the cloning process. If you clone your objects around another location, you might have serious problems with alignment.

There are only a few controls but they give you a great deal of flexibility. Cloning can be a very useful tool for creating repetitive effects such as posts of a fence, stairs, ladders, and even the spokes on a bike wheel. In fact, since we're on the subject of cloning uses, let's take a look at how you build a model using the Cloning tool.

A Cloning Walk-through

In this walk-through we'll be making a wooden ladder for Chuckie's bunk bed. Yes, he's a bit young to be climbing a ladder, but it will be there when he's ready. The ladder makes liberal use of the Cloning tool to create the rungs and the dowels that connect them. Let's get started with the walk-through.

The first step is to create the support beams to hold the rungs. These are simply vertical boxes as shown in Figure 9.40.

The support beams have been beveled on the top and bottom, but not the sides, since the holes for the dowels haven't been cut yet. This is a ladder for a child, so we want to avoid using any elements that might be a

FIGURE 9.40   *The ladder support beams*

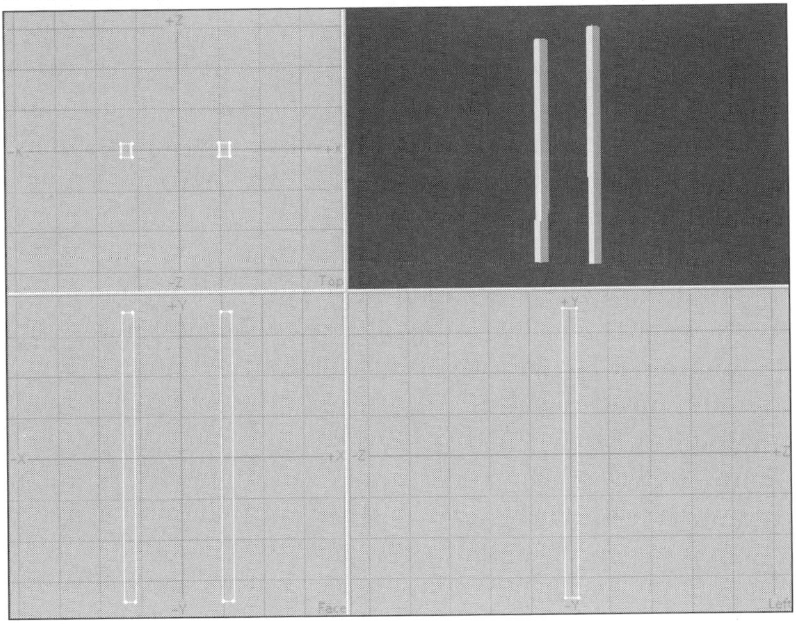

hazard. Attaching the rungs with wooden dowels is a safe solution. The next step in modeling the ladder is to create two tubes that are centered along the sides of the support beams as shown in Figure 9.41.

These tubes are the modifiers that will be used to cut the dowel holes in the ladder support beams. Now it's time to use the Clone tool. The modifiers need to be cloned along the Y axis. They are cloned six times with an offset value of 8 inches along the Y axis, creating the configuration seen in Figure 9.42.

These modifiers are now located where the rungs will be placed in a few moments. The next step is to cut holes in the support beams by using a subtractive boolean. Once the holes are cut, the sides of the support beams are selected and beveled to smooth the edges of the holes. The support beams now look like Figure 9.43.

OK, now it's time for the dowels, which are created by beveling the ends of the modifier tubes and placing them in the support beams, as shown in Figure 9.44.

Notice how the dowels are flush with the outside edge of the support beams. You don't want them extending beyond it because they will be a hazard. It would also be a bad idea to inset them, since little fingers could be stuck in the holes. If you want to create believable objects, you have to make sure they make sense to the viewer.

FIGURE 9.41 *The modifier objects for the dowel holes*

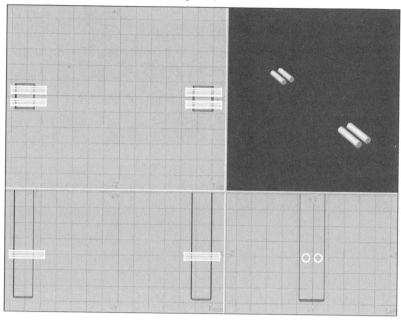

FIGURE 9.42 *The cloned modifiers*

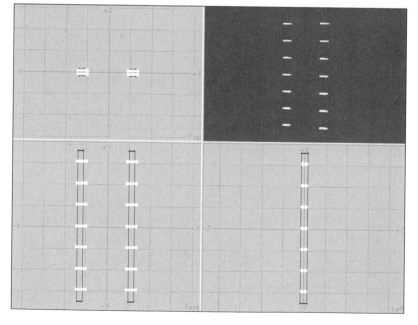

FIGURE 9.43 *The support beams with dowel holes*

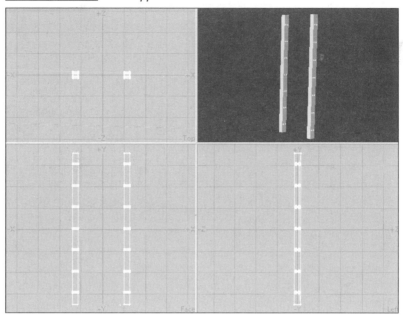

FIGURE 9.44 *Placing the dowels*

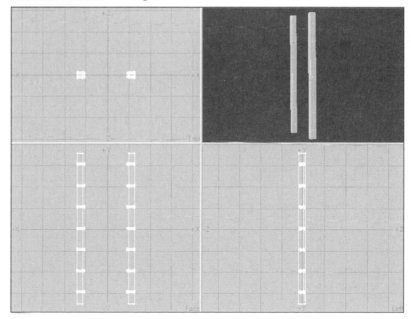

OK, now the last step is to create the actual rung, which is merely a rectangle that has beveled edges. The rung is lined up with the first set of dowels, then cloned using the exact same settings as the dowel modifiers to create the row of rungs seen in Figure 9.45.

Now the last step is to combine the runs with the support beams to create the finished ladder seen in Figure 9.46.

As you can see, the Cloning tool was instrumental in creating this object. You could have manually placed the modifiers and rungs, but that would have taken more time and wouldn't be nearly as accurate. The Cloning tool placed each object at exactly the same distance apart. If you try to manually eyeball the separation, you'd likely have some discrepancies.

This is just one of the many ways cloning can save you time and headaches. Of course, there are other variations of object cloning such as arrays, which can be used to create different cloning effects. Let's take a look at how arrays are used.

Array Cloning

An array is a 3D volume cloning tool. It clones the object along the X, Y, and Z axis in a cubic manner, unlike the Clone tool that only makes copies of an object in a linear fashion. It's a unique tool than can be used to create some great effects, though the most popular uses only really involve two dimensions. Let's take a look at the array settings to see how they are used to create 3D cloning.

- **Array Type:** There are two types of arrays, rectangular and radial. The rectangular array creates the clones on all three axes, while a radial array only rotates the clones around one axis. Radial Array is more of a two-dimensional cloning tool. Figure 9.47 compares a rectangle and a radial array.

  The group on the right was created with a rectangular array and the group on the left with a radial array. Notice how the rectangular array created the clones in 3D space while the radial array only created its clones in 2D space. Also, the radial array rotates the objects around the axis, while the rectangular array has no rotation.

- **Dimension:** This is a rectangular array setting. It controls the number of clones along each axis. To create the cube of clones seen in the previous example, the X, Y, and Z dimensions were set to 3.

- **Number:** This is a radial array setting. It determines the number of clones to be created.

FIGURE 9.45   *The ladder rungs*

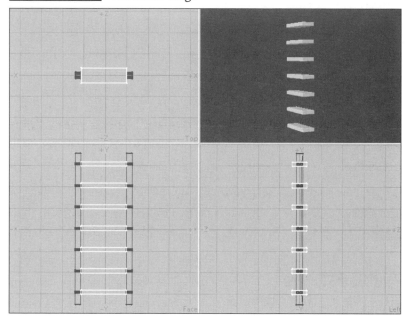

FIGURE 9.46   *The completed ladder*

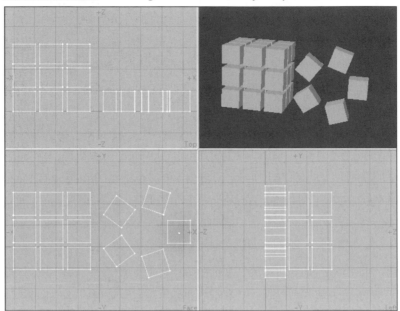

FIGURE 9.47 *A rectangular and radial array compared*

- **Axis:** This is another radial array setting. It determines the axis the clones will be created around. The Rectangular Array tool doesn't have an axis setting, because this is controlled by the Dimension setting.

- **Offset:** This is a rectangular array setting that controls the spacing between the clones. It's usually measured in percentages but sometimes uses actual real-world measurements such as centimeters and inches. A setting of 100% would place the clones directly next to one another. Figure 9.48 shows the result of setting the offset to 200%.

- **Jitter:** This is a unique tool that adds a little chaos to the array. The Jitter setting moves the clones around based on values you enter for the X, Y, and Z axes. Figure 9.49 shows the effect of using a jitter of 1 foot on all three axes.

As you can see, the cubes are now chaotically arranged. This can be a fun tool for creating chaotic arrays for object such as blocks in a stone wall, or even randomly cloned weeds for your 3D garden.

The Array tool can be very useful for creating objects that have plenty of redundancy. To get a better idea of some uses, let's explore a walkthrough for both rectangular and radial array modeling.

FIGURE 9.48 *An offset value of 200%*

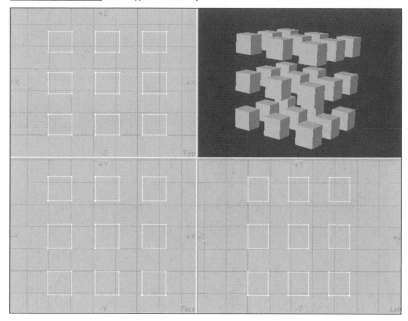

FIGURE 9.49 *Using the Jitter setting*

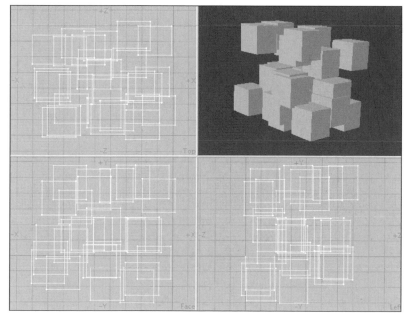

An Array Walk-through

We'll start the walk-through by taking a look at how to create a Duplo fort with the Rectangular Array tool. This is actually amazingly simple to do, yet it would take you the better part of an hour to complete manually.

The Duplo fort started with a single Duplo model like the one in Figure 9.50.

This piece is then cloned using the Rectangular Array tool with the following settings:

- **Dimension:** 6 units for X, Y, and Z
- **Offset:** 100% on the X, Y, and Z axes

This creates the cube of Duplo blocks shown in Figure 9.51.

Notice how the blocks are just sitting on top of one another. They aren't actually connected, as they normally would be. Well, this was done deliberately because poor Chuckie doesn't have the strength to push them down on one another. He has to wait for his dad to do it. Of course, if you really wanted to build them properly, you'd use an Offset of 80% on the Y axis so they would be stuck together like the ones in Figure 9.52.

FIGURE 9.50   *The Duplo model*

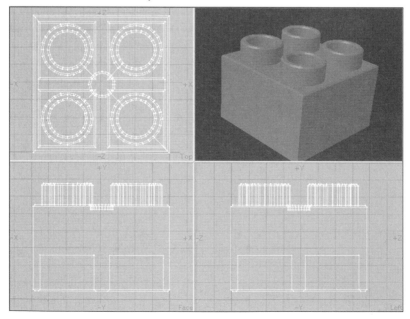

FIGURE 9.51 *The array of Duplo blocks*

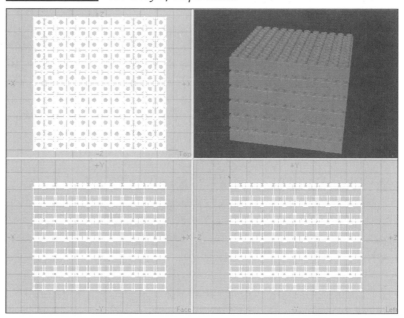

FIGURE 9.52 *The Duplo array with a Y offset of 80%*

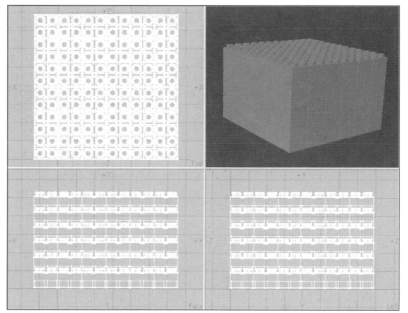

Notice that they're nice and snug against one another. This is how they would normally appear, but for the sake of our walk-through we'll be using the Chuckie version that isn't tight.

Now for some liberal use of the Delete function. To create the hollow center of the fort, the blocks in the middle are selected and deleted as shown in Figure 9.53.

To create the towers on the corners of the fort, all of the blocks except the actual corner ones are selected and deleted as shown in Figure 9.54.

The next step is to create some windows so Chuckie's Little People can see out of the fort. This is accomplished by selecting blocks on the sides of the fort and deleting them. On one side no blocks are deleted, so the door can be added later. Figure 9.55 shows the window holes.

OK, the last step is to select the blocks on the front of the fort and delete them to create the door seen in Figure 9.56.

See how quickly a complex object can be created with the Array tool? You could have manually placed the Duplo blocks, but it would have taken a much longer and probably caused countless headaches. The Array tool can be very useful for creating three-dimensional clones.

FIGURE 9.53   *Creating the interior of the fort*

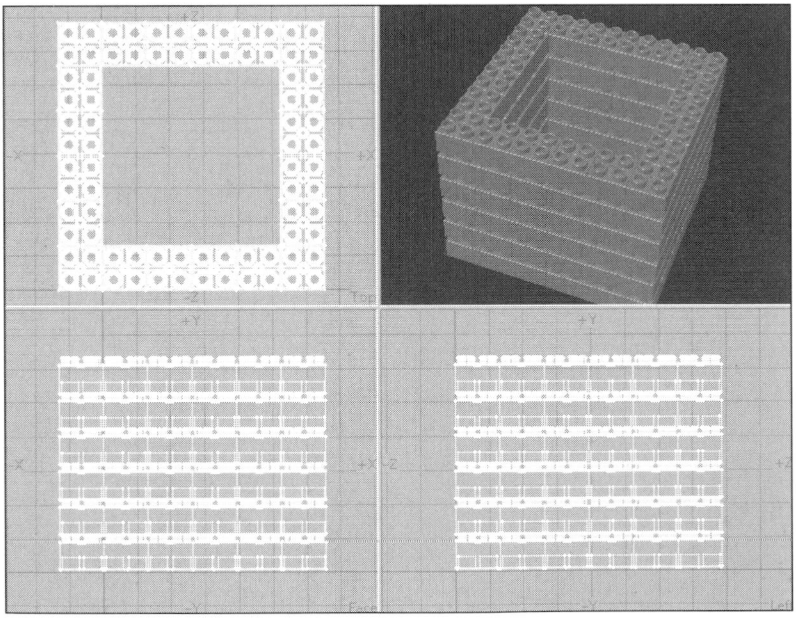

FIGURE 9.54 *Creating the towers*

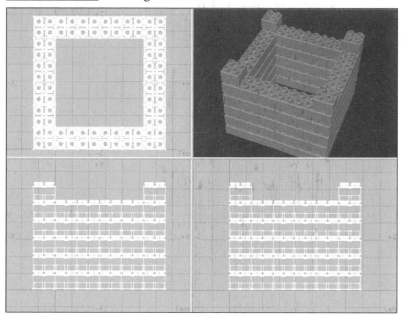

FIGURE 9.55 *Adding the windows*

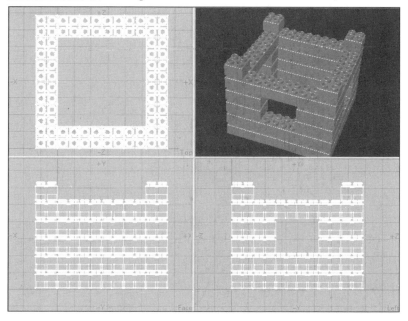

FIGURE 9.56   *The completed fort*

OK, now for a look at the Radial Array tool in action. We're going to see how the spokes on a wheel for Chuckie's tricycle were created using the Radial Array tool. It's really a very simple process, taking a mere two steps.

The first step is to create the spokes that will be cloned. Figure 9.57 shows how the spoke was created using the wheel as a template.

Now the spoke is cloned using the Radial Array tool with the Axis set to Z and the Number set to 24, creating the finished wheel seen in Figure 9.58.

It took only two steps to create spokes for the wheel. Doing this manually would have taken twenty-four times as long. Sure, it would only take a few minutes, but that's much longer than the ten seconds it took with the Radial Array tool. Each little minute adds up when you're working on detailed models. A few minutes saved here and there will add up to hours in no time.

FIGURE 9.57 *Creating the spoke*

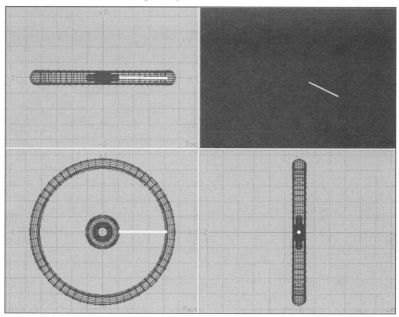

FIGURE 9.58 *The completed spokes*

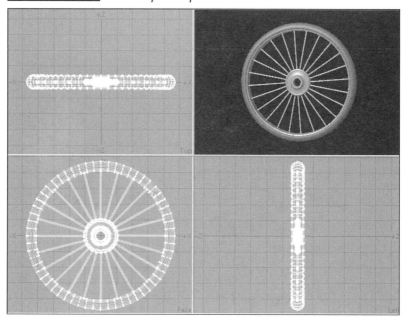

Wrap-up

Well, that does it for our discussion on modeling tools. Although there are a large number of actual modeling tools, the ones we covered in this part are the most useful. Taking a look back at what we've discussed, it's easy to see how you can model literally anything with the tools described. It's all a matter of selecting the right tool for the right job. Planning is everything when you embark on a 3D modeling project.

You know, it looks as if we're finally finished with the modeling segment of this book. We've covered a lot of ground in the last nine chapters. What's important is that you focus on the "Where and When To Use" sections of the chapters. These will aid you in making your modeling decisions. When you're about to start a modeling project, consult these sections to find out what tool is best for the object you're modeling.

Now that we have a handle on the modeling aspect of 3D graphics, we're ready to take a look at the surfacing aspect. This is the point where the models spring to life with vivid detail. Surfacing is a critical part of the 3D process, so we'll be covering it in great detail. Let's get started.

PART IV

Surfacing Techniques

Once you've modeled your objects, you'll need to surface them so they can be rendered. Surfacing is the process of adding the colors and textures to the object. It's the step in the 3D process that can make or break your object. A poorly developed model can be improved with quality surfacing, but bad surfacing can destroy a great model.

Surfacing is one of the most challenging aspects of 3D graphics. It's typically the step that throws most artists. There are many things to consider when you surface your model, which we will be covering in this part. In fact, we'll be exploring the two different types of surfacing: procedural and image maps. We'll take a closer look at the different image map types such as planar, spherical, cylindrical, cubic, and projection. Finally, we'll dig deeper into the surfacing attributes such as color, specularity, luminosity, transparency, reflectivity, and bump.

Yes, it sounds complicated—but as long as you have a handle on what these items are and where they should be used, you'll be fine. There is much to consider when surfacing your objects, and we will explore most of it in the following two chapters. We'll start by taking a look at the different surfacing methods.

CHAPTER 10

Surfacing Methods

What is surfacing? Well, when you create a model you are defining a surface, which is the part of the model that you can see. It's the polygons or spline patches. When you surface an object, you are applying attributes to it such as color and bump. You are creating the visual effects on the object. It's basically the same thing as painting a clay sculpture in concept, but a great deal more involved and challenging. I'm not saying it's a nightmare, but it does take some getting used to.

In the real world, most of the surface attributes are handled for you by the material you're using to paint with. Your paint has shininess, surface texture, color, and reflectivity. In the 3D world, your paint only has color. You need to add the shininess, texture, and reflectivity yourself. This adds some work and requires you to think a great deal more. You need to be not only a painter, but an alchemist as well. Well, it's not all that bad—but you do need to thoroughly research your surfaces before you start creating them.

Before we get into the actual surfacing methods and attributes, let's take a look at how surfaces are created on your model.

Creating Surfaces

A surface is a specific region on the model that will bear unique attributes. When you create a model you need to assign surfaces so you can give them attributes such as color and texture. Most models incorporate more than one surface because they need specific details. For example, take a look at the toy block model in Figure 10.1.

Notice how the letters on the block in the OpenGL preview window are all different colors. That's because they are different surfaces. The block is all one color because it's another surface. Each letter on the block needed to have a unique color, so each was assigned a different surface. When you create a surface, you assign it a logical name. For example, the block surface would be named "wood block" while the letter P would be named P. It's that limited. You need to name your surfaces properly so you don't get confused later on. When you have a scene with many models in it, you're bound to have a large number of surfaces. If you don't name them properly, you'll have a hard time identifying them.

You'll also need to give each unique surface a different name so they won't overwrite each other when you load objects in a scene. If you have different objects with the same surface name, the last model loaded will overwrite the surface attributes of the first one. It won't actually save it to the file, but it will change them in your rendering program. Unique names are paramount.

A surface is created by selecting specific regions on the model and assigning them a unique name. These regions can be either polygons or splines, depending on the modeling method you choose. You simply select them and give them a new name. When you name the surface, you often have the opportunity to assign a color. This is important because selecting different colors will help you identify them. These colors are not the surface attributes, but rather a color to designate the different surfaces. It's always a good idea to keep them organized so you don't get confused, particularly when working with a scene full of unique surfaces such as the one in Figure 10.2.

Here we have a typical scene with our little friend Chuckie. As you can see, there are a large number of surfaces in the scene. Keeping track of these would be a nightmare without proper names and different colors. Let's take a close look at the scene and explore the reason behind a few of the surface selections.

- **Chuckie:** Chuckie has a number of unique surfaces, such as skin, diaper, shirt, and hair. All of these areas need different attributes. The shirt needs to be yellow and wrinkled, the diaper white and crinkled, the

FIGURE 10.1   *Surface selection*

FIGURE 10.2   *A scene with multiple surfaces*

hair yellow and glossy, and the skin beige and soft. To surface all of these areas with unique attributes, you need to assign them different surface names.

- **Dog Dish:** The dog dish has two surfaces, the dish and the food. Since we want the dish to be a hard plastic and the food to be a soft, squishy surface, we need to assign them different surface names. The last thing we want is a soft and squishy dog bowl (though I don't think Woof would mind).
- **Broom:** The broom has several segments: the wood handle, metal clamp, and straw bristles. All of these areas have completely different surface attributes, so they need unique surface assignments.

As you can see, it's really not that difficult to determine the proper surface selections on your models. It's really quite logical. You just need to think about all the different areas on the model and how their surfaces might differ.

Once you have your surfaces assigned, you need to need to select a surfacing method. There are two methods for surfacing your objects: procedural textures and image maps. Both have their advantages and disadvantages. The important thing is to know what they are so you plan around them. Let's start by taking a look at procedural textures.

Procedural Texture Surfacing

Procedural textures are mathematical algorithms that create surface effects in 3D space. Simply put, procedural textures are computer-generated surfaces. They are 3D versions of the fractal noise that you might have seen in such computer paint programs as PhotoShop and Fractal Design Painter.

When you work with procedural textures, you're given the opportunity to enter parameters that will affect the outcome. For example, you can determine the size, color, bump, and randomness of most procedural textures. Of course, procedural textures are the least standard surfacing method. The settings vary widely from one program to another. Image maps, by contrast, are relatively standardized, with consistent settings. With any luck we'll see procedural textures standardized sometime in the near future as more 3D programs begin to incorporate them.

There are two classes of procedural textures: limited and extended. The majority of 3D programs have incorporated the limited procedural textures, which include the two most common ones, fractal noise and fractal bump. Let's take a look at how both of these work.

- **Fractal Noise:** This procedural texture spreads a color across the surface in a chaotic manner. It typically has settings for the size of the noise and the frequencies, or number of times it's repeated. Fractal noise is somewhat similar to the clouds that cover a blue sky. The sky is your surface and the clouds are the fractal noise. The size of the fractal noise determines how much of the surface is covered. Typically you'll be able to see your surface color through the fractal noise, as shown in Figure 10.3.

The original surface is white and the fractal noise is black. As you can see, the fractal noise covers the surface like clouds. Fractal noise has a number of uses. It's typically used to add dirt to surfaces, as seen in Figure 10.4.

The surfaces of the tunnel were created with layers of fractal noise. The great thing about most procedural textures is they can be layered to create unique effects. The tunnel has three layers of fractal noise with different colors, which create a great effect. Fractal noise can be a great surfacing tool, but the effects it can create are limited, since you can only change the height and width of the noise.

FIGURE 10.3 *Fractal noise*

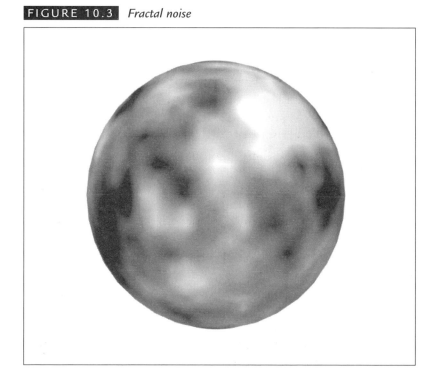

FIGURE 10.4   *Creating dirt with fractal noise*

• **Fractal Bump:** This procedural texture creates chaotic bumps on a surface. It uses the same technique as fractal noise, but translates the color
into a bump. All procedural textures are based on colors. In the case of
fractal bump procedural textures, the level of the color determines the
altitude of the bump. We'll talk more about this topic in Chapter 11.
For now, let's take a look at a typical example of fractal bump, shown
in Figure 10.5.

Notice the chaotic bump on the surface of the ball. These bumps
can be varied in size and amplitude to create a wide variety of effects.
For example, they were used to create realistic metal for the objects in
Figure 10.6.

Take a look at the lock and you'll see it has tiny, brushed lines on
the surface, which were created by making the fractal bumps very
wide. It's a limited trick, but the result is very convincing. You can see
that the fractal bump procedural texture can be used to create some interesting effects. Of course, fractal bumps are limited in their application. You can only change the shape by making them taller or wider,
which is great for some effects such as metals, but limited for most others. To create extended shapes, you'll need to utilize extended procedural textures.

FIGURE 10.5 *Fractal bump*

FIGURE 10.6 *Realistic metal created with fractal bumps*

There are a variety of limited procedural textures, but these two are the most popular. Your 3D program might also have other limited procedural textures like the ones in Figure 10.7.

(A) Wood: This is a relatively limited wood texture that can be used to create surfaces for furniture and wood floors.

(B) Checkered: The checkered procedural is a great way to quickly add checkered squares to floors or even racing flags.

(C) Marble: The marble procedural texture creates the chaotic lines commonly seen in marble.

(D) Crumple: This procedural texture creates crinkled ridges on the surface. It can be a great tool for creating rough surfaces and even effects such as the choppy waves of ocean water.

It's easy to see that a number of possibilities can be achieved with the limited procedural textures. These limited procedural textures are found in nearly every 3D program. Of course, if you really want to blow minds, you'll need to get your hands on some extended procedural textures. Let's take a look at how the extended procedural textures work.

FIGURE 10.7   *Other limited procedural textures*

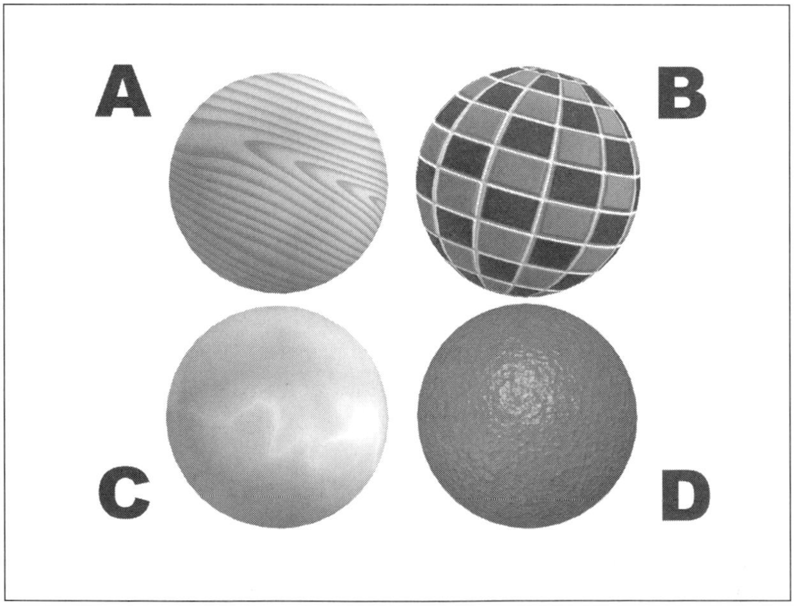

FIGURE 10.8 *Creating rust with extended procedural textures*

Extended Procedural Textures

What makes a procedural texture extended? Well, extended procedural textures have more tools at your disposal. They typically combine the color and bump effects into a single procedural texture so you can create detailed color effects with corresponding bumps. This is a real asset when you're creating effects like the rust seen in Figure 10.8.

This realistic rust was made in seconds using an extended procedural texture. This soda can really looks old, doesn't it? OK, so I rusted an aluminum soda can. I couldn't find my model of a steel can. If you look closely, you will see a bumpiness that matches the color of the rust. This is a distinct advantage of an extended procedural texture. You can combine color and bump effects because they are both a part of a single procedural texture. Another advantage of the extended procedural textures is that they typically have several fractal color settings in a single procedural texture, which allows you to created detailed effects like the variations in the rust colors.

The true power of extended procedural textures is in the diversified control. Many will have options for creating varied bump and color effects. The rock in Figure 10.9 was created using three different extended procedural textures that were combined in layers.

FIGURE 10.9   *A procedural rock surface*

Now that's a realistic surface. Notice the subtle surface details such as the chaotic large bumps combined with smaller pores in the surface. Now take a look at that splendid color chaos that perfectly matches the bump effect. This is a truly detailed surface that looks like a photograph of a rock. To get a better idea of how extended procedural surfacing works, let's take a look at how the rock surface was created.

A Procedural Texture Walk-through

Creating realistic procedural textures requires experimentation. If your program does come with predefined procedural textures, they are usually less than realistic. It's important to realize that a single procedural texture rarely does the job. Surfaces in reality are loaded with a variety of chaos. The colors vary dramatically, along with their dispersion. The bumps are chaotic and occur on two levels: a small consistent surface bump and random, larger chaos. This means real textures are layered, just like a good procedural surface. When creating detailed procedural surfaces you'll need to experiment, combining different procedural textures to create unique effects. The walk-through we are about to take will give you a better idea how to go about creating detailed procedural surfaces.

The first step in creating the surface is to give it a base color. The rock surface was given a yellow-beige color, as shown in Figure 10.10.

The next step is to apply the first procedural texture layer. It does take some experimenting to find the right texture, but that's actually part of the fun in using procedural textures. You'll create a number of cool textures before you find the right one. The great thing is that you can save the texture to be used later. The first layer of the rock was created with a dirt procedural texture. The variation in the surface detail and colors were set to a small value to create the swirling surface shown in Figure 10.11.

This swirling base created the foundation for the rock surface. Many rocks have swirling patterns on them. They don't look this obvious because they're broken up by the surface bump texture. Well, the same thing was applied to the procedural rock surface. To create more surface chaos, a crusty procedural texture was added to create the effect shown in Figure 10.12.

You can see how the rock now has more colors and a bumpy surface. The crusty procedural texture has three settings for fractal colors, which allows you to add some nice color variations to the surface. You can also still see the dirt pattern underneath the crusty effects. This is the power of layered procedural textures. They can be combined in layers the same way you combine layers in graphics programs such as Photoshop.

FIGURE 10.10   *The base surface color*

FIGURE 10.11   *The dirt procedural applied to the surface*

FIGURE 10.12   *The crusty procedural texture applied*

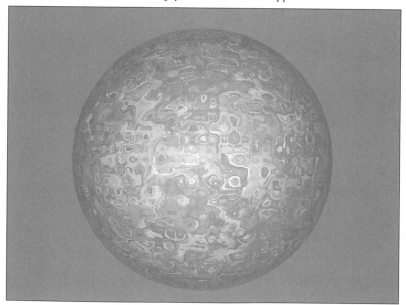

The final step in creating the rock surface is to add a crumple map with very small settings to create the lumpy, porous look on the surface of the rock, as shown in Figure 10.13.

Notice that the surface now has tiny little holes in it. This is a trademark of stone. It's these little details that really make the surface realistic. I'm sure you've also noticed that the surface doesn't exactly match the one we saw on the stone in Figure 10.9. Well, that's because the stone was larger than the sphere being used in this demonstration, so the details appear smaller on the stone.

You have complete control over the size of procedural textures. You can scale them to any size you desire and they will hold their quality. This is one of the main benefits of using procedural textures. Another benefit is the wide variety of extended procedural textures that are available in a program that uses them. There are literally endless combinations you can create. Just take a look at the old ball bearing in Figure 10.14.

This ball bearing has three layers of procedural textures, just like the rock, but each procedural texture has slightly different settings. With just a few procedural textures you can create thousands of variations. All of the objects we've discussed in this section have been surfaced with the Dirt and Crumple procedural textures, yet the results were all different because

FIGURE 10.13 *The crumple procedural texture applied*

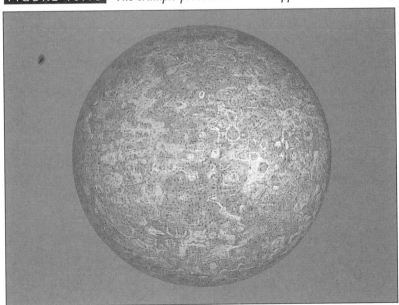

FIGURE 10.14 *A ball bearing surfaced with extended procedural textures*

they utilized different settings and additional procedural textures to create unique details. Layering procedural textures is the greatest benefit of using extended procedural textures.

Unfortunately, the sad reality is that only a handful of programs have extended procedural textures. These program include Imagine, Strata Studio Pro, Alias, and SoftImage. Of course, the last two are high-priced 3D programs that aren't often used by 3D enthusiasts. As with the simple procedural textures, more 3D developers are starting to incorporate them, but it will be a while before extended procedural textures become a mainstay of most 3D programs.

Now that we've covered the practice behind surfacing objects with procedural textures, let's take this opportunity to examine their pros and cons.

The Pros and Cons of Procedural Textures

Procedural textures can be a real asset in your surfacing efforts, but there are several things to consider. Let's take a moment to examine the pros and cons of using procedural textures.

Procedural Pros

- **Infinite Resolution:** Procedural surfaces are algorithmic, so they can be infinitely scaled. An image map is of a fixed resolution, so it can't be scaled without losing quality. You can zoom in infinitely on a procedural surface and it will always hold its quality.

- **Completely Random Effects:** You can create unlimited random effects over the surface. Since they are algorithms, you can simply add a random noise factor and the surface will never be identical in two places. On the other hand, an image map is fixed in size, so it will repeat very frequently over large surfaces.

- **Low Memory Use:** Procedurals use little to no memory. In fact, it's completely negligible. You can have thousands of procedural surfaces on an object and you won't even notice the effect on your memory.

- **No Seams:** You won't have seams with procedural textures, because they are an infinite surface that never repeats. This is a very nice benefit because surfacing seams found in image maps can be a real pain to correct.

- **No Mapping Coordinates:** You won't have to align your procedural textures to any particular axis because they are 3D volume surfaces. They extend in all directions, infinitely.

Procedural Cons

- **Slow Rendering:** While procedural textures use very little memory, they use plenty of CPU time. There is a great deal of math involved when you create procedural textures. In fact, the more procedurals you have on your surfaces, the slower your render times. There is a price to be paid for the infinite resolution of procedural textures.

- **Limited Specific Details:** Unlike image maps, which can have very specific details in specific regions, a procedural texture is continually chaotic. They aren't designed for small, localized details. For example, if you wanted to add a ring of jam around the underside of the lid on your jar of jam, you'd have to use an image map because procedural textures would cover the entire surface with jam. Of course, you may *want* a jar covered in jam—but you get the idea.

- **Nontransferable Surfaces:** You can't share procedural textures between 3D programs because they are all custom developed for the specific program you're using. On the other hand, an image map can be used by every program. All you need to do is save the appropriate file format.

As you can see, there are a number of pros to procedural textures, and very few cons. Of course, the cons that are present are relatively great. You couldn't label that jar of jam with a procedural texture. You'd have to use an image map for that job. Speaking of image maps, let's take a look at how they are used to surface 3D models.

Image Map Surfacing

Image maps are nothing more than pictures you apply to the surfaces of your model. You apply them in a similar fashion to wrapping a gift. Think of an image map as the wrapping paper and your object as the gift. There are a number of ways you can wrap a gift, and the same applies to image maps. To get a better idea of the concept, take a look at Figure 10.15.

Here we have a 3D pumpkin and its associated image maps. The different colors on the pumpkin indicate the two surfaces. The floating pumpkin skins are the image maps, demonstrating how they are applied to the pumpkin. It's not a lot different from gift-wrapping. Well, except that the pumpkin would make an unusual gift.

FIGURE 10.15   *Applying image maps*

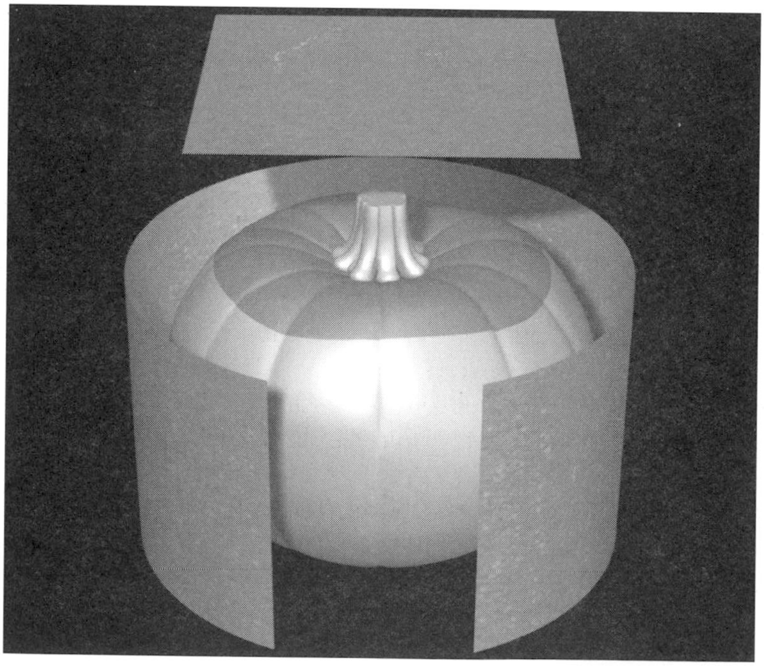

Image maps are two-dimensional, so they need to be applied to the object with specific mapping methods and coordinates—unlike a procedural texture, which is 3D in infinite space. Speaking of infinite space, an image map is limited to being applied to a surface with a specific, two-dimensional mapping method. Let's take a look at the different methods for applying image maps.

Applying Image Maps

There are two different image map application techniques, projection and UV. It's important to understand the differences so you can properly surface your models. A projection map works just like a film projector casting an image on a screen. You project the image map on the surface. The shortcoming of a projection image map is that is doesn't stick to the surface.

Why is sticking important? Well, if you plan to animate the model, you'll be changing its appearance. For example, if you have a character that is walking, its body changes with every step as its arms and legs move back and forth. If you surface the character with projection maps, it would literally walk out of its skin, since the projection map doesn't stick to the model. This does look bad for projection maps, but they aren't really that bad. You just need to know where to apply them. A projection map is fine for an object that isn't going to deform, such as all of the static objects in a room. Your TV won't deform during the animation unless it's possessed.

Projection image maps aren't that common any more. There are some programs such as Strata Studio Pro that still incorporate them, but most programs have converted to UV image maps. A UV image map is glued to the surface. It uses a coordinate system to lock the image map to the object. Think of it this way. You use tape to stick your wrapping paper to the gift box. Well, a UV map uses coordinates to stick your image map to the model. This is the best method for surfacing all of your objects. Think of the points in your object as magnets. A UV mapping systems uses these points to lock the image map to your object. All 3D programs today use the UV mapping method; even Strata Studio Pro has a UV mapping option.

When you animate an object, such as a character, using UV mapped surfaces, the skin will stay connected to the body as it moves. This, of course, is a desirable effect. You're better off surfacing all of your objects with UV mapping so they're prepared for any circumstance. You never know when your TV will jump of the stand and attack. Remember, we're talking 3D graphics here—anything can happen in a 3D world.

Now that we have a good idea how image maps work, let's take a closer look at the different methods for applying the image maps to your models. We'll start with the most common method—planar mapping.

Planar Image Maps

Planar image maps are the most frequently used image mapping method, since the majority of objects have relatively flat surfaces. A planar image map projects the image onto the surface of the object just as a movie projector displays an image on the screen. For this reason, it's best to use planar image maps on flat surfaces such as TV screens, boxes, walls, or floors. Figure 10.16 illustrates how a planar image map is applied to an object.

The TV screen is being surfaced in this example. Notice how the image is projected against the relatively flat screen. The thumbnails to the right illustrate how a planar image map is applied to each of the three axes—X, Y, and Z. Most image maps are applied to a particular axis. The only exception would be a cubic map because it's simultaneously applied to all three axes. To get a better idea of how planar image maps are used on an object, take a look at Figure 10.17.

Both the wall and floor in this image were surfaced using planar image maps. The wall was surfaced on the Z axis and the floor along the Y axis. Their image maps are shown in the small floating windows on the image.

Planar image maps can be used to surface many of your objects, but what if you need to surface a round object? Well, then you would use spherical image maps.

Spherical Image Maps

Spherical image maps are probably the least frequently used image mapping method. This is mainly because they tend to pinch the image map at the top and bottom of the surface. This is a by-product of the way they are mapped. A spherical image map wraps a flat image around the object in similar fashion to gift-wrapping a basketball. Have you ever tried to wrap something that was round with a flat piece of paper? It just doesn't work that well, because you always have too much paper at the top and bottom. Well, this problem doesn't happen with a spherical image map, because it pinches the image at the top and bottom, so you don't have any excess material. Figure 10.18 illustrates the spherical image mapping method along the X, Y, and Z axes.

Notice how the image map wraps around the globe from the top and sides. This is how a spherical image map works. Of course, it does create a problem. The image map will tend to pinch at the top as it's compressed to fit the smaller space. This can make your image map a real mess if you

FIGURE 10.16   *The planar image map*

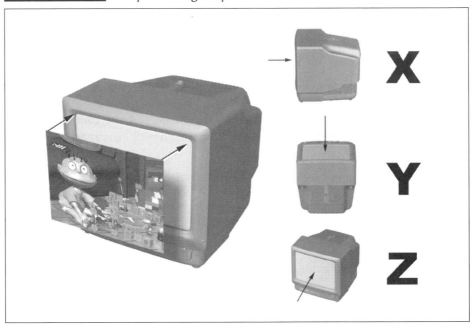

FIGURE 10.17   *Where to use planar maps*

FIGURE 10.18   *The spherical image map*

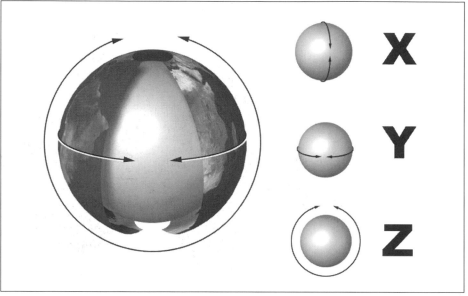

have any specific detail at the top of your model. Spherical image maps are best used on objects that don't have any detail on the top and bottom, such as the collection of Chuckie's play balls in Figure 10.19.

Notice how the faces are nicely placed on the object, yet there is no stretching at the top or bottom of the balls, This is because a solid color was used in these regions. You can compress a solid color all you want and it won't pinch. For the most part, you want to avoid using a spherical image map to wrap images that are highly detailed. If you do need to map a relatively round object with extreme detail, you should break it up into separate surfaces that can be mapped with different techniques, as we saw in the pumpkin example in Figure 10.15. The pumpkin is round, so to avoid pinching a planar map was used to surface the top and a cylindrical map was used to surface the sides. Speaking of cylindrical maps, let's take a look at how they're applied.

Cylindrical Image Maps

Cylindrical image maps are frequently used to surface tube-shaped objects. A cylindrical image map wraps the image around an axis the same way a can label is wrapped around the can. Cylindrical image maps are great for surfacing objects such as soda cans, batteries, tree trunks, baseball bats, or any other cylindrical object. Figure 10.20 illustrates the cylindrical image mapping method along the X, Y, and Z axes.

FIGURE 10.19A good example of where to use a spherical image map

FIGURE 10.20The cylindrical image map

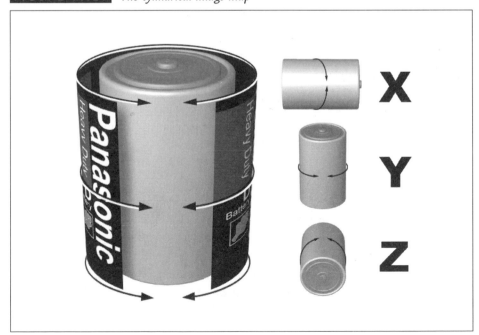

You can see how cylindrical mapping is very effective for mapping tubular objects like batteries. Of course, as with all image mapping methods, there is a drawback to using cylindrical image maps. Cylindrical image maps suffer the same fate as the spherical image map: They pinch at the ends of the model. The battery label was fine because that particular surface doesn't have a physical top. This is how you need to organize your surfaces if you're going to use a cylindrical map. Figure 10.21 show a great example of where to use cylindrical image maps.

As you can see, the soda can label looks very natural on the object. It also doesn't have a top to its surface, so there is no stretching or pinching. It's important to select the surfaces on your model so the image maps can be applied properly. Planning is everything. If you don't select the surfaces properly you'll end up with a very sloppy surfacing job.

Now we have just one more image mapping method to cover—cubic image maps.

Cubic Image Maps

Cubic image maps are probably the most versatile image mapping method and the least used—not because they aren't understood, but rather because

FIGURE 10.21 *The proper use of a cylindrical image map*

 *The cubic image map*

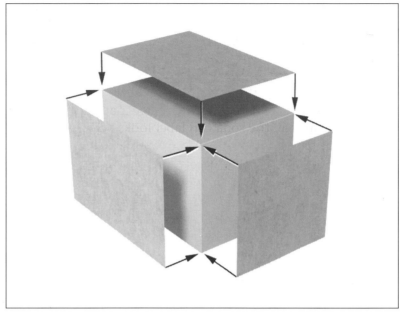

not every 3D program has them. Cubic image mapping is great for organically shaped objects. A cubic image map is essentially a planar image map that is simultaneously applied to all three axes as shown in Figure 10.22.

As you can see, cubic image maps can be useful for quickly surfacing objects that have the same image map on all sides, which makes it a great alternative to planar mapping each of the sides individually. Of course, they are only really useful when you need the surface to be the same all over the object. You can't apply unique details to specific areas of the surface with cubic image maps, since they repeat. Of course, they are a lifesaver when it comes to surfacing objects that require surface consistency, such as the sofa in Figure 10.23.

As you can see, the sofa has the same details over the entire surface. Creating this same surface with any other image mapping method would be very difficult. You can think of a cubic image map as the closest thing to procedural textures you'll get with image maps.

Of course, there is one thing to consider when using cubic image maps: They don't repeat very well on really organic objects. Take a look at the rock in Figure 10.24.

The seams have been highlighted so you can see them better on the printed page. These seams appear because a cubic map will surface each

FIGURE 10.23   *A cubic mapped sofa*

FIGURE 10.24   *Cubic map seams*

axis with the image maps. This works well on flat surfaces where the sides meet on a linear seam, but an organic object has constant changes in the surface so there are no straight seams. This means the seams will appear in the middle of the image map, which isn't seamless.

When you create image maps that are going to be repeated on your model, you make them seamless. This means their borders will blend when they are tiled on the surface. Of course, when the image map is tiled on an irregular surface, blending is impossible because the surfaces will often meet in the middle, not the edge that was made seamless.

OK, now that we understand the different mapping methods for image maps, let's take a look at the image map pros and cons.

The Pros and Cons of Image Maps

Image maps are the most powerful surfacing method, but they do have their shortcomings. It's important to understand the potential of image maps as well as their drawbacks before you use them to surface your models. Let's take a look at the pros and cons of using image maps.

Image Map Pros

- **Specific Detail:** Image maps are painted surfaces, which means you can add as much detail as you'd like—you're only limited by your imagination and your patience. The detail can also be very specific, such as creating the jelly stains around the lid of a jar of jam or placing rust on specific region of a soda can.

- **Precise Control:** With image maps you can place the details exactly where you want on the surface. This is close to impossible with procedural textures, since they're infinite surfaces in 3D space. You can't limit the procedural texture to a particular portion of the surface in most cases. If you wanted to place dirt on the edges of your tires, you would need to use an image map, since the procedural texture would cover the whole tire with dirt.

- **Transferable Surfaces:** Since an image map is merely a picture, you can transfer it to other programs. This is a great plus, particularly if you use more than one 3D program. Also, you can purchase libraries of image maps on CD-ROMs that are compatible with all 3D programs. This can save you a lot of time you might otherwise spend creating them yourself.

Image Map Cons

- **Surface Seams:** The main problem with image maps is surface seams. These can be very annoying and troublesome to correct. When you surface a complex object with image maps, you need to break it down into surfaces that can be properly mapped with a planar, cylindrical, spherical, or cubic map. The problem is that not all surfaces conform to these exact shapes. For example, to surface the rock we saw earlier, we'd have to use a cubic image map, since it has similar details on all sides. This creates a problem because the rock isn't shaped like a cube.

- **Repeating Details:** This is a common problem when working with large models. In order to surface a large model with an image map, you need to repeat it to cover the model. Well, since the details are fixed on the image map, you're now repeating the details. Reality doesn't have a great deal of repetition, so your 3D model tends to look abnormal with repeating details.

- **Stretching and Pinching:** Image maps are two-dimensional, so they have great difficulty conforming to curved surfaces on detailed models. When they attempt to conform to a curve, they're either stretched or pinched, either of which creates a very undesirable effect. Figure 10.25 shows an example of image map stretching.

    Take a look at the wood board, which has an image map applied with planar mapping from the top. Notice how the image map has stretched through the wood on the end. Although the end of a board has wood grain, in reality it's not stretched. Now look at image map pinching in Figure 10.26.

    Notice the tight, pinched lines around the top. This object was surfaced with a cylindrical map, which is great for the sides, but as the object gets smaller the image map is pinched to fit. These are common problems with image maps.

- **Fixed Resolution:** Unlike a procedural texture that has infinite resolution, an image map is fixed to the resolution of your actual image. You can only zoom in so close on the object before it begins to break up and become pixelated. Of course, you can create larger image maps, but that presents another problem—memory usage.

- **High Memory Use:** Image maps exhaust a great deal of system resources. If you have an object that needs a great deal of specific detail, you'll need to create a number of image maps, which can be very hard on memory, since the file size of the image map is loaded into memory. If you are using high-resolution image maps for close-ups, you'll use up your memory quickly.

FIGURE 10.25　*Image map stretching*

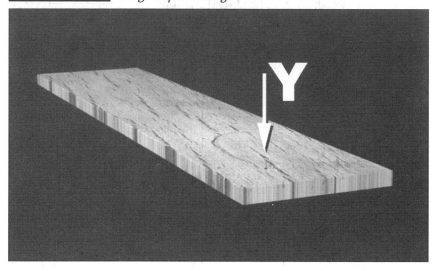

FIGURE 10.26　*Image map pinching*

You might think image maps are a poor surfacing method because they have so many cons, but the cons are greatly outweighed by the pros. Image maps are the predominant surfacing technique because of their flexibility. To get a better idea of how image maps are used, let's take a look at an image map walk-through.

An Image Map Surfacing Walk-through

The first step in surfacing your models is to define the surfaces and their surface mapping method. The way you select your surfaces can have a profound impact on the quality of your finished model. In this walk-through we'll be taking a look at how the surfacing was applied to Chuckie's favorite food—hamburgers. Actually, his favorite food is anything within reach, but he does prefer hamburgers like the one shown in Figure 10.27.

The hamburger and all of the other elements in the image were surfaced with image maps. Image maps can help you to achieve some amazingly realistic results. We'll be taking a look at how the top hamburger bun was surfaced in this walk-through. Let's get started.

The first step is to assign the surface to your model. The hamburger bun has an organic shape, so it needs to have multiple surfaces assigned to avoid image stretching and pinching problems. Figure 10.28 shows how the hamburger bun was broken into three surfaces.

The side of the bun has been given a surface so it can be surfaced with a cylindrical map. It's basically cylindrical in shape, so this is the best mapping method. The top of the bun has a separate surface to avoid the stretching that would occur if we surfaced it as a part of the sides. The last surface is the inside of the bun, which will need a different surface to simulate the rough bread center.

To apply images to these surfaces with accuracy, you'll need what is called a painting template. This is a representation of the surfaces you're painting. Painting templates are typically created by taking a screen capture of the surface from your modeling program or rendering out a template of the surface. Figure 10.29 shows the painting template for the top of the bun.

You'll want to be sure that your painting template is taken from the direction you intend to map the surface. The top of the bun is going to be mapped from the Y axis, so the direction of the painting template needs to match. Also, when you create a template it must be cropped the very edge of the actual surface so your image map will line up with the model's surface.

FIGURE 10.27   *A 3D hamburger*

FIGURE 10.28   *Assigning the surfaces*

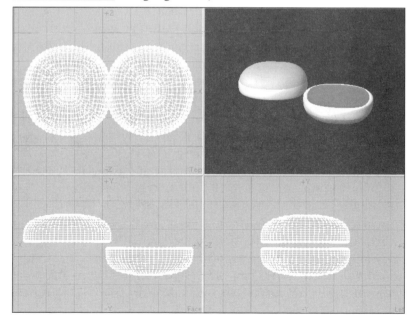

 *A painting template*

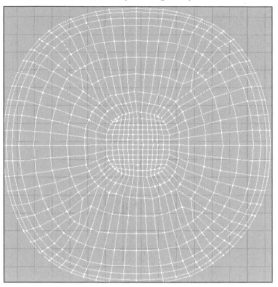

Once the templates are created for each surface, you begin painting the image maps. In many cases, such as the hamburger bun, you can scan in portions of real-world objects to create the surface. Painting detailed surfaces can be very time-consuming, but a scanner makes the job a matter of minutes. To create the hamburger bun top, side, and bottom surfaces I scanned in a real hamburger bun and touched up the image maps. Figures 10.30–10.32 show the three image maps I created for the hamburger bun.

Once you've created the image maps, you need to load them into your 3D program and apply them to the model. Figure 10.33 shows how these image maps were applied to the burger bun model.

The sides of the bun were surfaced with a cylindrical map, as we discussed earlier. The top, on the other hand, was surfaced with a cubic image map. Why? Well, it's not quite flat enough for a planar image map, which would create stretching downs the sides of the top that aren't quite flat. The solution was to use a cubic image map. The reason this doesn't create a noticeable seam is that the sesame seed image map is relatively consistent over the entire image, so it can blend more easily than if it had unique surface details in the center of the image.

As you can see, surfacing the hamburger bun wasn't that difficult, now that we understand the different mapping methods and their limitations. Surfacing your object with image maps is made a great deal easier if you take the time to define the proper surfaces.

FIGURE 10.30 *The bun top image map*

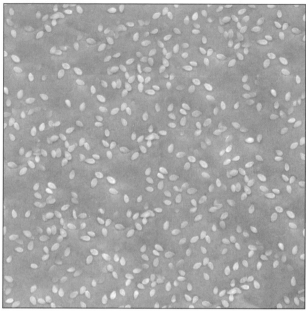

FIGURE 10.31 *The bun bottom image map*

The bun side image map

Applying the burger image maps

Now that we have a handle of the surfacing methods, let's take a look at where and when we should use them.

Where and When to Use the Surfacing Methods

Both procedural textures and image maps are useful surfacing techniques with their positive and negative sides. The important thing to know is where to use these different surfacing methods, and also when they should be combined. You can combine both methods on the same surface to create very detailed surfaces. Let's take a look at where you should use each surfacing method.

When to Use Procedural Textures

- **Large Objects:** Procedural textures are great for surfacing large objects because they don't repeat or have surface seams. If you were creating rolling hills of dirt or grass in the background of an image, you wouldn't want to use an image map because no matter how seamless they are, they will still show obvious repetition of details.

- **Organic Objects:** Procedural textures are awesome for surfacing organic objects like the rock we discussed earlier. They can be used to create very realistic detail, since they are infinite in 3D space. Of course, if you want to surface an organic object that requires specific surface details like a creature or the hamburger we discussed earlier, you'll need to use image maps.

- **Surface Texture:** This is an example where procedural textures and image maps work together. When you create models that need a small surface texture, such as machined parts, plastics, or metals, you won't want to create an image map to make the texture. A better idea is to apply the image maps for the specific details and leave the small bump details to the procedural texture.

When to Use Image Maps

- **Complex Surfaces:** Here is where the image map shines. If you wanted to place labels on a cereal box, you couldn't use a procedural texture, since the label needs an abundance of details, such as text and pictures, laid out in the proper manner. This can't be done with procedural textures. The same applies for creating organic surfaces such as creatures and characters. If you need to surface your object with an abundance of variations, you'll need to use image maps.

- **Specific Details:** Creating specific and unique surface details is nearly impossible with procedural textures because they are designed to be never-ending through 3D space. There are some procedural textures that can pinpoint specific details, but the image map is still king in this arena. Creating the soft blends between the dark brown top of the hamburger bun and the light area on the very edge would be very difficult with a procedural texture, yet it only took a few minutes with an image map.

Knowing is everything in the 3D world. Knowing the proper use of surfacing methods will save you many hours of wasted time trying to use the wrong method. Surfacing is a very complex issue that requires a good deal of experimentation to get just the right look. Don't be fooled into thinking it's a matter of simply applying procedural textures and image maps to get the job done. There are many other attributes to consider, which we will explore in Chapter 11.

Wrap-up

OK, that wasn't too bad. Surfacing your objects can be both a challenge and fun, depending on how well you know the different methods and where they should be applied. Of course, not all 3D programs are created equal, so you'll need to explore your tools to see the options at your disposal. Everything in 3D graphics is about experimentation. Even the professionals learn something new every day, usually by trial and error. If it doesn't work the first time, don't give up—just take a breather and approach it from a different angle. A little perseverance always pays off.

Now that we have a good idea of the two surfacing methods, we can take a look at the surface attributes, which determine the appearance of the surface.

PLATE 1 *Chuckie Snack*

PLATE 2 *Chuckie Playtime*

PLATE 3 *Reading Time*

PLATE 4 *Jacuzzi Chuckie*

PLATE 5 *Daredevil Chuckie*

PLATE 6 *Big League Chuckie*

PLATE 7 *What's That?*

PLATE 8 *Biker Chuckie*

PLATE 9 *Cookie Time!*

PLATE 10 *3D Lunch*

PLATE 11 *Platinum Comic Cover*

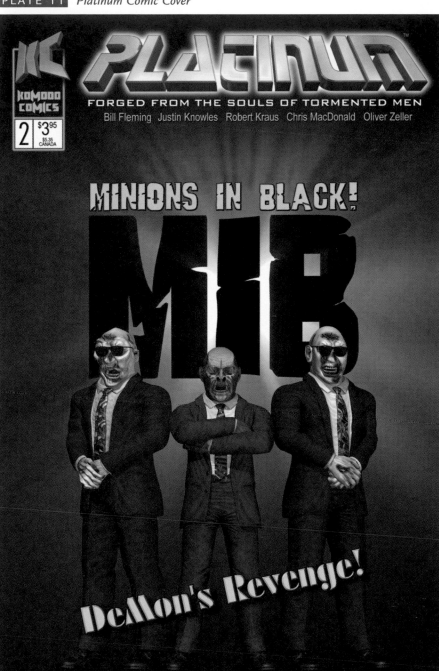

PLATE 12 *It's Alive!*

PLATE 13 *The Power Team*

PLATE 14 *Soul Attack*

PLATE 15 *3D City*

CHAPTER 11

Surface Attributes

Surfaces in reality contain a number of attributes. These attributes are mirrored in 3D surfaces. The significant difference is that when you paint a surface in reality, the paint comes with its own surface attributes such as color, specularity, transparency, bump, and glossiness. In the 3D world you need to manually create each of these attributes for your surfaces. I know it sounds like a lot of work, but it's really not all that bad, once you get the hang of it and fully understand how each attribute works. In this chapter we will be exploring the following surface attributes:

- Color
- Bump
- Specularity
- Reflectivity
- Transparency

These are the most common attributes you'll find in 3D programs. They are also the most relevant attributes, since they are the main components of surfaces in reality.

We'll be taking a look at each of these attributes in detail, and in order of importance. Before we get into the actual attributes, let's take a look at the common settings for attributes.

Attribute Settings

Each attribute comes with a number of settings. These settings determine the placement, size, rotation, and repeating nature of the attribute. Now, each program has subtly different ways to name the settings and apply them, but they are all basically the same. Let's take a look at each major attribute setting and what it does.

- **Texture Type:** This setting determines the mapping method for the surface, either image map or procedural. If you select image map, a requestor will pop up letting you determine the method of choice, such as planar, spherical, cylindrical, and cubic. If you select procedural textures, you'll be presented with a requestor where you can enter the settings. All programs handle their interfaces differently, so don't expect them to all operate this way.

- **Texture Axis:** This determines the axis you will be using for the attribute. If you're using an image map, this is where you would determine the axis it will be mapped along.

- **Automatic Sizing:** Some programs automatically size the surface for you, while others require you to either do it manually or select an automatic sizing option. Typically, only image maps are automatically sized. Procedural textures are usually loaded containing the default settings, which are unrelated to the size of your surface. Figure 11.1 shows a simple sphere with an image map automatically sized to the surface.

  Notice how the image covers the entire sphere. That is because the sphere is a single surface. Automatic sizing is a great setting because it saves you the time and effort of sizing your images to the surface. The majority of the time you'll want your image maps automatically sized.

- **Texture Size:** This setting determines the size of your texture. In the case of image maps, it will determine the size of the map on your surface. Figure 11.2 shows the same image we saw in Figure 11.1 reduced to half its original size.

  This can be a very useful tool when you're using cubic or repeating image maps. When you repeat an image map, you typically don't want it to be the exact size of the surface, but smaller so you can see the repetition. Speaking of repeating textures, let's take a look at the Repeat setting.

- **Repeat/Wrap Amount:** This setting allows you to repeat an image map across the surface of your object. You have the option of determining the number of vertical and horizontal repeats. Figure 11.3 shows the image map repeated three times vertically and horizontally.

FIGURE 11.1 *Automatic sized image map*

FIGURE 11.2 *A resized texture*

FIGURE 11.3   *Repeating image maps*

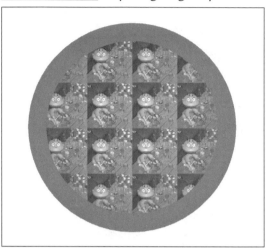

This is the setting you'll want to use when surfacing large floors, walls, and other objects that need an image map to be repeated to fully cover the surface. You could build a huge image map to cover these objects, but that would eat up way too much memory. Repeating is a fast and economical method to cover a surface with an image map.

- **Texture Center:** This is the center axis for the texture. It's the point of reference when you move and rotate the image maps and procedural textures. It's also the point where your surfacing begins. Speaking of rotation and movement, let's take a look at those settings.

- **Rotate:** This setting rotates the texture axis, which in turn rotates the procedural texture or image map on the surface.

- **Move:** This setting moves the texture on your surface. In the case of an image map, it moves the image to a new location on the surface. This is accomplished by moving the texture axis we just discussed. Figure 11.4 shows the result of moving the texture axis.

- **World Coordinates:** This is a unique setting. By default, all surfaces use the actual object coordinates, meaning the object axis is the control for the surface. If you select world coordinates, the world center axis in your scene is the control for texture editing.

All of these settings are provided to make your surfacing job easier. Of course, the way these settings are applied changes radically from one program to another. For example, most 3D programs provide you with a bounding box for editing the texture axis, like the one shown in Figure 11.5.

FIGURE 11.4   *Moving the texture axis*

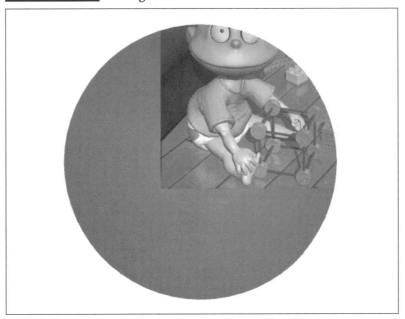

FIGURE 11.5   *A texture axis editing bounding box*

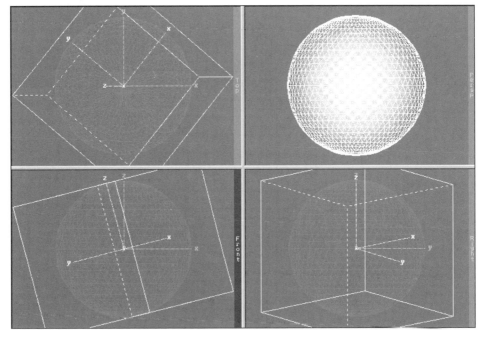

This is an invaluable tool for properly aligning specific details on your surface. If you want to place a label on the front of a wine bottle, you'll need to have visual control over the rotation, size, and movement of the texture. Unfortunately, there are programs such as LightWave that don't use the bounding box, so texture axis manipulation is a total crapshoot. You may not need to edit the texture axis all that often, but when you do you'll really appreciate a bounding box editor.

OK, now that we have an idea of the setting, let's get started with the surface attributes.

Exploring Surface Attributes

Surface attributes are the elements that define the appearance of the surface. They do more than simply change the color—much more. Surface attributes define the hardness, shininess, bumpiness, reflectivity, and transparency of a surface. They are all major components of every surface in reality. To accurately replicate these surfaces in our 3D worlds, we need to understand how these attributes work. We'll be taking a look at each attribute and what it does in the following section. We'll begin with the color attribute.

Color

This is a rather obvious attribute that we have covered many times already in this book, so I'll keep it brief. The color attribute determines the actual visible color of the surface. There are a number of things to consider with the color attribute. You can create color with image maps, procedural textures, or a combination of both. The color attribute is where the surfacing begins. It's the most detailed of all the attributes, so it deserves most of your attention.

We have already discussed the ways to create procedural texture colors, but we've only briefly touched on image maps. Let's take this time to explore color image maps in a bit more detail.

You have a number of options at your disposal for creating color image maps. Let's take a brief look at each method and its merits.

- **CD Image Map Libraries:** There are a number of companies that offer CD-ROM libraries of image maps you can use with your 3D programs. These are a fast and cost-effective means for acquiring image maps. Most come with a variety of seamless, tileable woods, bricks, dirt, and other assorted image maps. Figure 11.6 shows a wood texture acquired from a CD-ROM image map library.

FIGURE 11.6 *An image map from a CD-ROM library*

As you can see, the quality is great. These are usually scanned in from very high-resolution photographs. You could scan your own, but I think you might have a difficult time trying to fit a tree in your studio.

Appendix A in the back of this book lists manufacturers that produce CD-ROM image map libraries.

- **Scanned Images:** If you have a scanner, you can create your own image maps by scanning in photographs or things lying around your house. I've scanned everything from a rug to tree bark. In fact, Figure 11.7 shows an image map created from a rock I scanned.

  You do need to be careful when scanning heavy objects, though—you don't want to break your scanner glass. Once you've scanned your images, you can retouch them in a paint program, and you're ready to go.

- **Texture Creation Programs:** There are some new solutions on the horizon for 3D artists to create their own unique image maps with automated software. These programs use complex algorithms, such as procedural textures, to create textures that can be exported as image maps. DarkTree Textures from Darkling Simulations (www.darksim.com) is

FIGURE 11.7   *A scanned image map*

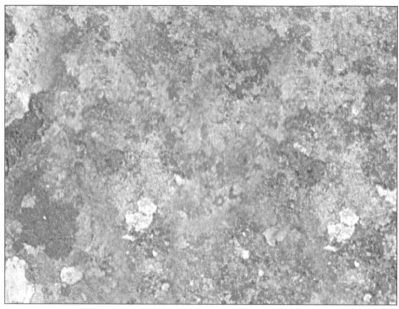

one of these. This program produces a wide variety of procedural textures that can be exported as seamless image maps. Figure 11.8 shows an example of a textile image map created with DarkTree Textures.

- **Painting:** This is the most complicated method of creating image maps. Painting image maps is definitely a fine art. You can't simply throw paint on the screen and pray it works. It can take some time to hone your image-map painting skills, so have some patience. It's not like you need to paint a Picasso—just replicate a few of the details you see in real surfaces. The most popular program for creating 3D image maps is Photoshop, but some artists use Painter and Corel PhotoPaint. Figure 11.9 shows some wood boards I painted with Photoshop.

    Painting image maps with this level of detail takes time and practice. You need to have a thorough understanding of painting techniques. I could barely paint a smiley face a year ago, so you can definitely create great image maps after only a little time.

As you can see, there are a number of ways you can create color image maps. It all depends on your painting skill level and the image map you need. I probably use my scanner just as often as I paint them myself. No matter how you come by your color map, it's the defining element of your surface. Speaking of definition, let's take a look at how we define some altitude changes on the surface with bump maps.

FIGURE 11.8   *A procedurally created image map*

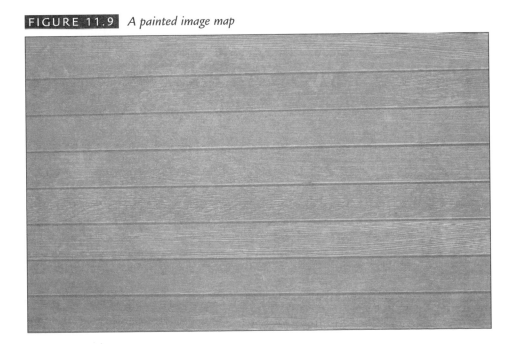

FIGURE 11.9   *A painted image map*

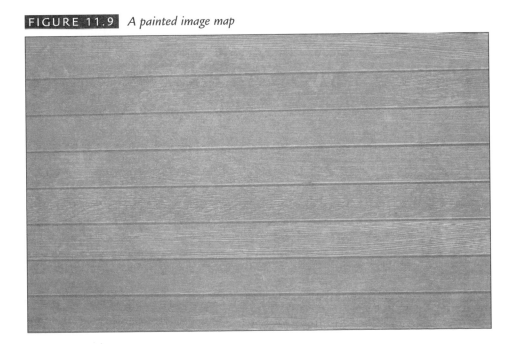

Bump

The bump attribute gives your surface physical texture, something you could feel if you touched the model. The bump attribute either raises or lowers details on the surface, depending on your settings. A bump attribute can be either a procedural texture or an image map. When you use image maps, the program translates your colors into values of depth. The maximum number of colors in a bump map is 256 shades, which are read in grayscale values, so it's rather pointless to have a colorful bump map. A good rule of thumb is to always use grayscale images for your bump map because they are one-third the size of a color image, so they use less memory.

When using an image map for your bump map, white represents the maximum height, while black is the maximum depth. To get a better idea of what a bump map looks like, see Figure 11.10.

This bump map creates the recessed text on top of a soda can. The text is black so it creates a dent in the surface. Figure 11.11 shows the effect of applying this bump map to the soda can.

You can see that the text is clearly recessed on the lid of the soda. Creating the proper bump map can be a bit challenging. It all depends on the effect. For example, if you wanted to dent the soda can, you could apply a cylindrical bump map to the sides to add dents. This image map would probably look a little like Figure 11.12.

FIGURE 11.10 *A typical bump image map*

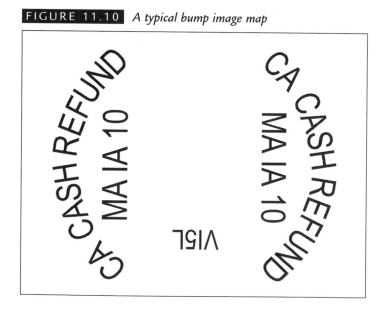

FIGURE 11.11   *The bump map applied*

FIGURE 11.12   *A dent image map*

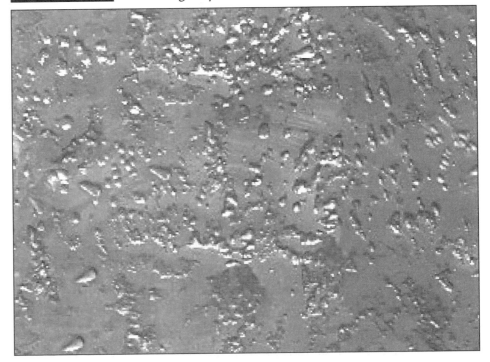

Notice the dark spots on the image map and how they blend into the gray surface color. This will create a smooth transition on the edge of the bump. In most cases it's important to ensure that there is some level of smoothing on the bumps or they will look too harsh. Let's take a look at what the dent bump map looks like on the soda can shown in Figure 11.13.

As you can see, the soda can is now heavily dented and looks a great deal older as a result. This can has definitely had a bad day.

The bump attribute in 3D program comes with a setting called Level, which controls the intensity of the bump. Typically this is a value from 1 to 100, but some programs let you go into the thousands, which can create some really large bump effects. The level controls the actual heights of the bump effect. A low setting of 10 would create very little bump, while a setting of 100 would create the largest bump—that is, unless you can go higher than 100. LightWave allows you to go all the way up to 5000%, which essentially creates a bump 50 times that of 100%. Yes, it's a bit excessive, but it can come in handy for creating really serious bumps.

Bump maps really add a lot of character to your models. Figure 11.14 shows how a bump map was used to create the effect of wound tape.

Notice how the top of the tape has small ridges that represent the layers of tape that have been wound around the cardboard core. This was a simple effect to create with the bump map shown in Figure 11.15.

FIGURE 11.13   *The dent bump map applied*

FIGURE 11.14   *Creating wound tape with bump maps*

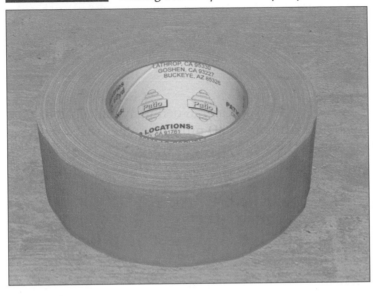

FIGURE 11.15   *The duct tape top bump map*

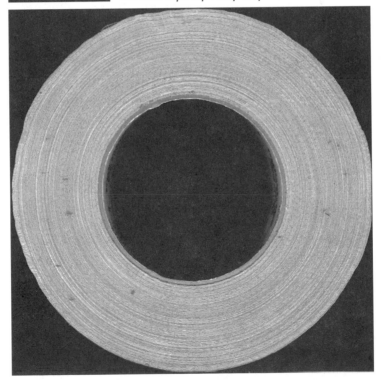

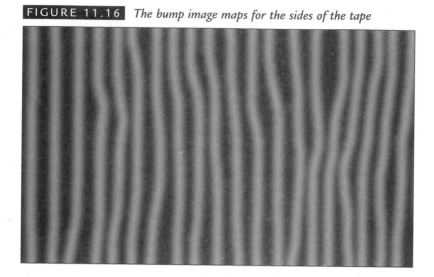

FIGURE 11.16   *The bump image maps for the sides of the tape*

In fact, this tape has plenty of other bumps maps. Take a look at the sides and you'll see small dents on the edge of the tape and wrinkles on the sides, which are all trademarks of duct tape that has been thrown around the shop. These details were created by the two image maps seen in Figure 11.16.

The bump image map on the top was used for the wrinkles and the bottom was used for the little folds. In addition, another bump map was used to create the tiny divots. You can see how bump maps are instrumental in creating detailed surfaces. Bump maps are second to color maps in the order of importance, but specularity comes in at a close third. Let's take a look at how specularity works.

Specularity

Specularity is defined as the reflection of a light source on the surface. It's that little white spot you see on shiny objects. Most man-made objects in reality have some form of specularity as a result of the material they are made of. For example, plastic objects have a moderate to high level of specularity because they're hard and shiny.

Remember when we spoke about specularity in the chapter on Bevel modeling tools? Specularity is one of the key attributes for creating realism. For us to believe an object is hard plastic, we'll need to see a specular highlight on the surface, which is often referred to as the "hot spot."

3D programs provide you with several ways to set the specularity of your surface, such as a global setting, procedural textures, and image maps. The global setting fixes the entire surface to a single specularity value. This is great for consistent surfaces such as plastics, but not so good for metals or even human skin. If you want to change the specularity of specific areas on the surface, you'll need a procedural texture or image map.

You can easily create realistic metals by applying a procedural fractal noise texture to your specularity attribute. Figure 11.17 shows an example of realistic metal with variations in specularity.

Take a look at the metal tools in the image and you'll see that the specularity varies over the surfaces. That's because a small, fractal noise procedural texture was used to break up the specularity. Metal has a low specularity that is rather chaotic. To create realistic metals you should use a procedural specularity texture.

On the other hand, if you need very specific specularity changes, you'll need to use an image map. When using image maps, the colors of the image map represent the levels of specularity. The same rules apply as for the

FIGURE 11.17 *Procedural texture specularity*

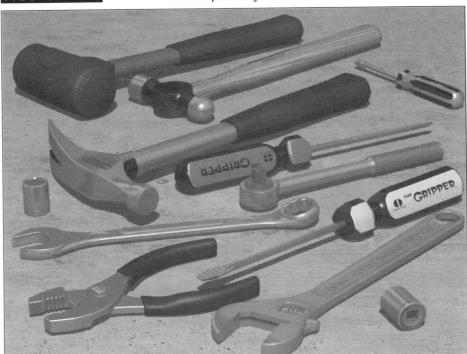

bump map. There are 256 levels of specularity, one for each shade of gray. White is 100% specular, while black is dull with no specularity. Porous rubber would be a great example of a surface with very low specularity.

Specularity image maps have a number of uses. One in particular would be applying varying levels of specularity to a human head. The face has many different levels of specularity. The forehead, nose, and chin have a higher level of specularity because they contain more oil than the other parts of the face. Wet surfaces are more specular. Figure 11.18 shows a character head and its corresponding specularity map.

Notice how the area around the forehead, nose and chin on the specularity image map to the right are whiter than the rest of the image. This increases the specularity. You can see how the specularity on the character face to the left really brings him to life. Specularity image maps are a real asset when creating organic objects.

OK, now we've covered the common attributes of every object. There are two more common 3D attributes that show up in a number of real-world objects, but not all of them. They are reflectivity and transparency. Let's take a look at both to see how they work in the 3D world.

FIGURE 11.18 *A specularity image map*

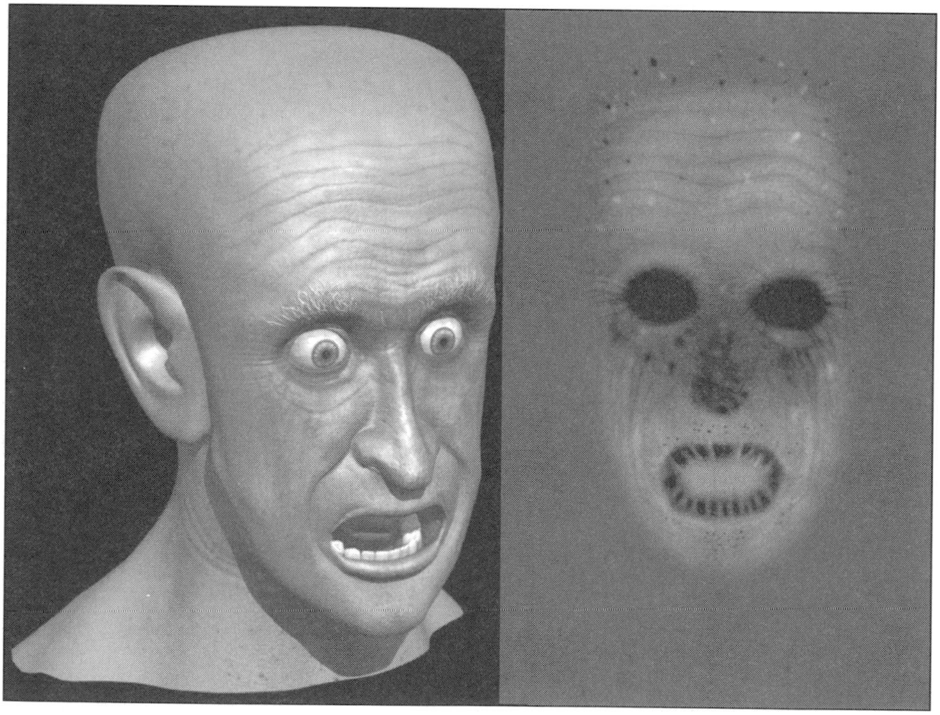

Reflectivity

Reflectivity is the attribute that determines how much of the environment the object's surface will reflect. Reflectivity mirrors the environment on the surface of an object. Common reflective surfaces are metal, plastic, and any other surface that might be polished or wet. Water is very reflective, so wet objects also become reflective.

The reflectivity attribute can be determined by a global setting, procedural textures, and image maps. The global setting is good for rather plain surfaces such as mirrors and glass. On the other hand, if you want to make more detailed surfaces like metals reflective, you'll need to use procedural textures. The wrench in Figure 11.19 was made reflective with a fractal noise procedural texture.

Notice how the wrench looks reflective, but the reflection isn't very clear. This is because the fractal noise procedural has made tiny parts of the surface nonreflective to break up the reflection so it looks like a chrome alloy metal. While procedural textures are great for creating random details, they can't be used for specific details. In these circumstances you'll need to use an image map.

Image maps can be used to create some incredible reflection effects. For example, take a look at the battery in Figure 11.20.

FIGURE 11.19 *Fractal noise reflectivity*

FIGURE 11.20 *A battery made reflective with an image map*

This battery uses a reflection map to give the plastic and metallic plastic surfaces of the label different levels of reflectivity. The metallic plastic is almost like chrome, while the rest of the label is much less reflective. Let's take a look at the image map that was used to create this effect. Figure 11.21 shows the reflection map for the battery.

You can see several areas with different shades of gray on the image maps. These varied levels of gray represent the different reflective areas of the battery label. The chromed plastic area needed to be about 50% reflective and the plastic areas about 12% reflective. This means the chrome areas on the reflection image map were made a light gray and the plastic dark gray. If you look closely, you'll notice that the text in the middle of the chromed area is darker in the reflection map because it's not very reflective.

You can see how an image map can be used to create very specific reflection effects. You can do some great things with the reflection attribute if you use the proper tools. Before you apply the reflectivity attribute, take a moment to consider the kind of reflective detail you'll need.

OK, now were ready for the last attribute we're going to discuss—Transparency.

FIGURE 11.21 *The battery reflection maps*
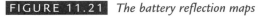

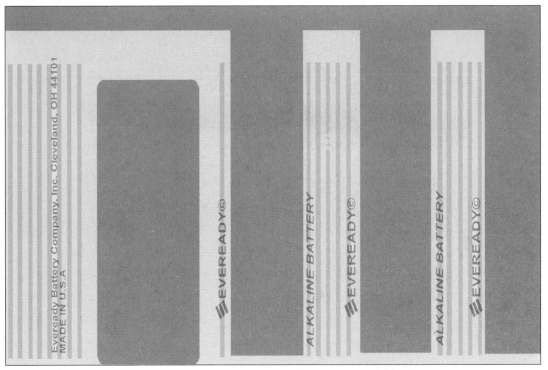

Transparency

This is just like it sounds: A transparency attribute makes the object transparent. If you wanted to create a glass bottle, you would make the bottle surface transparent. This attribute can be a global setting, a procedural texture, or an image map. You should use the global setting to make glass surfaces transparent as long as they are clean. If they are supposed to be dirty, you can add a fractal noise procedural texture to make certain areas of the glass less transparent.

Of course, it you wanted to apply an extreme level of detail to the transparency of the surface, you would have to use an image map. When using image maps, the colors of the image map represent the levels of transparency. The same rules apply as for the bump map. There are 256 levels of transparency, one for each shade of gray. White is fully transparent and black is opaque.

You can use image maps to create very detailed transparent effects. For example, if you wanted to make a window with stickers on it clear, you would use an image map to filter the window portions and leave the sticker portions opaque.

There is one thing to consider when making your surfaces transparent—index of refraction. Transparent objects refract (bend) light as it passes through. Since we don't actually see colors in reality, but rather the light reflecting off the object, we get a distorted view through glass depending on the angle of our viewpoint.

3D programs will provide you with an option for setting the index of refraction for your transparent surfaces. Some will have preset values for particular surfaces such as glass and plastic, while others will leave it up to you to decide. To make your life a bit easier I've included a table in Appendix B that lists the index of refraction values for many transparent objects. Figure 11.22 shows an example of a refractive transparent 3D object.

All of the objects in this image are computer-generated. The ashtray was given a glass surface and an index of refraction value of 1.6—which is the value for a thick glass object such as Coke-bottle nerd glasses. Notice how the cigarette box behind the ashtray is distorted through the glass.

FIGURE 11.22 *A refractive transparent object*

This is a defining element of the scene. It's a very natural effect when looking through thick glass that is rounded.

That does it for the surface attributes. As you can see, they are not nearly as complicated as they might first seem, but they can be used to create some amazing effects. Once again, it's all a matter of knowing how they work and where to use them.

Wrap-up

Well, that does it for the basics of object surfaces. It's a lot of information to take in at one time, so you might want to read through this part a few times. In fact, reading the entire book a few times might not hurt.

Modeling and surfacing are the backbone of 3D graphics. If you take the time to master these areas, you'll find the rest is quite simple. Yes, animation seems daunting, but getting to know the limitations of your model will help you to better understand the limitations of animation.

This book has laid the the groundwork for the next book, *3D Staging, Lighting, and Animation,* in which you'll have the opportunity to see Chuckie walk and talk. In addition, I'll include a detailed chapter on "Software Products and Career Choices." You'll find out which program is best to learn for a particular career choice. You won't want to miss this chapter.

I hope you've enjoyed this book, and I look forward to working with you in the next book.

Index of Image Map Collections

On-line

Serious 3D Free Image Map of the Day	Serious 3D Magazine	www.serious3d.com
Links to many on-line texture databases	3d Café	www.3dcafe.com

On CD-ROM

Seamless Textures You Can REALLY Use	Marlin Studios	www.marlinstudios.com
Seamless Textures Collection	Artbeats, Inc.	www.artbeats.com
City Surfaces	Artbeats, Inc.	www.artbeats.com
Exteriors	Artbeats, Inc.	www.artbeats.com
Wood and Paper	3d Café	www.3dcafe.com
White Puffy Clouds Hi-Def	3d Café	www.3dcafe.com
Water Textures	3d Café	www.3dcafe.com

Texture Generation Programs

Darktree	Darksim	www.darksim.com
Imagine	Impulse, Inc.	www.coolfun.com

Index of Refraction Values for Transparent Materials

Material	Index of Refraction	Material	Index of Refraction
Vacuum	1.0000	Emerald	1.5700
Air	1.0003	Glass, light flint	1.5750
Carbon dioxide, liquid	1.2000	Lapis lazuli	1.6100
Ice	1.3090	Topaz	1.6100
Water	1.3333	Carbon disulfide	1.6300
Acetone	1.3600	Quartz 1	1.6440
Ethyl alcohol	1.3600	Sodium chloride (salt) 2	1.6440
Sugar solution (30%)	1.3800	Glass, heavy flint	1.6500
Alcohol	1.3900	Calspar1	1.6600
Fluorite	1.4340	Glass, dense flint	1.6600
Quartz, fused	1.4600	Methylene iodide	1.7400
Calspar2	1.4860	Ruby	1.7700
Sugar solution (80%)	1.4900	Sapphire	1.7700
Glass	1.5000	Glass, heaviest flint	1.8900
Glass, zinc crown	1.5170	Crystal	2.0000
Glass, crown	1.5200	Diamond	2.4170
Sodium chloride	1.5300	Chromium oxide	2.7050
Sodium chloride (salt) 1	1.5440	Amorphous selenium	2.2920
Polystyrene	1.5500	Iodine crystal	3.3400
Quartz 2	1.5530		

Index

Note: Page numbers in italics refer to the figure on that page.